C000213363

A Funny Old Quist

A Funny Old Quist

The Memoirs of a Gamekeeper

EVAN ROGERS

Edited by Clive Murphy

ELAND

London

First published by Dobson Books
First published by Eland in 1986
This edition published by Eland Publishing Limited
61 Exmouth Market, London EC1R 4QL in 2009

Text © Clive Murphy & Evan Rogers

ISBN 978 1 906011 12 3

The cover shows Evan Rogers © Mary Hancox
Map © Reginald Piggott

Printed in the UK by MPG Biddles

To Mary and Charles

By the same author

The 'Ordinary Lives' series,
recorded and edited by Clive Murphy

The Good Deeds of a Good Woman
The memoirs of an East End hostel-dweller
BEATRICE ALI

Born to Sing
The memoirs of an East End mantle presser
ALEXANDER HARTOG

Four Acres and a Donkey
The memoirs of a lavatory attendant
S. A. B. ROGERS

Up in Lights
(originally published as *Love, Dears!*)
The memoirs of a former chorus girl
MARJORIE GRAHAM

Oiky
The memoirs of a pigman
LEN MILLS

At the Dog in Dulwich
The memoirs of a poet
PATRICIA DOUBELL

A Stranger in Gloucester
The memoirs of an Austrian in England
MRS FALGE-WAHL

Dodo
The memoirs of a left-wing socialite
DODO LEES

Endsleigh
The memoirs of a river-keeper
HORACE ADAMS

This story from the West Herefordshire countryside is not for the squeamish – nor for those who disdain the concept of 'loyal service'. But who would dare dismiss in their entirety the attitudes, the warnings of an octogenarian ever close to nature? Certainly not I.

CLIVE MURPHY

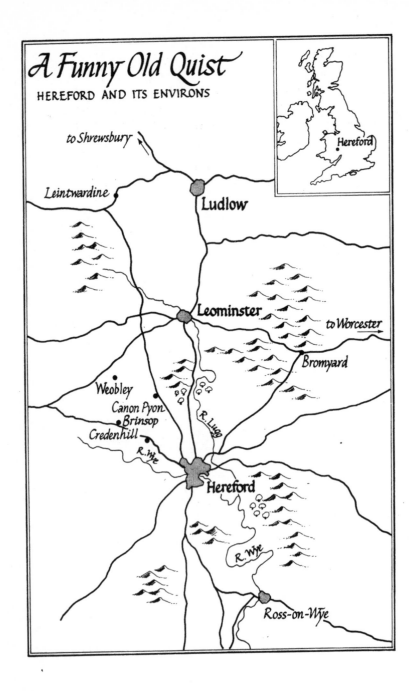

A Funny Old Quist

HEREFORD AND ITS ENVIRONS

to Shrewsbury

Leintwardine

Ludlow

Hereford

to Worcester

Leominster

Bromyard

Weobley

Canon Pyon
Brinsop
Credenhill

R. Lugg

R. Wye

Hereford

R. Wye

Ross-on-Wye

One

A gentleman told me one day when I was out shooting, he said, 'Do you know what you are, Rogers?' I said, 'No, sir. Not exactly,' I said. 'More a broken-down keeper or next door to it!' He said, 'No, you're not,' he said. 'You're a gentleman's gentleman!' My present master, too, Sir Derrick Bailey, he said to me once, he said, 'If you'd had the schooling my sons had, do you know, Evan,' he said, 'you'd be riding about in a big Rolls Royce, smoking a fat cigar?!' I said, 'Yes, and I'd be bored stiff!!'

I've had a lovely working life, a lovely country life out in the fresh air; it's been wonderful—sixty-eight years of it at Brinsop Court, not counting the Great War. To be correct, it's sixty-eight years up to October last. I don't know of another man in Herefordshire that have worked sixty-eight years on the same estate. I should love to know have I broken the record for the rest of Great Britain as well. Perhaps I'm blowing my own trumpet too much but I feels, 'Did I really do it?' When Sir Derrick first came here in 1947 I used to have rows with him, but in the end I told him where he got off and he always respected me after, and I've never looked back, doing the work I love—making sport for others, picking up two pound off one gentleman, five pound off another and hearing, 'Thank you, Rogers, for the nice day.'

I'm eighty-one—born 25th March, 1897. I've got false teeth; I've got glasses; I've got a double truss on—if I took them all off I'd fall to pieces! But my only *real* trouble is low blood pressure. If I walk fast I get out of puff and the whole world starts to go round—and if I go on faster I'm on the ground and I've got to wait till I recover. About six years ago I was with Sir Derrick in the garage yard and I heaved forward and he'd to call two men and have me lifted to my cottage, Ivy Cottage here, up the Arbour. So I only work a few hours a day now, I've got to take it reasonable. Sir Derrick says I can please myself whether I work or not; if I don't feel like working, not to worry. He's been a dear good gentleman in my life. His sons are very good, too. I like them all. But we don't always see eye to eye. They've got new ideas, I've got the old ideas and can't break my habit of them. 'Oh have you heard of the new idea of so and so and so and so? We'll try that.' And of course you've got to stop *your* old fashioned idea and you're lost. Young Master Tom, his son as is running half of Brinsop since Sir Derrick went to the Channel Islands, he was only talking to me the other day. Most game is reared by electric but I've never done it, I've hatched them under bantams and hens and from now on I won't be able. 'Don't worry, Evan,' he said. 'There'll be plenty of birds for what we want. We don't want to go out shooting at pheasant as if it's a farmyard,' he said. 'If only we gets two or three nice shots in a day, *that's* sportsmanship! The place is well stocked with wild hen birds,' he said, 'and as long as you kills the vermin we can always shoot on a place like this.' So I'll just *feed* the wild game for him still and kill the vermin and organize the yearly shoots—the four pheasant shoots, the two or three duck shoots, the partridge shoot, and the pigeon shoot after the game season's over.

My daughter, Mary, she says, 'If you don't think you can manage it any longer, Dad—I know this has been your life— there's always a home with me in Poole.' But it'd be like catching a fox and putting the poor bugger to live in a box because I'd go down into a strange vicinity and I wouldn't know a soul! All there'd be is me and the ruddy dog. With Mary and Charles, my son-in-law, at work I should be stuck in the house on my own from day to day and life wouldn't be worth living. Oh Poole's a beautiful *place*! I could recommend anyone to go there for a holiday. And Bournemouth nearby, it's got what I term all the 'cream' living there. There's beautiful houses and gardens all the way down to the seaside, all kinds of shrubs in the avenues. There's great big patches of lawn and a big bandstand half way down one of them with about a thousand chairs, and you pay sixpence, I think, and you can sit in a chair for an hour and listen to the band only about two hundred yards from the water, and then you can go straight out onto the sands and there's seats again. . . . But no, I shouldn't be happy. Although it's such a beautiful area, I'd miss Ivy Cottage because I've felt always that I was part of Brinsop Estate and keeping it going, it's been my own 'place' as you can call it. It's nice of her to ask but here I can enjoy my work and have my freedom. Of course I may *have* to go. You see, since my dear old wife, Ann, died in January I've been mostly alone. Mary and Charles come nearly every other week-end and the Home Help comes twice a week and Meals on Wheels on Tuesdays and Thursdays, but what I needs is some dear old working class lady as have lost her husband. If she'd look after me, I'd look after her and give her a damn good home. One thing I detest is housework. I shall never make a housewife. It's no good. It's impossible. I did the housework after my first wife died and I've done it now after my second wife have died and I've just about had enough of it. And there's the loneliness, the stillness of the air in the house. When I'm outside I can hear birds and lambs; the life outside is going on. But when you come indoors and shut the door you've got the stillness—and as for Television, well, you can have the lot.

Oh I miss a female in the house! It's not the same! Take me now of a morning. Sometimes I oversleep, and I haven't got a wife to say, 'Evan! Come on! Wake up!' Then I come home from work a bit tired and I've got to go and light the fire and boil the kettle, boil an egg and cut some bread and butter, or maybe sponge over the floor with a mop where I've dirtied it with my boots. It all goes against the grain. I've never done it, you see; I've never *had* to do it and it takes some getting used to. It's like in another world. I'm damn nearly too lazy to change my

11

shirt. And I hate tinned stuff, see: I'm a terrible man in the spring of the year for my new potatoes, new peas, all vegetables out of the garden, a few carrots growing big and fresh. But I don't know how to cook them! My wives or housekeepers or Mary have always done it! You've to put them in some water and boil them, but for how long I don't know. Only recently I had a little joint of pork given me. The person who gave it me, she said, 'All you do,' she said, 'is score the rind, sprinkle some salt in the rind, and rub the salt in the rind, and then you get those nice little crisp pieces, the craunchy bits.' Well, I had it in the oven one night and I forgot it and I burnt it all nearly to a cinder. There's the remains of it in the pantry now [27th March, 1978]. I gave the dog a piece of it; it's too hard for me to bite. But I've got to get used to this. I've made a regular order with the grocer in Credenhill, and if I run out of anything I get on the phone and I say, 'Oh please add so and so to the list—a pot of mustard and two pounds of sugar more please; a tin of corned beef. Thank you very much. Goodnight,' and he delivers everything Friday four o'clock and I'm here to meet him. It's making life harder for me because my job keepering follows on like a farmer's. Month after month there's the right thing to do. You've got to be 'with it'. You lose a week and you'll never pick that week up. A gentleman asked me one day, he asked me a difficult question, he said to me, 'When is the busiest time of a keeper?' Do you know what I told him? I said, 'Never a dull one. He's *never* idle!' You can't sit on your back-side. This being interviewed will be the longest spell that I've had sitting down for the last seven years, do you know that? It's marvellous, isn't it?, what we can make our lives do, or what we can do *with* our lives, I should say! I don't want to bore you stiff with my silly nonsense but it's true. People want Saturday and Sunday, Christmas Day and Boxing Day and Easter and Whitsun and the rest of it for holidays, but there's no holiday for a keeper. You advertise for a keeper like me and see how many answers you'll get! I've been here in my time seven years on one stretch and never off the place, not so far as to have my hair cut! And in one respect you're more at risk than a policeman because you're away out of the sound of the population. No one sees you in the woods; you're on your own; and if there's anyone poaching after your boss's game they can come up and shoot you and you can lie there for weeks, or they can shoot you dead and you may never be found. But I love the work, I've never been in fear of it. I'd do it all over again if I had the chance.

Even as a boy I was always fiddling with the guns what Father had from when he was keeper at Wormsley. My father was keeper for Squire Knight of Wormsley Grange, you see, before he retired from keepering and took the farm where I was born on Nupton Hill in the Parish of Canon Pyon. I'm the only one left of my family now. My father and mother and brothers and sister are all gone and I shall go one of these days but we don't know when, do we?, and it's a good job too! Not that I'm afraid of death—I wouldn't mind if I went tomorrow. I think I've done a nice little job while I've been on this earth but I don't believe there's a heaven and I don't believe there's a hell either. I'm only saying what I think—I'm not in a position to give insights; I've only had my education in a little country school. No one has never come back to tell us they've been in the next life. It could be a myth. What the soul consists of I do not know. But when the breath has gone out of the body and the heart stops beating, what are we? How do our souls go to heaven? How this? How that? How the next thing? No man can tell! I don't think there's any scientist have ever fathomed anything out to that extent. In my view, and it may be a poor view, there may have been a mighty *man* and they may have called him Our Saviour, Jesus. I've never pondered about God but I will say this, that from going to church you get easement of mind. The vicars I've met, they've all been as I term genuine living men; I haven't known one of them disgrace himself. Probably they don't believe a lot of what they're saying—they do it for a living, and a poor one at that. Maybe they do it to keep the peace, to hold the nation together. What would happen if Christianity was done away with?! There's enough trouble, God knows, with the bit of laws we've got! When I look at the youngsters today and see them running about my heart aches for them. For all young children I think church is a grand thing. Father made *us* go and we were glad to get out of his way! But I think most vicars could put more into their work than what they do. Which reminds me of an old tale. There was an old tramp went to a vicar's house and he knocked at the door and the vicar come. 'Yes, my man?' he said. 'And what can I do for *you*?' 'Please sir, have you got a crust of bread?' 'Certainly, my man! I'll go and have a look.' So he went in to the pantry and he brought him a half a dry loaf. 'Here you are, my man!' he said. 'I'm giving it to you not for my sake, not for your sake, but for God's sake!' 'Well then, Guvnor,' said the tramp, 'for God's sake put a bit of butter on it!' . . .

My earliest memory is of a vicar, the vicar of Canon Pyon as christened me at Canon Pyon Church coming up with his son to have tea with Mother at Nupton Hill Farm. I was only about five and I was wearing a little blue blouse with white stripes in and little short corduroy knickers and stockings up to just above my little shoes, and I had to wear a big wide straw hat because the vicar was coming, and there was a couple of ribbons hanging down behind and I hated the sight of them. A big tree had blown down, and me and the boy, we was playing by this tree and we quarrelled over something and all of a sudden this vicar's son, he cut me right across the face with a stick . . .

But I was telling you about my father's guns. I remember one Wednesday when I was about ten and Father and Mother was in Hereford I got two cartridges out of Father's ammunition box and I was just able to open his double-barrelled gun and I loaded it and went out through the front door. There were some railings in front of the little lawn in front of the house and I put the barrels down between two of the battings on these railings and I balanced them up until I got them poking towards a cock pheasant. Then when I pulled one trigger the old gun come back and knocked me out! My sister, Mabel, she carried me in and put me on the sofa and then she went out again and picked up the cock pheasant. That was the first cock pheasant that ever I shot in my life. I had a bruised shoulder, I tell you—*and* I had a smacked bottom when my father come home that night!

My mother, Esther Jones, was born at Cadoxton, near Cardiff, and my father, Arthur John Rogers, was from Taunton in Somerset. They met when he came back from Africa in Dinas Powis where she and her sister, Jemima, were running a little farm, going out in the meadows together with buckets and carrying them back on their heads after milking the cows. He'd been batman to Lord Roberts—I've got an old meerschaum pipe Lord Roberts gave him out in Africa. It's in a leather case; It fell one day and the meerschaum inside cracked and I tried to have it repaired but no tobacconist would take it. As far as my knowledge goes Father was in two or three occupations before becoming a keeper, one of them in India. He was called Hell Fire Jack because he didn't trouble about anybody or anything. Like me, he wasn't educated that fully. He was a rough old covey, a six footer—almost exactly the same height as I used to be—and in the end he grew a beard. I've seen him come out of a public house and catch hold of two men by the scruff of the neck, bash their two heads together and drive his toe in their bottoms and then say, 'Come on! Get up and I'll give you some more!' I've seen three policemen try to put cuffs on him outside a public house and in the end be afraid to touch him. He drank very seldom but when he did he always had too much and he always got nasty with it. We was all afraid of him, so we couldn't love him like we loved our mother. Mother was small featured, about five foot eight or nine, very slim and always pale looking and always in an old black apron and always gentle. One day when he was thirteen or fourteen my brother, Arthur, went with my father, they went down to see a farmer over buying a colt and when they come back my father, he heard Arthur telling

Mother something what he did at a public house. He caught hold of Arthur and took one of his walking sticks out of the drainpipe with red paper roses pasted on it by Mother in the corner of the hall, and he thrashed that boy . . . Well, talk about weals! Mother had to have the doctor. He said, 'I'll have that man put in behind bars!' She said, 'No, you won't!' She went on her hands and knees to him. From that day on we was all afraid of Father. We'd jump through the eye of a needle out of his sight. Hear his voice and we was gone. Arthur was fastened in his bedroom up at the old home—this is true and if my sister was alive to tell you she'd tell you now—Arthur was fastened in his bedroom for two days without any food for doing some little thing like throwing a cat out through a door. Mabel, she went in the pantry, for some Welsh buns, put them in a jug, went in the garden and got the clothes-prop, put it in the handle of the jug and tapped Arthur's bedroom window. Then she went back into the pantry with the jug when he'd put it back on the prop for her, and she pushed him up a jug of milk. The Boer War and his time in India must have affected my father's attitude of mind. He'd come in with a big stick and wallop you, think nothing about it.

There was one thing all of us boys suffered for. We had a patch of turnips right by a patch of corn, and one Sunday afternoon we had to line ourselves out to let the sheep graze the turnips because we hadn't got sheep-netting to stop the sheep going over the corn. Well, we was that interested in playing, we never noticed the sheep go just off this patch of turnips into the corn, and he come out and caught us chasing the sheep back into the turnips. Oh, he was like a madman because we hadn't done what he told us to do! I can't understand parents beating their children, there's no need for it. It's the same as with a dog. If you can't train a dog by kindness, you're not going to train him with a big stick, I'm telling you. Try the kindness first. Try other methods after, if you know them. But Father never had the patience to try anything. He was straight off the mark and you never knew what he was going to do next.

You couldn't cope with him. It's a wrong thing for me to be telling you stories like this about my father, but they're as true as God made heaven—'if there is such a place' as Sir Derrick has said to me many a time.

There's always people worse off; there *might* be someone with a worse father! He had his kind moments, I suppose, but they was very few, *very* few. *I* can't remember *any*. He was bound to have been kind *some* time in his life to marry my dear old mother because she was an extraordinary dear old person, a lovable old soul. He never hit her, but he wasn't kind to her in *my* eyes, not as how I've seen him on a Sunday with a cooked dinner on the table—lovely roast pork, cauliflower, gravy, apple sauce. Perhaps he was late, been out round the sheep, a-ewe-lambing or something. He'd come in, 'I don't want that bloody stuff!' and chuck it straight up the chimney. He was what I term as a very *false* man. A stranger come along and he 'sir'-ed them and all the rest of it. Say a lady was to come up to the door. 'Oh yes, my lady! Yes, my lady!' He'd go on his hands and knees to her nearly and then he'd go in to Mother and say, 'What does *that* bloody thing want?!' And with us boys when we got married he made a hell of a palaver. 'Oho! It's a blessing they're going to get married' and all the rest of it. Yet he wouldn't come to my first marriage, and he wouldn't let Mother come. She obeyed him to the last item, though I don't say she loved him. She was a marvellous woman, a marvellous woman.

She saved his life when he was keeper for Squire Knight at Wormsley Grange. That's where my brothers Arthur and Edwin were born—in The Pool House. Mabel was born before that at Kingsthorn village. Bob and I were born at Nupton Hill. There was Mabel Mary, the eldest; Arthur John (the same names as my father) next; Edwin James next; Robert Henry next; and me, Evan Abraham, the baby of the family—about eighteen months between each. . . . At Wormsley, Squire Knight had a big rabbit warren, where they bred hundreds of rabbits, an enclosure of about eighty acres of derelict land—rocks and trees, too uneven for cultivation—with a wire fence all the way round; once they killed over a thousand rabbits to ten guns in one day. Well, the poachers went there one night, just before a big rabbit shoot, and run nets in the warren. Twelve o'clock right up on the boundary—it happened to be on Nupton Hill where he went to farm when he retired keepering—Father heard a rattle at one of the gates. He went to investigate and he woke up in a ditch next morning with his jaw out of joint and broken ribs. A cowman found him. What had happened was one of the poachers gave his big St Bernard puppy a clout and it limped home to The Pool House and my mother thought, 'Oh, my husband is in trouble up the rabbit warren!' and ran about a mile and a half and contacted the bailiff. It amounted to my father going in to Hereford General for seven months. The doctors gave him up, they sent him back home. Mother was giving him brandy, and any liquids she could make up, with a teaspoon. All of a sudden one day his jaw come natural and he said, 'Mother,' he said, 'give me a lump of bread and cheese!' and he ate the lump of bread and cheese and he recovered. Dr Hart-Smith of Leominster was amazed that Mother cured Father and saved his life.

The Christmas after—I've heard my father talk about it many a time—Tweed, the old keeper on the Foxley Estate adjoining Wormsley, came to my father, he said, 'Do come up and give me a hand,' he said. 'I'll be bound to have the poachers.' Every Christmas Eve the poachers used to go on his estate and defy him to come out of his cottage. So Father went up after it got dark to the cottage just under Nash Wood—I know every inch of it there—and they had a glass of whisky. Bang, bang, bang! 'They've come!' Tweed said, and opened the latch of the door. Someone shouted out in his garden, 'Don't come out! We'll shoot you!' So he banged the door shut and as he banged it two charges from a twelve-bore gun come against the door, and the lead is in that woodwork today; you could cut the bits of lead out with a knife though it's been painted a dozen times since then, and that's over eighty years ago; you can see the little rises of the lead where the paint goes

18

over them. That was the poachers in those days. They'd have
their haul of birds and away they'd go in their ponies-and-traps.
Now they come with a pick-up or a lorry where you're rearing
game. And they still defy you to go out of your house! They
watch you, and God help you if you go out. They'd kill you.
We had a keeper round here shot dead the year before last.
They couldn't care two hoots. They come with shot guns,
revolvers, truncheons, any weapon they can get hold of. This
Christmas they've been coming for game in gangs of ten and
twelve . . . And it's the same with these big turkey-factory
places—*they've* had raids on their turkey houses and all.
They take turkeys by the score, couldn't care less! Here only
three months ago—on a farm not far away—two bullocks were
killed, eleven hundredweight each, their heads and their skins
and their bowels left on the field and their carcasses gone—
live animals at midnight! And sheep! Twenty at a time they'll
take. What can you do? It's getting unbearable. That's what's
happening now, these days, this present moment!

I'm thankful to my father for one thing in particular—
during my childhood he taught me how to work. *All* his
children had to work. We'd to work while we was going to school
and in the holidays—no, Robert didn't live with us at Nupton
Hill so he only helped us in the holidays. Mother was poorly
when he was small and he was fostered by people the name of
Warrington in Hereford, a retired policeman and his wife.
He went to the Blue Coat School, Hereford, and the
Warringtons used to bring him out and he used to stay with us
for however long the holidays were in the country. How we
prepared for when he came! It was marvellous. We tried to
assist him in every way. He was a town boy, you see, so we
made everything as easy as we possibly could. I tell you, we had
a lot of explaining to do. He'd hardly seen flocks of sheep, or
big flocks of poultry like my mother's. It's amazing! First of all
we had to entice him to come for walks—he wasn't used to
going through woodland and meadows. We had to watch as he
didn't get in danger, fall down steep gulleys and holes, when

he was going about the woods. 'Now be careful, Bob! Don't go and step down there or else you'll get strangled!' And of course we always let him have the best so as to make him know it was his home, his real home. If we had anything shared given us we always seen that he had his helping first. Perhaps it was a basket of plums come off the tree—'Come on, Bob! Pick the nice one! It's good!' I don't know, I've noticed it in my life that townspeople seem to be a bit more greedier than we are in the country. He'd always put two or three of the ripe gooseberries or anything like that in his pocket and have another in his hand. He never seemed satisfied. As I look at it there was no big gardens or orchards for them in the town. Us boys in the country, if somebody had an orchard and they had a decent tree of apples, well, on the way home from school, over the hedge we'd be and lift one or two up the trunk, and up they'd go and give the bough a shake and we'd all help ourselves with apples off the floor and put them in our school-bags. And sometimes the old farmer'd shout, 'Hey! Come on! I'll get the bobby here for you!' and away we'd go helter-skelter. Now a townsboy would know nothing at all about that, you see, or a tree of plums. Rows of plums we used to have from the orchards around here, lovely great big egg-plums. One large plum would be nearly half a pound. Well, you had a meal if you ate one of those.

My father rented Nupton Hill Farm for very little rent from a very nice gentleman called Mr Careless. It was very, very rough, nearly all woodland, on a hill eight hundred somewhat feet above sea level with a big six-roomed stone house at the top. There was a nice little ash-bed, of clean ash poles grown very closely together, and my father was a wonderful axeman. I remember us boys tushing poles right down over the hill to the bottom for the hopgrowers to come for them with a big trailer and traction-engine all the way from Bromyard. One load would be two thousand poles. We tushed them down in bundles, three or four at a time with a bag on our shoulders to stop them rubbing; our little shoulders was sore. Then we had five acres of spring oats which we used to harvest for the cattle for feed for the winter—all by hand, no machinery. That's why I'm such a good scythesman.

There was always *something* for me to do. Mother baked bread for the whole family on a Saturday about once every three weeks so I had to collect as much wood for her as I could in about two foot lengths. I used to love making a roaring fire. On the Saturday morning we'd open the old baking oven, ram in the wood, ram in the Hereford Times underneath it, light it, and away it would go and, when we'd got a lovely heat there and all the cinders were down on the bottom of the oven, we levelled them out so as to heat all the brickwork. Mother many a time had to put a cloth on the big iron handle of the door because it was too hot for her to hold. Then I had to get what we called a 'hoe', a scraper with a long handle to it, and I reached to the back of the oven and raked the cinders into a shovel when they had only just gone a dull black and the heat was all in the brickwork, and I brushed out the bit of ash left with a damp brush because otherwise the brush would go on fire. Then we used to put the tins with the loaves of bread in the back of the oven with a long flat piece of board on a six foot long handle—what we termed as a 'peel'. I used to love sliding the tins in to the back of the oven, putting them in rows; and when they was all in, cakes and all, Mother used to close the door up and time them—she was always worrying about the clock and looking at it on the mantelshelf to see she hadn't made a mistake; she was a real professional. At last, out would come these lovely crusty loaves with a large bottom and a small top.

She also made skimmed milk cheese, fresh milk cheese, sage cheese, all in little vats. She had a cheese press in the dairy, a big room at the back of the house with a sloping roof. There were muslin cloths over each vat and each vat was perforated with little holes. Mother had her milk in a two gallon bucket and put in a small teaspoonful of rennet and rolled up her blouse sleeve and put her arm in and stirred it all up and it

21

would all turn to what we termed as 'whey'. Then she'd pour the whey into six vats and place them inside one another and there was a big iron press that came down on top and you had to screw it down a little at a time—many a time I've gone in the dairy and screwed it down, and all the juice run out into a tub and was given to the pigs with some meal in and they did well on it to make our little porkers to go to market. When Mother took the vats out of the press she used to rub the skins of the cheeses—six different sizes—with salt and when they dried she used to stack them in a little spare hat-room and I've seen that little hat-room in one winter as full as you couldn't open the door to go in! People used to come from as far afield as Wales and London for Mother's cheeses. For her sage cheeses she used to get the sage in the summer when it was in full green and hang it up in the attic for it to dry and she'd powder it and put it through a sieve and then when she'd be mixing the whey she'd add in so many ounces and stir it all up thoroughly and it gave a kind of blue vein all the way through the cheese and people loved it.

Many a time when Mother's bread was just cooling off and was lovely and soft, I'd pull off the top of one of her loaves and go into the dairy and cut a V-piece out of a cheese before it dried and I'd go with a pint mug straight into the cellar where we made our cider and then sit out in the woodyard on a log and eat and drink my fill. I drank our home-made cider from the age of nine years old!

We'd about seven acres of apple trees, and Father used to sell about three hogsheads a year—about a hundred and fifty gallons—to a big cider merchant in Canon Pyon village who then sent it all up to London after it was bottled, and took first prize with it! My father didn't mind in the least as long as he was given the cash he asked for. Those hogsheads that he sold paid the rent of Nupton Hill Farm so you can guess we had to work like niggers to get the cider made. We used Fox-whelp apples. They make a lovely cider. We shook them and put them in bags or put them in a big heap and covered them over until cider-making in the autumn—never before October and the apples was going soft. We had a big troughing made like a roundabout with a huge great stone in—we called it the 'mill'. Us boys, we had to have towels to wipe ourselves down after shoving this stone, about two ton. It went round and round, and to keep the musk in when we were grinding we had a little kind of wooden oar so as to keep rowing it down in this trench for the stone to crush it till it was all sloppy. Then Father had twelve what they called 'hairs' like four-bushel sacks split in half and opened out. These hairs were put with musk in in a frame and folded over, like you was building up cheeses, and pressed—Follow me? All right, sir?—and the cider· run out of the framework through a spout into a tub below, and you carried your cider to a barrel and poured it in through a tun-pail. You always carried cider in a wooden bucket and the tun-pail was wooden and the barrel was wooden—otherwise you'd turn the cider black. Then you'd throw the dry musk out to the poultry and the wild pheasants in the coverts—they loved the white kernels of the apples—and you'd wash the hairs and put them away for next year.

Apart from the cider-pressing, the baking, the cheese-making, the pole-tushing, we helped with the pig-killing. We always used to kill two sixteen-score pigs and sell them to cover the expense of the feed of the pigs we kept to sell alive. Another job of mine was to go to the special sitting house for my mother and lift off all the hens. She'd have eight or nine in a row sitting on ten or twelve eggs each. Twenty-one days it takes for chicks to hatch. Mother always liked to get the hens to hatch over a week-end in term-time if she could so that us boys was at home to carry the hens and take the chicks to the little coop and the little run out on the meadow right in front of the house. From the time I was nine or ten, if Mother was dressing young poultry, I used to drive her to town on a Saturday in a little pony and trap—we called the pony Dotsy; a stiff little cob she was—and, do you know what Mother got for her chickens? One and ten-pence or two shillings each at the outside! And eggs then was thirty a shilling! She sold chickens, eggs, butter, but she never took the cheese to market; she had too many customers at home for it. We also sold about ten ton of King Edward potatoes to the baker to put them in the flour for the bread—he's still alive to tell the tale now—so I was helping planting them, and digging them, sorting them, bagging them and storing the seed. Then there was swede-pulling, lambing, planting the peas . . . You took everything in its season. This had to be done; that had to be done. It all took time. Never an idle moment.

I didn't have much life outside school and the farm, though I took part in the little sports which were free for anybody in each village. I did well in the hundred yards—*and* in the mile after I was twelve; my time was four minutes and thirty-eight seconds for the mile. And I could jump to my chin—a side-jump; I always ran at a gate sideways, not straight at it, because my legs got in the way for the simple reason I'm a little knock-kneed; and I can't straighten my arms either.

There was always sports in Canon Pyon on the afternoon of the Club Walk—racing, jumping, skittles, egg and spoon race, sack race, obstacle race, musical chairs. Anyone could sign on for those but the club was for elderly men. My father joined it—it was called 'The Oddfellows' Club'—and on a Sunday in the spring of the year, about May, they had a 'benefit' and they'd call it a Club Walk. The Oddfellows, they all went to church behind a big band from Hereford, starting at the public house about ten o'clock. It was beautiful. Arthur, Edwin and me and my sister, we used to go down two of our meadows and we could see Canon Pyon Church and the road all the way down and we used to watch the band—bang bang bang, bang bang bang bang bang bang, the music playing; the sound nearly always came up on the wind. It was a real musical Sunday for us to see the Oddfellows marching to church. When they come out of church they'd march all the way down to a big marquee pitched with tables and forms to sit on, and they had a big spread of a dinner.

Books never interested me. I could never follow sentences, I

24

don't know why. I'd stop where I shouldn't have stopped, where there wasn't a comma or anything, if you follow me, and, after I'd read it, I wouldn't know what a sentence was about because I'd stopped in the wrong place. Now today I can pick up the Hereford Times and I can understand it line for line.

From the age of about seven I went to Brinsop School, three and a half miles from home. My brothers and my sister—not Bob, of course—all went to the same school. That was seven miles a day we'd to walk for a start, sometimes picking our way from those tall trees on top of yon Nupton Hill down through the Brinsop Estate and back again through snow up to our knees. I was always tired! The school's been closed years now. There's another school at Credenhill and they're talking about closing that one. What's happening today, you see, because of the declining population, a bus comes all the way from Weobley at eight o'clock in the morning collecting the children, drops them at the one school and half past three takes them back home again. We used to wear clogs made of alder in the winter-time—snow sticks to leather but never to a board. When there was no snow you could hear the rattle of a little boy coming down the road a hundred yards or more away—clinkety-plonk plonk-plonk-plonk. I didn't care a lot about school so when I was between ten and eleven my mother bought me a little pony to encourage me to go, and I used to ride it to a little small-holding by the school—the Glebe House farm buildings— and put it in the stables. It didn't take me above ten minutes or a quarter of an hour to trot there. After school I used to bring the pony out and the children would crowd round me. One would say, 'Oh give me a ride, Master Rogers!' They called me 'Master' because I owned a pony! Sometimes I brought two home at a time, one in between my legs and the other holding my waist from behind. I used to trot up the road and go across the meadows to their houses and then scoot across and up through the woods to Nupton Hill Farm. Oh I had a bit of fun while I had the pony! Before then, I was very lonely, you see, when I was the only one of the family left going back

25

home through the woods of a night. The pony made all that much difference. She used to follow her track and I was home in no time. There was one little occasion when I was on my own and before I had the pony. We had an old English sheep dog, a great big strong old dog. You've seen the dog I mean—their hair comes all down over their eyes and blinds their sight; grey-haired dogs they are, very good sheep dogs, very good cattle dogs and lovely companions. Well, that dog when I was at home and not at school, he never left me and, when I was coming back from school one afternoon, I heard a dog going uh uh uh uh, wincing through its nose, at the top of one wood where there was a little gate going through onto our first meadow. I looked through the gate, and there was the old dog with half his kennel and his chain and collar and all on! He'd come across two meadows to greet me with half his kennel stapled to his chain! He was that strong—I was quite ten years of age—that I was able to use the boards as a kind of sledge. He dug his clees in and tushed me home along the ground.

Mrs Jones, the headmistress of Brinsop School, was what you'd term as an ordinary farmer's wife. She always looked spick and span and more or less like a dairy-maid; her husband had a farm in Mansell Lacy—called 'Nancy Lacy' by the Americans in the last war. There was about thirty-eight of us, all in one room, bar the little toddlers—they used to go into a little lean-to with the under-teacher to be taught. Mrs Jones taught the rest of us arithmetic, writing, everything, till we were twelve years old. We was all in classes—Two, Three and Four, and the highest class was Number Five, I think. There was the top class in one part of the room, the next class in another part of the room—not divided off at all—with about twelve or four-teen big desks with pens in little grooves and inkwells. Mrs Jones, she used to come along from one pupil to the other and see how we was getting on, or she could watch every pupil while she sat by the harmonium by the big fire we had in winter-time.

One winter, my father, he fell a big ash tree and after he fell it there was a hollow in the bottom, it was starting to go rotten in the heart. Us boys was down there with a hacker and little axes cutting off the boughs or anything that would make firing for the home, and there was a lovely little nest in this hollow and I pulled it out and I heard 'Teet! Teet! Teet!' 'Hello!' Father said. 'What have *you* got, Evan?' I said, 'I've got a little mouse.' 'It's a *dor*mouse, boy!' he said. 'Take it up home! Put it in a box!' Which I did. I put this dormouse in a wooden box with a little bit of wire netting in front. Oh I had him quite twelve months. Went to school one day—two days before we was breaking up for Christmas—and somebody brought a little kitten. 'We'll have a lesson over that,' said Mrs Jones. 'Anybody else got any pets?' Evan put his hand up, I said, 'I've got a little dormouse at home.' 'Have you really?!' she said. 'Bring it to school! I'd *love* to see it!' I said, 'Very good, Mam.' So next day I puts this dormouse (hibernating in its nest) in a cardboard Quaker Oats box and carried him gently off to school; 'Here you are, Mrs Jones!' and she put the box on the shelf over the fire before she played the morning carols. Come about eleven o'clock—we'd all been out to play—she said, 'Now then, we'll have the dormouse.' She took down the box and she looked at me and she said, 'Evan,' she said, 'there's only the nest left in the box!' she said. 'The mouse is gone!' I said, 'Well, it was there when you put it on the shelf, Mam.' She said, 'Was this hole in his box when you brought him here?' I said, 'No,' I said. 'He must have thought it was summer with the heat of the fire and woken up. Where can he be?' We turned that school upside-down and, as we was breaking up for the Christmas holidays that evening, I had to come home without my dormouse. Went back to school at the start of the next term. 'Morning, children!' 'Morning, Mam!' 'Join round the fire and we'll have the first hymn!' I'll always remember it. We got all the hymn books and passed them round, and Mrs Jones started to play. 'What's up with the thing?!' she said and she was working the pedals and rattling away with her fingers on the keys and she couldn't get a sound out of the harmonium. Then her

27

eldest son, Oliver, he said, 'Mother!' he said. 'There's no baize on the back of the organ!' Would you believe it?!—that mouse had gathered every thread and packed it underneath the keys! When we took away a piece of the woodwork, there was my little dormouse rolled up in a ball of green baize!

As I've said, I didn't care a lot about going to school so, when my brothers and my sister left and I was the last one going, I often used to dodge it and stop in the woods. But where I got beat, I hadn't got a watch and I didn't know what time to go back home! Oh I loved the woods! Edwin dodged with me before he left. Edwin and me was inseparable. What I had, he had. We was a happy pair of boys. Arthur, Bob and Mabel always seemed distant from me, being as I was the baby, I suppose. Unfortunately he had epileptic fits and you could pick him out of a thousand in appearance because the centre finger on his right hand had a lovely parrot's beak on after an accident with the dairy-door latch. He left me a silver watch when he died about ten year ago in an Old People's Home in Ross. His wife was already dead but they were parted and they'd no children.

We was always with the North Hereford hounds when they come fox-hunting in our district. The hunting people would send a card to my father to stop all the fox-earths, to stop the foxes going to ground so as the hounds would keep running. Well, when we understood the game, me and Edwin, we used to have a bit of fun. We used to go in the stable on a hunting day, get a couple of chains and when we'd hear the hounds coming— we generally knew which way the fox would run; it all depended on the wind—we'd hide somewhere near a gate. And here would come the hounds and perhaps we'd see the fox, and we'd shout 'Tally ho!' and of course the man in the red coat would come full gallop. 'Which way have they gone, Tommy?!' 'Straight on! Straight on, sir!' So whenever he'd gone through the gate and the hounds perhaps would be a hundred yards up in the wood above him, we'd swing the chains round the gate post and the head of the gate and fasten them in a knot. Up would come the followers on their horses and they'd say, 'Where have they gone, Tommy?!' and we'd say, 'Straight over here into Southhall's Rough, sir! Hold on a minute, sir!' And there was my brother, he'd get his cap off and hold it out, and I'd be struggling with the chains and undo them. 'Thank you, Tommy!' Shilling off one, sixpence off the other! We had shillings and shillings off them! That's how we made some money in the wintertime, and we valued what we bought with that money because our parents never gave us a penny.

The vicar of Brinsop used to come down to the school to sign the Register about once a month. He came to school one morning and he said to Mrs Jones, he said, 'I want a word with the old keeper's sons that live over the way,' he said, 'up Canon Pyon.' He said, 'You've got three of his boys coming to school, haven't you?' So Arthur went out of the class and talked to the vicar and the vicar said, 'Do you think,' he said, 'your father could get me a fox?' he said. 'I want to get a fox skin for my wife to make her a fur of.' 'Yes, I'll get you a fox,' my brother said. So Arthur, Edwin, and me, we caught this fox in a trap and carted it unskinned to the vicarage about two hundred yards up from the school, early in the morning so as to get to school on time. We carted it in a big cumbersome market basket about two foot square. The vicar come down in the lunch hour and thanked us very much for taking the fox, how much was it?, and I think he gave Arthur ten shillings. Arthur had this money and at the end of the school day he said to Edwin, 'Here you are,' he said. 'You carry the basket across this meadow,' he said, 'and Evan will carry it across the other meadow, and then we'll all carry it down the road and then when we start to go up the hill we'll take it in turns.' Arthur was very domineering. My brother Edwin, of course, obeyed him. When it come to me, 'Here you are!' said Arthur. 'Your turn to take the basket!' He pushed it to me. I said, 'Carry it yourself!' He said, 'Come on! Do as you're told!' I closed my fist and I knocked him out for six. Me and Arthur could never get on. Because he was the eldest and strongest of us and although Father was so hard on him, Arthur was the apple of his eye. He was blinded in one of his own after he left school, when he was about fifteen, I think. Until the war Mother had a servant girl, Edith Bethel, to help her with the work in the farm house and one day this servant girl went out with Arthur picking sloes to make sloe gin. She was holding the end of a bough down to pick the sloes off and drop them in a bucket when she accidentally let it go and it went up—swish!—and it hit my brother in the face. Now the boughs of a blackthorn have very nasty spikes to them, very sharp needles like gorse more or less, and one went right in the ball of his eye and blinded it. Arthur married four times. He died five years ago. His son and his daughter both died before him of T.B.

Talking about blindness, mother's sister, Aunt Jemima, she went completely blind in about 1938. After Mother got married, Auntie lived on her own for a while at Dinas Powis and then she come to live with us at Nupton Hill. She was about five foot ten, rather thick built—she wasn't no little dwarf, I tell you! Sometimes when we came back from school, she and Mother, they'd be sat down in the kitchen talking and, whenever we entered the room, if they was in the middle of a sentence and it was something secret they didn't want us to know, they rattled off in Welsh and of course we was diddled. Auntie paid about ten shillings a week for her keep and helped Mother with the washing of the clothes and mending the socks. They got on lovely together, the two sisters. She taught me 'The Farmer's Boy':

> The sun went down beyond yon hills
> Across yon dreary moor
> When, weary and lame, a boy there came
> Up to a farmer's door.
> He asked if he could be employed
> To plough and sow, to reap and mow
> And to be a farmer's boy. . . .

And she told me the story of a gentleman whose gardener died in the spring of the year. He put an advert for a new one in the paper and after a week or two a gardener turned up to apply for the job. The gentleman said, 'There's cabbages there,' he said. 'My old gardener before he died,' he said, 'he got the ground ready,' he said, 'so all you've got to do is plant them fifteen inches apart,' he said. 'But I want you to plant them leaves down in the holes,' he said, 'and the roots up in the air.' So the poor gardener pulled some new plants and started to plant them the right way. 'That's enough, my man!' said the gentleman. 'I like a man that'll do what he's told, and you're doing the reverse to what I've told you!' So that man had to go. A second one come and he done likewise so of course *he* had to go too. But there was an old tramp come looking for a job one day. The gentleman said, 'Can you do gardening?' 'Oh yes!' he said. 'I can do it!' 'Well, there's cabbages there,' the gentleman said. 'Where that line is down now,' he said, 'I want you to put the cabbages fifteen inches apart,' he said, 'and the leaves down in the holes and the roots up.' So this old tramp, he made his first hole and he started to ram the leaves down in the hole. 'Ah!' said the gentleman. 'You're the man I've been looking for!' he said. 'You're doing what you're told! Now turn that cabbage round,' he said, 'and plant it the right way!' And that tramp was with him for years and, when he got too old to work, he was given a cottage and a pound a week for the rest of his life.

That's one thing *I*'ve nearly always done in life: I've done what my masters told me—though I've expected them to take the responsibility.

Two

Going to and from school through the Brinsop Court Estate all through my schooldays, I got to know the two keepers there —Jim Lapage and George Bromage. Not only did they know *me* well, they knew Father well, too, because he used to buy rabbits on the estate and sell them to a Mrs Carter of Eign Street, Hereford—one and eight a couple—and very often they used to call at the farm and have a glass of cider and a chat with him.

Brinsop Court was owned by Mr Dearman Edwards. Though the surrounding land was about a thousand acres—six hundred of farmland and four hundred of woodland, much as it is today—it was only a small residence then with no more than about eight bedrooms. These two keepers, they was two even keepers—what I mean is, they wasn't one above the other; they worked together. They was employed by Sir Charles Pulley of Lower Eaton who had the shooting. Bromage—a small, stout, fat-faced man with a moustache—he looked after the one beat up near our home : Red Bar Wood, Vallet's Wood, Round Oak Wood, Badnage Wood. Lapage—a clean-shaven, thin, tall man, a six-foot two-er—he looked after the two woods, Merryhill and one-third of Credenhill Park called Sally Coppice.

Well, soon after I left school—and I was very happy to leave school—I started with these two keepers at two shillings a week. That was in 1909 when I was twelve years old. I've worked on the Brinsop Estate ever since.

It was February, just after the shooting season, and my first job was to help the keepers put down pheasant-catchers in the woods—a pheasant-catcher is a little cage with a tube a hen pheasant creeps in through—and take the hen pheasants as we caught to a big laying-pen built on top of Merryhill, a hundred yards long and fifty yards wide. There was little conifers planted in it for the hen pheasants to run under in case of alarm, and before we released them in this pen we brailed them on one wing so they couldn't fly away. To make them produce more eggs we fed them on Eggfo, a meal from Spratts Patents Limited, which we mixed with mash. Each day I'd to carry buckets of water up to them from a spring at the bottom of the hill, and examine the wire netting to see that no foxes or dogs had been scratching. The netting was ten foot high but the pen was never covered at the top so as the cocks could fly in and do their mating. When we had sufficient eggs we took the wing brails off, opened the gates and let the hens out and they laid a second time for us in the wild.

In one of the sheds at the Court we kept shallow egg-trays of sawdust out of the way of the frost. When the birds started to lay I'd to go up to the pen every afternoon with a basket and collect the eggs and take them down very gently to this shed and put them on the sawdust in rows. The shed was always kept locked. Lapage had one key and I had the other; no one else was allowed in. I'd to spend about an hour and a half a day then, reversing every egg to keep them fertile, to keep the yolks on the move.

Lapage lodged in Park Cottage down below Merryhill and opposite the second drive, the drive running through Brinsop Park. I myself was to live there later. Well, at the top of the garden of Park Cottage, in the hatching pen, there were rows and rows of sitting boxes and I had to put earth in the bottom of each and a nice little bit of hay and then dummy pheasant eggs to keep the farmyard hens sitting till you put the real pheasant eggs under them to hatch in April (it takes the eggs twenty-four days to hatch). I'd to go round at night with a pony and float to everybody that'd got fowls and borrow all their

33

broody hens. I've brought as many as twenty back in one night. You can put up to twenty-two eggs under a big hen. A bantam isn't large enough to cover more than ten; she's better for little partridge eggs. But she's the better mother : she isn't so clumsy : she doesn't crush the chicks ! Many a morning I've found about three dead pheasant chicks under a big hen; she's put her foot down and she hasn't heard them cry and she's squashed the life out of them. You tethered the hens to a peg to feed them four at a time and you had to see as they did all their droppings before they went back to their nests. If they didn't, they'd make a mess over the eggs and spoil a clutch; they'd rise their bodies up because there was too much mess and that would cause the eggs to cool.

Whenever a chick is hatched, his head is always at the large end of the egg, and in the top of this end there's an air bladder that won't let the white nor the yoke go up near the top of the shell—that's where the chick gets his first breath of air before he can peck the crown off and wriggle himself out. . . . Anyway, when the hatching started we'd transport the chicks to coops in a meadow under the wood—one coop every twenty-five or thirty yards in rows—dozens and dozens of coops, each with about twelve pheasant chicks to a hen. The three of us, Lapage, Bromage and me, we'd take it in turns to watch them day and night. We'd a cabin to sleep in in the shadiest corner of the meadow in case it was windy. It would take you about an hour and a half at night closing in the chicks, walking from one coop to the other, putting up the shutters to stop the dogs or foxes turning them over. You had the coops out on that meadow for six weeks, from about the first week in May till the second week in June, then you carried them on stretchers when they were poults—a six week old chick is called a 'poult'—into a ride of the wood and after they'd been in there about a fortnight they'd start to leave the old hens and go up into the coverts to roost. This is the critical time of rearing pheasants. You have to see on a windy night that they don't get blown down off the branches or else along will come Mr Fox and he has a good cheap supper.

34

If they go on low branches, you just go along quietly before they get settled and shake them off and make them fly up higher.

As regards the feeding of the chicks, we had old fashioned boilers standing on the meadow and we cut wood to keep them going and trapped and shot and ferreted rabbits and boiled them. We bellied—or 'paunched'—the rabbits and skinned them and boiled them for an hour or more, and when the meat was cool we put it in a big wire-netting strainer and picked all the bones out and put it through a mincing machine like a mangle. We added meal to this sloppy meat as it come out of the mincer and crumbled it in our hands into our feeding baskets and the little chicks loved it, they used to grow like hop-bines on it.

We reared about seventeen hundred chicks a year in this way. To the best of my knowledge there's little open-air rearing in Herefordshire since the days of Lapage and Bromage. The chicks and the hens were at the mercy of the world; we'd put boughs over the coops for them to run under when there was danger, and the large ones with green leaves acted as a shade as well. Oh it was a healthy way of rearing game, better than them all being penned up! If you happened to be taken ill and missed a feed, there was a certain amount of insects for them to eat. You couldn't have it so much now because all the insect life is killed with chemical spraying. When the little wild ducks are hatched at the end of March, how many fly do you see hovering over the water on pools? None at all! Two thirds of the wild duck *always* die in Herefordshire because there's no insect life for them to live on. We had a helicopter here last week [week commencing 20th March, 1978] spreading the artificial fertilizer. Whizz wubble woo voo going back and forth way on top of you—it nearly hit the roof off. Oh it drives you up the wall—or it does *me*! The machinery, it's unbearable. And the chemicals are dropping in the air and blowing in the wind, going everywhere, over the hedges and woodland and all; you get them in your lungs. *We*'re in danger as well as the insects and the

35

wildlife. Years ago, there was a nightingale in Badnage Wood and many a night before I was first married I stopped out till twelve o'clock to hear that nightingale. He'd keep on whistling beautiful tunes, and I sat on the roadside and listened to him for over an hour at a time. But the nightingales with a lot of other birds have disappeared out of the country through farmers using these chemicals. We've this nice little lake, Harlands Pool, in the valley in the centre of the estate. Many a time when I've had wild ducks hatching I've got a board—a door if I can get one—and put on some feed-bowls with duck meal in and tied a rope to it and sent it flying out into the middle to keep the ducks alive. God, there's many and many a thing a keeper can do if he's interested!

In the old days, rearing the pheasants in the open, there was the danger of vermin, but if you were a good keeper and knew how to kill, it was jam. Up in Merryhill Wood we even used to rear turkeys, one farmyard hen to a coop, same as for the pheasants. When they were little turkey chicks with all their feathers, they went to roost with the pheasants and you whistled them and fed them like the rest on wheat from the granary till the first of October. 'Turk turk turk turk'; 'gobble gobble gob gob gob, gobble gobble gob gob gob'—they would come running round you like it was a farmyard. Oh it was a pleasure!

Under Lapage and Bromage the rabbits was so numerous that they gave me a bundle of steel traps one day to go and trap a hedge above a field of corn. Round Oak Wood was only about a hundred yards away; the rabbits was coming out and they only had to cross one meadow and straight into the cornfield; they'd eat off about twenty yards a night just as if you'd cut it with a scissors. What they sent me to do was take five dozen of these traps and, every hole in the hedge where the rabbits was running through on the cornfield side, I put a trap in. They'd taught me how to put a little stick straight across the plate in the daytime for the simple reason that when the pheasant come down to feed on the young shoots of corn and they tread on the trap, if the trap springs, it catches the piece of wood and doesn't lame them or take their foot off. Now George Waith, the bailiff, had put a cart in the middle of this field after the corn was planted so that the stones could be picked off the surface of the ground, and as I was going home midday for dinner after setting these traps I saw the wife of one of the general workmen who lived in a double dwelling at the top of the Arbour putting stones in a bucket to fill the cart. She had a little toddler by the side of her and she was expecting a baby. Do you know how much she earned? One shilling when she filled that cart! Her husband's wages was about eleven shillings a week—there wasn't a man on the estate getting more than fourteen shillings a week and some had families of four and five and six. Not that you could buy less with eleven shilling than what you can buy with £6 today. Sugar was three halfpence a pound and one ounce of tobacco was threepence halfpenny . . . Anyway, that cart was one foot six down to the bed and about three foot six wide by four foot six long and when this woman filled it full, that was a ton of stones. It used to take her about five days to earn her one shilling.

Well, I goes up in the afternoon just before teatime to take all the little sticks off my traps to prepare the set for the rabbits to come down out of the wood whenever it got dark. When I got half way down the field, there was that dear little child belonging to the woman sat on the bank. I thought, 'Good God! She's never in one of my traps is she?' And she was! A stick was holding her four little fingers in the jaws of a trap, and they'd started to swell! I pressed the spring down and I caught hold of her little hand and I put it right full in my mouth. I nearly choked, but I kept it there and she gave a little smile and I thought, 'It's all right! Thank God for that!' She was only about two years old.

Meanwhile her mother was on picking stones. I'd seen her empty the bucket into the cart, throw down the bucket, come to a lower part of the hedge and go back afterwards to continue picking stones. She'd been that busy she hadn't spotted me or seen her little girl caught in the trap. I walked along the hedge.

The little toddler had one arm around my neck; I could feel her little hand gripping it—and not one whimper all through the ordeal. Suddenly I saw something light in a brown apron underneath the hedge. And now the woman stopped her work and come to meet me. She was that giddy and that weak I could hardly hear her voice. She'd had a little baby underneath the hedge, rolled it up in her apron and left it there out of the wind and gone on picking stones! It's a marvellous story. It's un-believable. It's never left my memory. I'm bound to tell it: an ordinary country lass about twenty-three years of age, a dear little soul picking stones and having a baby in the field and me catching her little child in a trap while I was under the two keepers. I carried the child down to her back door for her and she took her inside with the baby and she come out and she said, 'Thank you very much, young Rogers' and I didn't tell a soul.

In 1911 Dearman Edwards sold Brinsop to Sir Richard Sutton of Benham in Berkshire who gave it to his mother, Lady Sutton, and his step-father, Mr Hubert Delaval Astley, a retired vicar. They'd got one little girl, Miss Ruth Astley—now the Honourable Mrs Humphrey Wyndham—and one son, Philip Astley, only a few days younger than myself. Lapage and Bromage had to leave because they brought their own head keeper, Harry Darling, and his wife, from Benham with them—they lived in Ivy Cottage where I lives now. He was in his forties, a nice little fellow, only about four foot ten—small, but he knew his stuff. He had two children, a boy and a girl called Georgie and Monica. With the Astleys came Ben Thomas from Bristol as head gardener. He wasn't much older than myself but he was one of the best gardeners I've ever met in my life. He was a five foot ten-er and when it rained all his curly hair went down flat.

One afternoon in the spring of 1912, Major Thompson, Lady Sutton's steward, a big gentleman as had been in the Life Guards with her son, come up to Nupton Hill Farm and he said to my father, he said, 'The bailiff down at Brinsop Court,' he said, 'has told me that you've got some sons up here and we've work for them.' At the moment I was cleaning our pigsty for Father and I heard the conversation, so I jumps over the pigsty wall and I went out in front of this gentleman, I said, '*Could* you find me a job, sir?!' 'Just the sort of lad we want!' he said. 'When can I start?' I said. He said, 'You come down Monday. I'll pay you eight shillings a week.' So I went down on Monday by myself—Edwin would have been incapable because he was having his fits so regular, and Father wanted to keep Arthur because he was the strongest and doing most of the farmwork. This Major Thompson, he put me on to dig his garden down here at Oak Cottage where Mrs Henzell lives now, a vicar's daughter as is in retirement. Oak Cottage was rebuilt for him and his wife with all the spare oak beams after two wings was added to Brinsop Court. There was a new wing on the east side for the servants' quarters with bedrooms upstairs and, underneath, the Servants Hall, the store room, the telephone room, the big kitchen and the scullery. On the west side as faces the lawn and the Black Mountains they built a loggia; then there was another loggia up on top of this loggia in line with the bedrooms, a balcony with a framework in front to let in the sun in the month of June. They had tea up there; 'We'll have tea on the balcony today,' and the butler and the butler's boy and all the rest of it had to carry everything up there for them—you know, the eatables and the teapots. Not only that—they turned the old granary into a banqueting hall and one of the biggest rooms into a library, and they repaired the big very, very old-fashioned oak-studded hall door, and in the centre—Brinsop Court is a square surrounded by moats— they put rosebeds with slab stones all round them. There was more than three hundred men working on the Big House when the Astleys arrived—all from the villages around, bar the head men, the contractors, who came from Soho, London.

The new Oak Cottage had flush lavatories. Before that, the occupants used to do their business between two big beams over a brook. Anyway, when I'd dug the garden there for the steward—it took me about a month forking it and making it clean, ready for planting—Ben Thomas come and had a chat with me. 'You come and work for me,' he said. 'I won't give you any hard tasks till you get used to me and used to the place.' So I thanked him and was switched to being gardener under him, still at eight shillings a week.

Ben Thomas and his men had enclosed an old hopyard as a kitchen garden for the Big House. My first job was to pull up about three rows of kidney-bean sticks, take the bind off the sticks and tie them up, twenty-five in a bundle, and put them up on end in a big open shed so as to keep them in the dry, ready for next season. That pleased Ben Thomas awfully. Then after, when he started all his little seedlings, not a quarter of an inch high, in little boxes in the greenhouse, I'd to get my riddle and barrow and fresh boxes and, when it come a wet day, I'd to fill these boxes about three inches deep, putting layers of tiles for drainage in the bottoms and then a bit of sand, before pressing down my prepared soil. Then I planted each little plant about two inches apart till the box was filled, about five dozen little plants in one box, then put them in the cold frame. I had some eighty odd frames to fill and about six or eight boxes in each of pansies, violas, antirrhinums, asters, stocks, Brompton stocks, ten week stocks, nicotianas. Lady Sutton was very fond of nicotiana—the tobacco plant, with purple or white flowers. They're a lovely scented flower. Just as evening mist is falling, you walk by a patch of those! Oh, it's a magnificent smell to it; they'll beat all your little blue violets. I took many a leaf home and rolled it when it was dry and soaked it in rum to make it flavourable, and smoked it. Then I'd to cut the lobelias out of the boxes in tufts like little bunches of cress and plant it as edging round the borders of geraniums. Then in Autumn I was dividing all the big Michaelmas daisies that had been growing four or five years in big large clumps. I'd to get two forks and press them down in the crown heart—back to back the forks. You get the one handle of one fork against your chest, catch hold of the other handle with your two hands and pull the two together. With forks you break the roots apart, never cut them—you must never chop them through with a spade, otherwise the plant will die. Ben Thomas taught me everything like that. Then I'd be helping the grown-up gardeners to plant the potatoes and sprouts and broccoli. They had a special pruner to prune all the fruit trees . . . But I don't want to go through it all. Gardening is gardening and everything has its season, you're busy all the time round. It's like being a keeper; you're never short of work if you do your job properly. I'm pleased to say the gardening didn't last more than about one clear twelvemonth—I'd been used to living up in the woods. But I learned a lot.

There was a water plant, very much like a polyanthus, called a Primula Bulleyana. He come up with one spike and he'd go up about two foot six tall and every four inches he'd throw out a circle of flowers. We always planted him around the moats by the terraces. And the beauty of him was, when the sun was out, if you was on the other side of the moats, all these spikes stood up with their different colours, red, yellow, cream, and you could see their reflections in the water, you had a lovely double section of colour.

I remember Mr Astley, he made a nice grass walk. I was sent out on a meadow with a turfing iron and a long plank and a turf-cutter, and I cut about seven thousand turfs, three foot long by a foot wide, and peeled them off one inch thick, and we hauled them with carts and we made this walk right from the bottom of the big lawn right up to the kitchen garden. The walk was over a hundred yards long and four foot wide. We rolled it down and it all took root and it looked just lovely. And then we planted shrubs called the cotoneaster in groups of five all the way up with spaces between them, and then about two thousand bulbs of the giant daffodil. 'Come on, Evan!' said Ben Thomas in October. 'I want you to come and plant these!' I had a proper bulb iron with a treddle on it. Well, I had all this quantity of bulbs and I thought, 'Now I'm going to have a bit of fun!' So I looked for three good spaces and down those

41

three spaces—I shall never forget it—I marked out an H with holes in one space, and in the next space I made a D and in the next space I put an A. I popped along with my bag of bulbs and I put a couple of bulbs in each hole and I put the blocks back as soon as I could, and there was nothing said. The following spring when the bulbs come up and they all come in bloom, I'd got a lovely HDA—Hubert Delaval Astley—down the side of this walk. Do you know, I was told to go and dig them up straight away?! Mr Astley was horrified. I was fed up to my jaws.

I went down to work one morning shortly afterwards, and Ben Thomas was stood on his stool clipping a privet hedge near the cabin where we had our meals at a corner of the kitchen garden. It was three minutes past seven and I was supposed to be there at seven. So, as I went in through the gate, Ben Thomas said, and I realize now it was only jokingly, 'Don't start before you're ready!' I said, 'What did you say?!' He said, 'Don't start before you're ready!' I shouted to Jack Brooks—Jack Brooks was a gardener working down on the water gardens where we'd got water lilies in baskets on the pool by the outlet to the moat; he'd just hung up his frail of food in the cabin and caught hold of a wheelbarrow full of weeds to burn in the incinerators up the slope at the top of the kitchen garden—I said, 'Hey, Jack!' I said. 'What time is it?' He said, 'Four minutes past seven now, Evan.' I said, 'Thank you, Jack.' I went straight across to Major Thompson, the steward, and I said, 'Please let me have my cards!' 'What's the matter, Rogers?' 'I've been upset,' I said. 'Very much so, too.' I said, 'I was three minutes late—and don't forget I've got a mile and a half to walk,' I said, 'before I start work—and I was told not to start till I was ready!' 'Who by?' So Major Thompson went with me to Mr Astley who was going along the side of the moat to the aviary he'd built for foreign birds and he told him what Ben Thomas had said to me—not to start before I was ready. And I explained that what made it worse was, the night before, I'd left the garden at quarter to eleven because I was working the little fire engine so Mr Thomas could water the herbaceous borders, and for nothing extra in my wages, and when I got home my mother and father had gone to bed and I just had a cold snack, went to bed, got up, walked a mile and a half and was three minutes late, and to then get told not to work before I was ready . . . 'What would *you* have done?' I said. So Mr Astley said, 'My dear boy,' he said, 'what would you like to do if you don't want to stay in the gardens?' 'Well,' I said, 'my old Dad was a keeper,' I said, 'and I intend to be a keeper,' I said, 'and keepering I'm going to do. I must look out for a keeper's job, now,' I said. 'Oh!' he said. 'We're not going to lose you?! You're too important!' he said. 'You're the kind of young man we want on this place.' Along come Ben Thomas, the head gardener. 'You coming back Evan?' I said, 'Not on your life!' 'Are you willing to help on the farm in the summers?' asked Mr Astley. 'Maybe the keeper will have you for the rest of the year.' I said, 'Anything but in the gardens,' I said. 'I've done my duty while I was in the gardens and I've finished!' 'My dear boy, under the circumstances . . .' He turned round and said to the head gardener, he said, 'It was wrong of you, Ben, to speak to this laddie like that.' 'I'm sorry, sir.' 'Well, don't let it happen again.' Mr Astley was quite fifty-five to sixty when that happened. I dug his grave, dear old boy, when he died in 1925—*and* Lady Sutton's afterwards, *and* their son's.

So Mr Astley and Major Thompson wouldn't let me go, and I worked on the farm hay-making, scything gangways for the horses and binders, stooking sheaves and crop-hauling till October when I went up and saw the keeper, Harry Darling, who, as I've said, lived here at Ivy Cottage, this very cottage we're talking in today, and he took me on and had me as a part-time lodger for five shillings a week so as I could get away as much as possible from Father, and we went rabbit-catching mostly—trapping, snaring, long-netting, purse-netting with fer-rets—all through the winter. Only Harry used a gun—I wasn't yet old enough. We used the long nets at night. I've still got a couple of hundred-yard nets in the shed here that I used

43

in those early days, and they're still as sound as they were then because I've looked after them. You've a top line and a bottom line, and one of you runs him out where the rabbits run into the woods off your meadow while the other pegs him up, one peg every ten yards. The rabbits gets entangled in this net and you go along and kill them the humane way—just turn the nose up till the neck goes click. I've had to kill as many as eighty at a time in one net. Purse nets you use with ferrets at a warren. You put about five dozen nets down according to the size of the burrows—there might be ten holes to one and twenty to another. When the rabbit runs out of a hole he's caught in this little net about two foot by two. The ferret can get in and out through the meshes.

Every week we'd to take a dozen rabbits into the Big House for Lady Sutton because she was breeding and selling Pekinese spaniels and fed the little puppies on rabbit mixed with Nestlé's milk and honey. I'd to take these rabbits into the scullery and skin them. Then Mrs Cadman, the cook, she used to boil them, and the next day when they was all gone cold I'd to pick the bones out before she put them through the mincing machine. I wasn't allowed to have one skin. The kitchen maid, she had the perquisite. I thought it was very unfair. And the rest of the rabbits no longer went to my father like in the days of Dearman Edwards; they were sent direct to Hereford to Mrs Carter in hampers by the bailiff.

But I made some extra money in another way. I hired a float and charged a fruiterer a penny a pound for all the blackberries and apples and other fruit I collected round the cottages at his own quotations, and delivered them for him to Morton Station. Believe me or no, I was able to buy a little black-nosed heifer and a little shorthorn red heifer—both in calf—at £12 each (today a cow and a calf would make £180), and I also bought a colt for twenty-five guineas, and Mother said she'd look after them at Nupton Hill.

Harry Darling liked a pint. This one day just about a week before Christmas we finished early—about a quarter to one I expect it would be—at the end of Badnage Wood. There was an old farmer there—Matthews his name was—and he'd got three sons. They was three lads too!—Harry, Walter, always nicknamed 'Pie', and Jack. They made a nice lot of cider so the old keeper, he said to me, 'Come on Evin!'—he always called me Evin—'We'll go down and have a drink with this bread and cheese we've got in the ferret bag!' So out of the wood we goes, and down across the meadow to this farm at the end of our beat. We hadn't been there long, finished this lunch, when out comes the voices from their dinner of the three young men and we got chatting. 'Let's have a bit of shooting!' they said to old Harry Darling. 'All right,' he said. 'But what are we going to shoot *at*?!' One went into his mother's fowlhouse and collared the cockerel and we took him up to a meadow about fifty yards away just outside the cider house down the bottom of the lane and we pegged him out on the meadow with a piece of string round one leg, and the three young men and Harry Darling, they stood at the gate and started shooting blind-folded at this cockerel with an old muzzle-loader gun. One at a time they went on firing for about an hour, putting a shilling a go in my cap down by the gate post. I couldn't join in. Well, I was saving and I was only officially earning eight shillings a week. They'd be getting about sixteen or seventeen from their father and Harry Darling as head keeper was getting a pound. Well, out come old Mr Matthews and he said to me, 'Sonny,' he said, 'pop to The Bell,' he said, 'and get a bottle of whisky.' Whisky in those days was only 2/3d a bottle, a pint and a half. When I come back he poured this bottle of whisky in a gallon jar and filled it up with cider. 'Come and have a drop of my special!' —he was handing the glasses round. One or two strangers had appeared; there were six or seven of us. Oh we were having a time of it!

It was getting on, starting to get dull. Still they were firing at this cockerel and still they were missing. 'Well, Evin,' said Harry Darling, 'we'll have to go.' 'What about Evan having a shot?' someone said. 'He can load for himself.' Another

45

round of drinks. Then I overheard: 'No need for him to be blindfolded. We'll draw the wad and the shot when we're pretending to check the gun for him.' So I went and loaded the gun for myself while they was drinking. I put in some more powder, then I put in a wad and rammed it down, put in a measurement of shot, put in a wad, rammed it down, put in more shot, then another wad—right, the gun was ready for firing! They pretended to check the gun. 'Go on! Let him have a shot not blindfolded!' They didn't know I was one up on them with the extra wad and the extra shot. I said, 'Right!' Up there! Bang! The old cock dropped dead and I fell on my cap of money and I had four pound seventeen in shillings!

That was Christmas 1913. In 1914, when I was turned seventeen and all keepering was stopped in the country and Harry Darling was put delivering milk for a dairy because he was over military age, I said I was eighteen and joined the army. But before I went I set a trap quite a mile away from Nupton Hill Farm at the bottom of a birch wood what we called The Birches where something had been running through a bit of a channel and some stones. Well, I caught a polecat, that's an animal three times as large as a polecat ferret, the size of a full-grown kitten, with a black and grey face and a big black moustache; a very powerful and vicious animal with a black body and very strong hairs and very large glassy eyes like an owl's, that lives on young rabbits, pheasant chicks and all young birds—you don't want many of those to devour all you've got on an estate . . . But let me tell you the tale. I caught this animal by the middle clee of his five toes and I put on a glove to handle him and pull him out of the trap. I didn't kill him. I cut the middle clee off with my knife and I took him home and it healed up lovely. I put him in one of our spare ferret boxes, a box three foot by two and two foot high with wire netting and a little door, very strongly made with inch boarding all round at the bottom. I had it several months before I went in the army, and my brother, Edwin, said he'd look after him and give him bread and milk while I was away. There was no question of

46

him joining up because he was having those fits. Any little row with my father and off he'd go—I'd to help my mother to hold him down in bed with a blanket, she the one side and me the other. Well, when I went into the army, I heard from Edwin about three days before we was noted to go abroad that the polecat had eaten a hole in the ferret hutch and got away. I thought, 'That's the end of the polecat.' Do you know, at the end of the war—and it was over three years since I'd caught that polecat—I come back home and I set a trap in the very same ditch in The Birches and I caught the very same animal with the missing middle toe?! But this time I destroyed him because I reckoned he was now too old to keep and after taking him up to the house to show my parents and my brother Edwin, I threw him in the bushes.

Three

My brother, Arthur, had left home to be under-keeper at Wormsley Grange, and when the war started he couldn't go to fight because of his bad eye so he'd to work in the coal washeries in South Wales—at the Six Bells Pit, Abertillery. My brother, Bob, though, he had gone to the Dardanelles with the 1st Herefords. I thought, 'If Bob can do it, *I* can!' I went in to the Recruitment Office in Hereford and I signed on. They said, 'Age?' I told them 'Eighteen' and they took me. I was in the 3rds.

First I did my six weeks training on the Castle Green, Hereford, out on parade, learning to right turn, left turn, form fours —before ever we had a rifle put in our hands we had to use our feet and our heads to learn how to take a sergeant's instructions. I've seen the old sergeant tie many a red handkerchief on a chappie's arm to teach him which was his right arm and which was his left. I've seen fights over it. There was some men said, 'You dare touch my arm and I'll give you one of the best!' and the sergeant's had to withdraw putting on the handkerchief. Oh there was some fun, I tell you! I found out I'd one of the largest heads in the Herefordshire Regiment. They'd to send away to have a special hat made for me. But I wasn't going out there capless meanwhile on parade of a morning so as to look conspicuous in amongst my mates—I wore my civilian cap, and I wore it so often that I was finally rushed to the guardroom for about a fortnight for being improperly dressed.

Well, my hat come through, and we was transferred afterwards to Park Hall Camp, Oswestry. There was two railway stations there, Gabowen Station and Wittington Station, little side-line railway stations, one a mile from one side of the camp and the other a mile from the other side of the camp. You could catch a train from either and change at Shrewsbury for Hereford for your week-end leave. At Park Hall Camp we started stabbing sacks of sawdust for bayonet practice and jumping trenches for physical drill. We were there nearly six months when a message came through from the War Office to the old colonel in charge—the big noise, Colonel Symonds-Tayler—that the Lancashire Fusiliers had been blown to pieces out in Salonica. The whole battalion was out on parade and the old colonel had a big loudspeaker, he said, 'Boys,' he said, 'there's been a big calamity in Salonica. I wants one hundred of you young men that are nicely trained,' he said, 'to come forward and offer your services to go out to Salonica.' I was that cheesed off with the camp duties—emptying urinal buckets, cleaning the lavatories and, when I was orderly-man, getting the big tray of coffee and biscuits for those from my hut on night patrol—I was one of the first out in front of the colonel, and I could bring you ten witnesses to prove it. I thought, 'Get out of this, anyway! It can't be any worse!' There was about eighty volunteers, and we was told we'd be transferred in Salonica from the 3rd Herefords to the 12th Lancashire Fusiliers, the 22nd Volunteers Division. We'd had mock battles—they'd sent out a company on this hill and a company on the other; you couldn't see where you was going nor what you was doing and half of us would get lost; it was more or less what I termed 'exercising' us. But there was nobody as had been out abroad to see what we was going to see; we had no idea of what it would be like when we got to Salonica.

We went out on The Ballarat from Devonport. There was other contingents—so many from the Gloucesters, so many from the London Regiment, making up two thousand. I couldn't tell you which way we went—I tell you for why: all round the ship they had screens and we was travelling in darkness though on board the lights was on day and night. The first night, I was picked to go on guard up in a gangway of the upper deck. I don't know why I was on guard, I'm sure, unless there was going to be some squirmishes [sic] on board the ship, but, anyway, about twelve o'clock at night, here comes the old sergeant, he says, 'All clear?' 'Yes, sergeant. All clear!' I said, 'Sergeant, do you mind?' I said. 'One of the crew,' I said, 'told me to go in for a cup of coffee.' 'Did he?' he said. He said, 'Don't you leave this stand here!' he said. 'If I get you off duty,' he said, 'I'll have you up before the beak in the morning!' 'Oh!' I said. 'All right. Fair enough.' With that, this old boy, one of the crew of the ship, *he* come. 'Hello, sergeant!' he said. 'We wants this laddie,' he said, 'in the baking department. Can I have him?' So I seen the sergeant wink at him, as if to say, 'Yes, you can!' and the old boy said, 'Come on in, sergeant!' he said, and he gave him some coffee with some whisky in it, and in I goes, too, with my rifle and all my belongings to where they baked the bread, and I was in there baking for two thousand men, four hours on, four hours off, until we landed in six weeks. I was pleased to have something to do. I'd always been energetic doing everything and anything, and to be stuck there in an alleyway with a rifle by my side . . . Well, now I was given a little side-bunk in with the crew, and I had a little sack-cart where they had sacks and sacks and sacks of flour all stacked up, and I was bowling a sack of flour about every ten minutes down into a revolving kind of great round cistern, very bright and silvery, for making dough. Someone pulled a lever and all the dough used to roll out and the chaps with their white hats on and their big knives, they was carving lumps and passing them along on little trays to go down the side of the ship and be put in the ovens. When I left, the crew in the bakehouse had a little collection for me to land in Salonica with. It amounted to about £5 in franc-notes. In the army we had only pay books— sixpence a day, everything found.

We landed on New Year's Day, 1915, and I was out there two years and seven months, miles and miles up a wild country, with no big trees, only fig plantations, not a house in sight, thousands of us in scrapes in the side of muddy trenches, and a bit of maize bamboo to lie on, and as lousy as cuckoos. After being in the trenches for six or eight weeks at a time we got real crumby, with lice in the crevices of our shirts and all. Many a night I took my shirt off and turned it inside out and I've felt round the collar and I've had my nails full of lice where they was going from the outside to go back in the warm again. We were sent up new shirts about every twelfth week—otherwise we should have been eaten alive. When we was out for our nine days rest, a couple of platoons of us used to go down to a lake about two kilometres back behind the lines to have a good clean up and a bath. Lake Dojran it was called. We called it Doreen. There was a little side-line river leading into it and we banked it all up with sand-bags, made a wall so as to stop the water going down, and all of a sudden one day about eleven o'clock, when the sun was out beautiful and we was diving in and enjoying ourselves, here comes the Bulgarian monoplanes and they started dropping shells. My God, you should have seen us running naked to the dug-outs underneath the hills! I've never seen such a sight like it for naked men! And after the planes had gone you ought to have seen us running down and running back again, Tom picking up Dick's clothes, somebody with somebody else's shirt, a proper mix up!

It was amazing to watch the Greeks with their sheep on the hills. There'd be about four shepherds with, I should say, five or six hundred sheep. You'd see two of the men sauntering off to the other side of a hill, and then a whiff of smoke. They'd have put up a tent and were brewing up and, by the time they'd brewed up and had a sleep, the other shepherds with the flock grazing all the time would have walked round to where they'd pitched camp, and then they'd change over: those men as had had a rest took over the position of the others and could keep the flock on the move.

The mule, I'd been told, was one of the surest footed animals that lives, and, by God, he proved himself out in Salonica! The rations for each section that was up the front line was brought on the backs of mules. You'd see them coming up round the hills on the little rocky sheep-tracks, and controlling their steps with the men that were leading them. They'd come up to within, oh I dare say, a quarter of a mile of the front line and unload their packs—two big wicker baskets, one either side, mainly carrying Italian biscuits. We lived on Italian biscuits out there; very seldom did we get tins of corned beef, very seldom; biscuits was the main thing. And porridge—we had a lot of porridge for breakfast. Sometimes you'd get it what I call 'clotty'—it hadn't been stirred—and sometimes you'd get it half burnt, you'd have lumps of cinders in your mouth. Do you know, I never ate porridge again after the war?! Nor rice— we'd any amount of rice as well. No, thank you! I couldn't face it. Well, there was one hill called Machine Gun Hill—we named it ourselves. The mules would balance with a man leading them with a long rein in the dark. The men weren't allowed to have a torch, else Jerry would shell them and knock hell out of them—which they did one night. The mules come this night, they crossed a bridge the RE's built for them to come over so we wouldn't have so far to go to fetch our rations from the Depot, and one of the mule leaders, he struck a match and Jerry put a barrage over. You could hear them poor mules groaning. The chappies as went down to get our rations, they come back with half. They said there was about sixteen mules killed and their innards was hanging out as the shells was falling, and there was about three Tommies killed and about seven of them wounded—all leaders of the mules—and the rations was blown to smithereens.

The term 'barrage' means a lot of something coming at you: a barrage of shells explodes overhead and all the shot comes down on top of you. This one was concentrated on those mules because a chappie lit a cigarette at night-time. It was deadly. I could tell you worse tales than that but I won't, thank you, or else I shall be dreaming and jumping. Do you know, when

I was invalided home, from abroad, even five years after that, when I'd married my first wife, she could tell I was dreaming by the way I was knocking my arms about in the bed?! Many a time she caught hold of the tail of my shirt and pulled me back in bed—I was going over the top. That was the state of my mind when I came back from the army but I'll tell you no more for now because it was . . . Things happened out there . . . Men was struck dumb with fright . . . It ain't very often that anyone gets me to talk about the war. . . .

There is *one* little detail that don't upset me. It was a sight I've never seen since nor I don't want to see again. Our front line and the enemy's front line were about two hundred yards apart, parallel, and we had an observation balloon up two kilometres, about a mile and a half in English mileage. There was gas in this big observation balloon that held it up there, and there was a basket underneath and two men was in it using telescopes. Jerry got very annoyed. He came over with a plane one afternoon. We heard the old plane coming—oov a-woov a-woov—and he got within what looked like ten foot from the balloon because our anti-aircraft guns, they weren't there then, and he threw a kind of liquid fire on the balloon, and of course what happened, the balloon went up in flames and our two parachute men, they jumped out and we all . . . I think our hearts stopped beating because the two parachutes both opened and they looked like twenty yards apart in the air as they came down, and the remnants of the balloon on flame was coming down—they was three objects in line : our two men and the balloon in flames in the centre. Anyway, that was the end of that. The next clear day we put up another balloon. It was up in the air about half a mile attached to a large rope. Two more men was in the basket—you could see them with the naked eye. Here comes Jerry again just before dusk and, lo and behold, all our anti-aircraft are there about seventy-five degrees from the balloon, and all of a sudden : Bong Bong Bong. When a shell explodes in the air he makes a great dense ball of black smoke, and we seen this aeroplane come within ten feet of our

53

observation balloon, and this shell caught him right on the nose.
We seen the plane turn and, as he turned, so he went on fire and
the balloon went on fire at the same time. The two men in the
basket jumped out and the man in the aeroplane jumped out,
so there was the plane coming down in flames and the balloon
coming down in flames, as well as our two men and the Jerry.
That was the first Jerry I had any dealing with. I was one of
the Tommies as had to take him down for our interpreter to
speak to.

I was a private when I first went out there, then a lance-
corporal, then a full corporal. A few of our boys is killed and
of course they've got to be replaced by someone and I suppose
the captain of the company uses his brain and he also takes
notice of what the sergeant tells him, and then they have a
parade and say, 'From now on you're a full corporal from a
lance-corporal' or what have you. You *could* refuse. You could
stay a private if you liked; you didn't have to join the army at
all: you could be a conscientious objector. I knew several objectors. They're dead now. None of them ever explained to me
what they was implying. Before I met my first wife I was keeping company with a farmer's daughter and this conscientious
objector was rude to her and he had to marry her, you know
why. I told him face to face, I said, 'You wasn't very conscientious over that, were you?' Of course *some* of them may
have been genuine, no doubt about it. It's the same with these
people now over humane ways of killing. I'm one of those
people. There's nothing more ghastly than to see anything killed
cruelly. I like all the animals we eat—cattle, sheep, pigs and
what have you—I like to see them killed humanely, not as
they've got to linger and suffer. No, let's do things the proper
way if we've *got* to live on meat etc.—though if we became
vegetarians a cabbage wouldn't feel us cutting its head off before
we cooked it, would it? I've even invented a fox-trap which
I sometimes use to catch the fox alive and save snaring it and
trapping it and causing it bodily harm and pain. Catch it in
a cage and destroy it humanely afterwards if you must. Hunting

I don't mind. I've been connected with this estate for some sixty-eight years, as you know, and the hounds have been here during that period about twice every season and run through my coverts, and I've only known them to kill three times in that sixty-eight years! The fox has almost always beat them to it. The fox knows the ground, the hounds doesn't, and for gangs of people to go out and put scent down to distract the dogs from the fox is a fallacy: there's usually nothing for the dogs to kill anyway. Yes, I recall only three kills since I've been here. I was only at one of them and before you could say, 'One, two, three, four, five, six, seven, eight, nine, ten,'—three seconds—you never seen only just the head piece and the brush. When the first hound got that fox, there was then about ten other mouths on him and he was eaten up and finished. It's quicker than a punch-up at a football match when they're suffering and being tossed about with a policeman and hit with truncheons on the head. It's quite as fast as a bullet and more humane. Now, if these people that are such fanatics against the fox-hunting, if they went and stopped the job of bull-fighting, it would be capital. To say it's a cruel sport is a lot of poo-hoo; and it gives the horses exercise and people as are in offices, they has a lovely breath of fresh air, see the countryside. . . . This fox-trap of mine is six foot long and four foot square, a tube more or less with a rod across the top. The one end drops and the other's solid. You put a bait in, and whatever goes in pulls that bait and down goes the slide. And you don't only catch foxes, you catch farmers' dogs and all the rest of it at night-time. The farmers don't kennel their dogs, they just kick them out of their house, so if I catch one in my trap I know whose dog it is and I just pull up the slide, away goes the dog and he's not harmed. Since about 1952 they've been inventing 'new painless traps', but it's a lot of boloney because one trap is as painful as the other unless the animal is killed outright or isn't, like in my fox-trap, hurt at all. Now they've come to one with very high jaws which you put in a tunnel in the end of a hedge or by a gate-post to kill squirrels, rats, stoats, weasels, all small vermin. Admitted, it do kill those for the simple reason the little animal crouches to go in and, well, his body's low on the ground and therefore when the jaws comes up his heart stops beating and he's killed instantly. But if a full grown rabbit happens to go in, he gets caught in the legs just the same and he's in agony no less than with another trap. I've got some of these so-called 'humane' traps set out about the estate today and they'll kill about one in ten. If they catch the animals by the head, they squeeze them tight round the neck and they can't breathe; but if they don't, they're caught by the two legs or one foot—I've had them caught by the tail. The only thing about all this trapping business is to go round your traps in your coverts regularly and relieve the animals that are caught and still alive. It's illegal to set traps in the open without a permit—with traps exposed anywhere you can catch people's dogs, cats, birds, anything. When the *Second* World War was on we were smothered here with rabbits and I had to set traps in the open—they allowed me a permit for twenty-eight days, and after that twenty-eight days they come along to see as I wasn't using them. There was pheasant feathers in the fences and everywhere and little pheasants for about two or three years after, walking about on half legs. It was pitiful. The best way to kill a fox is in a snare—he'll choke his own self; he'll get caught up in the copper wire and khkhkh—he's gone.

I was a Mills bomber in the Great War. A Mills bomb is nearly two pound weight and it's made like a great big turkey egg and loaded with powder. There's a big ring on it about two inches in diameter and when you pull out that ring a spring strikes a detonator with a five-second fuse. You pull your ring. Right. Ready. Throw. I got that good at it with a dummy bomb in the practising area before we went in the line, I could drop a bomb in a pudding basin at forty-five yards. That's how I got my first stripe. When I'd got my two stripes I was in charge of a couple of men one night on a raid on an old mill. We'd about thirty men behind us with fixed bayonets, and our own fifty-four bombs, nine each side of us in pockets. Well, what happened, the lights was on in this old mill about seven hundred yards from our front line in No Man's Land between the two lines of trenches. We went and bombed the mill. I think there was three of the men inside killed and one was wounded and all the rest got away in the dark underneath where we couldn't see them by the big water-wheel.

As a Mills bomber you sometimes had to attack the trenches before the riflemen went in. But I'll go no farther than that, sir, please, or else I shall get out of control. You had to charge the enemy's trenches ahead of you, but before you entered you had to kill the men down in them . . .

When we were in the trenches the men from the country seemed to have more stamina than the citizens for the tasks we had to do. The citizens seemed to wrap up more than what we did; they was pale little office men and that; they hadn't been out in the fresh air. We was used to the country and the nights. No one could avoid malaria, though. I'd to go down to the hospital out of the front line with malaria fever about three times. I once had better teeth than these false ones, but I took that much quinine that it ate all the enamel off them. In the end I'd to go in front of a Medical Board and they marked me B. I didn't know what B meant but the names of about twenty-three of us was called on the Roll Call one morning, the last time I was down in hospital: we lined up, and they drove us down to the port and we was invalided home to Great Britain on the Prince George. At home when the sun come out in June it was the same as when I came from Salonica; I had relapses of malaria for about seven years. The men used to cart me off the estate and put me to bed and I was all right in a week or two. But it was in my blood system, you see. I've offered to be a blood donor but when they took a sample, No, it wasn't any good.

As a matter of fact there was one man that never got malaria. He was never ill to my knowledge for the two years and seven months I was abroad. Before we got on The Ballarat to go out there, we all had to be inoculated against diseases at Park Hall

57

Camp, Oswestry. But he stood out, and they arrested him and he had to go in front of the officers to give the reason why. He said, 'I've a healthy body and I can stand anything.' In the end they let him go. 'All right! Go on, then!'—they got fed up with him saying No. Believe you me, that man, when I was invalided home, he was still out there and he'd never been down to the hospital base : he'd never had an ailment. Every other man in that regiment was down one time or another with malaria fever or dysentery or what have you. But not that man. It's a funny thing, ever since, all through my private life, I've had to go to doctors with slipped discs and what have you, but I don't suppose I've got the faith in them that I should have. And as for these inoculations and injections put into your blood I do not agree with them nor I never shall. Of course scientists and all the rest of it, they *should* know, shouldn't they? I'm only one perhaps out of a thousand as looks at it that way. But that's been my thoughts ever since that man went through the war without a blemish.

Water was so scarce sometimes in the army that several of us had to shave with the same water. And we *had* to shave. We stuck the little periscopes for the end of our bayonets against the side of the parapet and you could just see your face and you pulled your razor out and you poured a drop of water out of your drinking-water bottle into a tin mug and dipped your brush in. You wasn't allowed to drink that drinking water in your bottle unless they ordered you to do so, else you had a court martial. But the saddest thing that I seen as regards restrictions was to do with the Irish Fusiliers. They was in a section adjoining us right by a fig plantation. Well, for a period, it thundered, lightened, poured down with rain. Everything and everywhere was flooded. Some of the trenches we had to give to the enemy; we had to come back because they were so full of water. Some places we had to go a little bit forward and be in danger. The Irish had to do the same as us. Now, there was one little Irish chappie of seventeen—he'd put his age on the same as myself to get abroad—and he was on duty in the trenches and he took his cap off to try and wring it and the sergeant, he ordered him to put it on and . . . This is only hearsay evidence that I'm giving you now, I got this out of one of the Irish; he told me that the little lad's hat was still wet through and running with water so he wouldn't put it on, and the sergeant pulled him up in front of an officer for refusing to obey an order and he had him court-martialled. We all see him shot against a fig tree as an example, and I went to that little lad's grave myself and his hat was on top of the grave. What happened next, all the Irishmen downed arms and come out of the trenches and stayed round about in the valleys. They took some quelling down. The Bulgarians could have had a walk-over. To find replacements, they had to phone down to the hospitals even and take every orderly. There was two orderlies from Tillington, the village near here, in the RAMC. *They* came up and helped to take over the position. And they'd never been taught how to fire a rifle! Orderlies out of the hospitals to fill up the line of the Irish! Finally, after eight or nine days, the Irish went back. If they hadn't, we'd have been put out to fight them and there'd have been Civil War. Was any of that published in our English papers?! Not damn likely!! There was never nothing printed in the English papers when we was abroad! We was off the map!

My own coat was drenched hundreds of times: it was saturated with water and too heavy for me to lift after standing in rain, snow, hail, with nothing over my head. To keep you warm on very frosty nights they gave you an issue of rum. And when they said, 'Double ration tonight!' we knew what was coming off. 'Look out tonight, boys!' It meant there was going to be a charge. We'd drink and sing to give us courage:

There's an isolated, desolated spot I'd like to mention
Where all you hear is 'Slope arms! Quick march! Attention!'
It's miles away from anywhere—by Gad it's a rum 'un.
A chap lived there for fifty years and never saw a woman.
There's only two lamps in the place—go tell it to your mother;
The postman has the one and the policeman has the other.

Now if you want a jolly night and do not care a jot
You take a ride upon the car, the car you haven't got.
For breakfast every morning, like old Mother Hubbard,
You double round the bloody hut and jump up at the cup-
board.

Sometimes you get bacon, sometimes lively cheese
That forms platoons upon your plate and orders arms and
stands at ease—

I can go on, but there's twenty verses to it. You say you've
a rotten memory—I haven't got a bad one, have I?! . . . When
we got the word up the communication trench—'Charge!'—
over the top you went with your rifle loaded and your bayonet
fixed, and hoped for the best. We was just like wild men. We
didn't know what we was saying because, when you were facing
the Hun and you got the order to charge, you didn't give a
damn. It was them or us. It was all softened down in the
Second World War because they had the big tanks with cater-
pillar wheels going ahead firing, and the infantry following
behind. There was no bayonet charging—*that* was fighting!
I've stood there with the shrapnel and the bombs and the
bullets flying overhead and the ground rocking under my feet!
Were we sent in this world for to be made shooting targets?
Never! And we didn't know the cause of the war. We weren't
told. We was just asked, 'Come and fight for your country!'—
that's all we heard! When you believe you're bound as a nation
to go and use firearms and destroy people, otherwise they're
going to destroy you, what are you to do? And it still goes on!
Why should we poke our nose into Northern Ireland? Why
should we use our English boys to get killed clearing the mess
up? It just about drives me up the wall! It says in the Bible—I
don't want to stress the Bible and religion but it says, 'Wars and
rumours of wars there always will be'. Well, I believe there
always will be wars, there's no one can stop them. It's sad men
have got to fight one another for leadership and because of
greed; it's all wrong. Oh, this is a lovely world, but it's the

people in it that makes it so awkward. One man jumps on an aeroplane and he holds all the passengers at bay with a little revolver or a sawn-off shotgun and demands a million pounds! Shoot him! Have done with him! It isn't worth spending the money on a court case over him, *or* sending him to prison. Look at the bombs going off in London—parcel bombs delivered by the postman! It's happening daily! It's wicked! How are they going to calm those minds and bring them to their level Christian senses? It's unbearable. Forgive me letting off steam! When I do let off steam like this I ask God to control my temper so as not to abuse my opponent. You can take so much . . .

But *I* was very lucky. I came away from Salonica on the Prince George with only malaria and a shrapnel wound under the chin—just a piece of red hot shrapnel hit me when I was in the firing line in the trenches. I had some wonderful escapes. My brother, Arthur, ended up working as gardener down in the Pensioners Hospital in Chepstow. I was down there twelve year ago and I seen men of my own age who'd fought in that war and they were still scatter-brained with shell shock or maimed . . . Terrible . . . Oh . . .

The Prince George called at Taranto in Italy on the way home. We was there for nine days and I didn't know that my brother, Bob in the Dardanelles had been wounded with shrapnel in the head and he was in Convalescent Camp at Taranto in the next compound to where we was when we got off the boat. They was putting in a silver plate. Before the war, he got a job as a printer's apprentice in Jakeman and Carver's, Hereford. When he come back out of the army he had a small pension and he got married to a Miss Hughes in Hereford. Jakeman and Carver's offered him his job back but they wouldn't give him the wage he wanted so he applied for a printing job in Northampton and he got it. He was only there three months, went home from work one day, lay on the sofa and died instantly. Just one stretch and he was gone. He'd been complaining of a headache. An abscess formed under his silver plate and exploded. He was only about twenty-three.

Back in England, this was controlled, that was controlled. On Hereford Station there was EAT LESS BREAD in damn great big red letters on a white wall all across the railway platform. I thought, 'Well, we've been eating Italian biscuits for the last three years, and now we've got to come home and eat less bread! Where the hell have we come to?! What the hell have we been fighting for?!'

I often look back at the Great War and think, 'Was it all worth it?' God knows. The country today is over-populated. What would it be like now if the thousands hadn't been killed in the First World War and the Second World War? But I've heard too many of the dear lads say, 'Oh God help me!' on the right of me and on the left of me, in front of me and behind me—and them was their last words. There's a shop in Tillington. Tom Jones, the father of the man that owns that shop now, was the only one out of the Gloucestershires that come back, and *he*'s dead and gone now like all the other ones and it's a certainty I shan't last for ever. In every church in every parish in Herefordshire the names of those who was killed and those who survived is on a Roll of Honour for everyone to see. My name's on the one in Canon Pyon Church. As a matter of fact in Brinsop Church I don't think we've got a Roll of Honour. We've got a Memorial Window instead, a big stained glass window that cost Lady Sutton £6,000, or so it was rumoured. She had it put up for her son, Sir Richard Vincent Sutton, the son as bought this estate for her and his step-father, Mr Hubert Delaval Astley, her second husband. It also mentions the lads killed in the service of their country as belonged to the Brinsop Parish—she left no one out. There was John Hugh Corbet and Cornelius Riley . . . Corny Riley went with me to school. It's a beautiful window. It's pathetic but it's beautiful. It's like a picture of the boys going over the top with their rifles, with the names of the dead all written in gold letters on the glass. The dates are 1914–1919 so Sir Richard may have died through the *effects* of the war. I don't think he died *in* the war. To lose the growing nation of young men—and especially those as was sent out with no one to lead them in front of the Germans in France and was mown down by guns like a machine cutting grass—it was horrible, deplorable! And they said, 'Oh, everybody will have an acre of ground and a cow!' Yes, we had some acres of ground and a cow, we did—those of us as come home! They even did me out of £92 gratuity money! They took away my Pay Book when I landed. I said at the Pay Desk at Park Hall Camp, Oswestry, before I came home on my twenty-eight days sick leave, 'I'm going to Nupton Hill Farm for twenty-eight days.' 'You'll be hearing from us in the near future.' Never heard a word! I had a solicitor in Hereford send three letters up to them: 'Please send me Rogers's Pay Book back'—it cost me pounds. But the Paymaster General knew nothing at all about it. Who had it?! Who drew my money?! Who drew the money from hundreds of others like me?! For all my services overseas I never got a penny! Never to this day as true as this pipe's in my hand!

I came home to Nupton Hill Farm on a Government Pass for a month and I had eighteen days of that month in bed. I hadn't got over the malaria; I was too weak to walk. My mother and my sister, Mabel, they changed my blankets; I was sweating like somebody had been douching me with water. Then I had a card from the Army to say, 'Report to the Depot at Bury in Lancashire for further services abroad.' I phoned them up at the Depot. I said, 'I'm not fit to travel. What am I to do?' They said, 'Report to the nearest hospital. If we don't hear from you in a few days we'll have to send a warrant for your arrest.' I said, 'Well, pack my few dods, Mother,' I said, 'and I'll be off.' Well, the pony was not fit to drive, she was lame and I went across three meadows to Molly my first wife's brother, Bert Rowberry, on the farm adjoining Nupton Hill and I asked him would he drive me to Credenhill Station, a whole mile away. Bert Rowberry is still alive, but, the dear old boy, he's laying at the moment on his bed in hospital.

It was either I had to go to Brecon Hospital or Hereford Hospital. All I had in my pockets was a half-crown. Half way to Credenhill Station I said to Bert, I said, 'Heads I go to Brecon. Tails I go to Hereford,' and it comes to heads so I went to Brecon. Up comes the train three o'clock and I was at Brecon Hospital eleven weeks under Dr Thomas. When I got better he gave me a note which I put in my tunic pocket. He said, 'Give this to your CO when you get back to your regiment,' and he sent an orderly with me down to the station and I was put on the train with my rifle and my haversack and a free voucher for the fare, and I reported at the barracks in Bury in Lancashire.

A provo sergeant was at the gates. He said, 'Who are you?' I said, 'Corporal Rogers.' 'Fall in Corporal Rogers! Take this deserter in the Guard Room!' I said, 'Hold on, sergeant, please!' I was an NCO so I was allowed to speak. I said, 'You was going to put me in the Guard Room?' 'Yes,' he said. I said, 'Not yet. Please take me to the CO's office!' 'Fall in the Guard!' He was afraid of losing me: two men with rifles came, one either side of me, when we went to the CO's office! 'Come in, sergeant!' In he goes. 'There's a deserter,' he said. 'Corporal Rogers.' 'Show him in, please.' 'Fall out the Guard! Quick march, Rogers!' In I go. Saluted the officer—with three pips, a captain. He said, 'Where have you been all this time?' I said, 'In hospital, sir. I'm sorry to tell you, sir,' I said, 'that your sergeant here,' I said, 'wanted to put me in the Guard Room.' '*Did* he?' he said. 'Yes, sir,' I said. 'I didn't like it at all, you know,' I said. 'I'm not feeling very strong. May I sit down, sir?' 'Certainly, Rogers,' he said. I said, 'Please read this note, will you?' It was in a sealed envelope. I gave it to him and he read it. 'Sergeant,' he said. I shall never forget what he said to that sergeant. He said, 'Take this man!' he said. 'Give him a good tea, order a couple of men to take his equipment and his rifle, and find him a bed—if they can't, give him yours! In the morning,' he said, 'he's got to go before a Medical Board and be advised by a doctor.'

I was travelling nearly all the next day and I'd to go in front of five doctors. They marked me B3 HS—HS meant Home

64

Service—and it was four months before the war ended so they put me in the Redcaps, the Military Police, still with the stripes I earned abroad. I was bringing prisoners of war, deserters, conscientious objectors, all sorts and descriptions of people not worth talking to, down by train from Oswestry, Chester, Newport, Barry Dock, and putting them in the old jail in Hereford, where the Bus Station is now. During that four months I think I brought about seventy prisoners down, and I always had a couple of men to help me, even if I was only taking one. I've got nothing against the Irish myself, but they're very hasty people when they're in tempers. In the Redcaps I've had Irishmen, half cut and stripped naked, coming at me in the hut through jealousy—just because I was English and they was Irish. That's just an Irishman all over. Not all of them. Some are better than I am, I dare say, though I've tried to lead an honest life or else I shouldn't have been here at Brinsop Court this sixty odd years as I have, working. In Barry I met an old man in the street, he said, 'See that doorknob over there?' he said. I said, 'Yes.' He said, 'Well,' he said, 'I was hall-boy in that house, and I used to clean the boots and polish that knob. That's where our Liberal Prime Minister lives.' Lloyd George lived in Barry. To the best of my knowledge it was Lloyd George who brought in the old age pension. I admire him for that. It was very sad when I was a boy. It was nothing to see three and four old men in a day, walking the roads looking for work, a big stick on their shoulder with a billy-can and a red handkerchief for their bit of tommy. They'd light a fire on the side of the road and boil a drop of water and put a pinch of tea in it and carry on again. Yes, I often think now what a wonderful old man Lloyd George was. He started to stir the country up. Not like the *present* Labour Government. They've made a hell of a mess of everything and try to grab every spare penny off the working class and off the nobility that the likes of me works for—most of the Big House is let off into flats; the banqueting hall and library are lying empty; what's the point in having the place? They're waiting for my dear boss to die so as they can get his Death

65

Duties. On the next estate to here they've sold thousands and thousands of pounds' worth of timber to try and get Death Duties paid. The Common Market never have acted yet and it never will. There's too many as wants a grab out of it. It's like this oil coming from the North Sea, isn't it? What's happening to that? Oh, it was going to make this country rich! *Has* it?! No—and never will! *You* won't have none of it anyway, the bloody Government will see to that. I'm going off the deep end, now. I shouldn't do. But look at all these young men going into the factories! They're just numbers! The master man don't know Tom, Dick, from Harry. God knows, you did have a number when you was in the army but you also had a name and they called it out every day to see as you was present and if you wasn't present they was after you! No, I've got no patience with this Government. It drives me up the wall. It more than drives me up the wall—it drives me up into the sky, so far up into the sky I can't get down again! I've worked for Conservatives all my life and *I'm* a Conservative in my way. Of course I'm not educated enough, or I *wasn't* educated enough, to understand Conservative, Liberal and what have you and what they stood for, but since I've grown up I've realized who was the best governors of this land. But we've got to go by the vote of the people. It's the people who choose, and this Government is the people's choosing, and they've got no one to blame because *they* put them there. Now they've got to suffer. You go into a public house for a half pint of beer or a glass of Guinness any day of the year now, and all you hear is grumbling. They did it theirselves. They made a rod to smack their own arse with.

When the war was over, there was sports in every little village, to have a rallying time. But it wasn't all so bright. There wasn't a family hardly in these little parishes that hadn't lost a son or two, some of them three. Some had lost fathers and sons. I only lost my colt and my two cows and that was enough—when I went home to Nupton Hill, Father had sold my colt for a hundred guineas and my black-nosed cow for £86 and my red one for £68! And do you know how much he gave me? Nothing! He told me to go to hell when I come back! *That*'s what I fought for? I left home for good. Would *you* stop at home with a father like that? *I* couldn't, whether it was Christianlike or no. I've seen him stand behind a horse in our stables and beat her till she kicked with her hind legs and knocked out the back of the stable. I've seen that with my own eyes! And I've felt at the same time like getting a hammer and giving *him* one and seeing what *he* would like! My sister, Mabel, she ran away also. She *had* to run away because my father would have killed her—she tried to poison him, he was such a brute. Mother helped her open a little shop in Tillington, and then she met a well-sinker called Davis and went to live with him in Birmingham. They had twelve children. He died about three years ago and she died after him. And Arthur, he went to work as gardener's boy for Mr Lewis of The Hollies, Llanyth, Monmouthshire. Only Edwin of the children stayed. There was Edwin, Mother, Father and Aunt Jemima on the farm . . .

Mr Astley knew I was home. He asked to see me straight away and appointed me as under-keeper—not just keeper's boy —to Harry Darling at ten bob a week. So, after the war, I went in through the front door at Nupton Hill and out through the back and returned to live with Harry Darling at Ivy Cottage, Brinsop—I re-joined the crowd. But I kept my eye on dear old Mother that she should never want while I'd got breath.

Four

Harry and myself, we celebrated the winter of 1918 in an un-
usual way. It was nearly mid-day, a fortnight from Christmas, and we'd been ferreting in Badnage Wood. We'd got our
quota of rabbits; in fact, I'd paunched them and put them on
a rail to carry home. Paunching made them lighter—it was a
long way to go and we'd also got the ferret bags and a gun each.
'Oh, let's have our lunch!' said Harry. Well, we'd just finished
our lunch and had a cup of coffee when he said, 'Listen, Evin!'
and I listened and I could hear an old sow down over the bank.
She was going nrghh nrghh nrghh and you could hear her
little pigs answering her. She'd pigged out in the wood and her
little pigs was about ten weeks old. She'd left Farmer Godsell's
farm and he'd never missed her. Anyway, this great blue and
white sow with big long ears and all her little pigs, whether she
smelt us or what, she come up the bank and into the ride and,
of course, we was amazed. Harry Darling said to me, he said,
'Look, Evin!' he said. 'Pork!' Up with his gun, Bang! He
knocked one of these little pigs over, killed it outright. I've never
seen an old sow pig run so fast in my life! She was going up
and down with her legs running in the gallop and her big ears
flopping, and her little pigs, well, they was gone before you
could say Jack Robinson.

My word, that little pig Harry shot weighed about thirty
pound! 'I can manage the pig and my gun,' said Harry. 'I'm
off as quick as I can,' he said. 'You can manage the rabbits,
can't you? Take your time!' and he hurried past Round Oak,

down across, and over a hedge half way along a meadow, and straight over the fence and into Ivy Cottage with this pig. I was following after with the eighteen to twenty rabbits, the two bags of ferrets, the spade and my gun. When I got home, the lean-to shed was full of steam. Harry'd got the boiler going, bellied the pig, put it in and scalded it. Later we chained him to the beam of the shed where I now keeps my nets, left him to hang there till he was stiff, then cut him up and had pork all over the Christmas —I shall never forget it. Harry Darling was down at The Bell over Christmas. In comes Farmer Godsell, and Harry tells him how he found his sow and piglets and sent them home to him. 'Do you know?' said the farmer. 'I've got that many pigs and piglets I've lost count of them. There's a pound note!'—he gave the old keeper a pound for sending his pigs home. Harry didn't tell him he'd shot one of them!

On the keepering side under Harry Darling I was still spending most of the time killing rabbits. Mr Astley wasn't interested in game. He was more interested in his aviary and his foreign birds—oh he spent thousands of pounds on birds. His son, Philip Astley—he was now a captain in the Life Guards—and me and Harry, we'd been four and five years away because of the war and the rabbits was uncontrolled. Don't say I don't know how to catch a rabbit!—the place was lousy with them till thirty odd year ago when we'd myxie, myxomatosis; you've heard of that disease, haven't you? I had a bet once with the keeper on the next estate to us, the Foxley Estate. A nice old man he was. He died in harness which I wish to do. We had a bet one day. I bet him a pound, I said, 'I bet you a pound,' I said, 'I'll kill more rabbits than what you can.' Well, I killed six thousand nine hundred and seventy-three rabbits here from October 3rd till March 25th—that's over a thousand a month. And, do you know, that keeper beat me?! He killed over seven thousand. I was very sorry in one way when rabbit-catching went because of that myxomatosis. It fed many a hundred families in the countryside. Families could live cheap on it. A rabbit, a few carrots out of the garden, a few onions chopped

69

up—they made a damn good stew. It was a beanfeast for them every day of the year. What's more, when Colonel Astley was in charge here—the Captain became Colonel in the Second World War so I always thinks of him as the Colonel—I used to take a brace of rabbits a week to every cottager on the estate. At one time there was twenty-two of them, so that meant forty-four rabbits a week. And the cottagers looked forward to it! But not today—people won't look at them with the myxie; even *I* won't eat one. There *are* rabbits, and I still kill them. I had about twenty ferrets here last year I'd got to feed. Every night I used to go out, just go up quietly under the hedge with a gun, pick two rabbits in the sights, Bang!, go and pick my two rabbits up. Night after night. The old jill that reared the twenty ferrets for me I got £5 for and I sold all the young ones for fifty shillings each. What would that be in this new coinage? It drives me up the wall and many thousand others at my age. I've had as many as eighty young ferrets a year in my time. But I'm not going on with them, it doesn't pay. You reckon up from April—April is the month that young ferrets comes into this world. Well, keep a dozen of them on from April till October. You needs a pint of milk a day easy for the dozen so there's seven pints a week. Reckon *that* item up! And that's without shooting them a rabbit or two, and a cartridge today is one and threepence where it used to be three halfpence.

Rearing ferrets was my hobby even as a boy. Say you've got four jills, four mothers, and they've been to their mate and they're all in young—right, you put them in four separate hutches; if you don't, they'll eat one another's young. In each hutch you have a little receptacle and you put in a bit of nice fine straw and some feathers, and the day they're going to have their young you can always tell because they'll catch hold of the straw and the feathers and they'll place them like a wild bird makes a nest, with just one little round hole—any ferret that's born today when they are full grown will go through a circumference of two inches. But you're deprived of seeing the young ferrets for nearly a month after the old ferret's had them;

you must never break the straw of their nest until you see those little young ferrets about two inches long and their eyes half split open crawling out of the nest. If you touch the nest, the mother, she'll go in straight away and snap the heads off every young ferret, kill them all. I never knew a ferret that wouldn't do it, and that's a lesson to anybody that is going to read this book. I'm telling secrets now. In my profession—and all keepers are like me—we keeps our secrets of what we find out during our life in the experience of gamekeeping to ourselves. People will say, 'Why don't you do it so and so way?' Well, I'll say, 'That's a secret of mine and I don't give it to anyone else' because otherwise it would be interfering with my living. Another secret about ferrets is you must only *moisten* the little chunks of bread with milk when you're feeding the young ones. If you puts bread in a dish of milk you'll have twelve little ferrets come out one over the top of the other and one pushes the other in the milk and they roll in it and they get what they call 'the sweats'—they fairly steam and you lose the lot, they die within forty-eight hours. I had it happen, so I know. Later on, you can give them milk on its own and rabbit flesh—you go round your vermin traps and come back with your hare-pockets full of rabbits and cuts out the flesh for them to suck.

A fellow I knew about twenty-seven years ago, he got a job as a keeper and he was rearing ferrets the same as I did and he come to me and I was talking to him and he said, 'Have you got any ferrets to sell?' I said, 'What's happened to all yours?' He said, 'Oh,' he said, 'I caught a blasted cat and I took it home,' he said, 'and to have my revenge back on the cat because he'd killed a lot of my pheasant chicks,' he said, 'I threw him into the box,' he said, 'to seven ferrets. I thought the ferrets would soon put paid to him. Next morning I went out and there was the old cat as brisk as could be and every ferret was dead.' The cat had killed all the ferrets. You couldn't have a worse enemy than a wild cat in your wood in June and July when there's little pheasant chicks running about. It'll devour up brood after brood, a wild cat will. The simplest way to catch one is to buy a raw kipper from your fishmonger. You tie a piece of string to it and drop it on a pathway in the wood where you've seen the cat and go along so far and so far . . . If she's in the vicinity and the wind is blowing in her direction, she'll smell it if she's a hundred yards away and she'll come out and she'll follow that trail. Well, a keeper never goes through his coverts empty-handed, and he's generally got a gun under his arm and that gun is loaded. Right. Up. Bang! It's instantaneous. Pussy, you're dead.

I used to use ferrets on rats underneath Lady Sutton's poultry houses—she'd five big poultry houses in the orchard. Colonel Astley and his sister, the Honourable Mrs Humphrey Wyndham, would come down on Saturdays from London, and I had to take two or three ferrets out to entertain them. They'd come out shooting rats with shot guns at about two o'clock after lunch. The rats would run from one fowlhouse to another across the orchard and I would use my ferrets to drive them out. I couldn't use the same ferrets as I used for rabbiting because those ferrets that I used for rats, it made them very savage. I've seen an old rat jump at a ferret and bite her and shake her, and I've had them gashed and bit in the face and their ears torn off. I lost several ferrets from rat bites, so I kept about half a dozen fitcher ferrets for ratting—they're a harder breed than the white ones. Oh, Saturday after Saturday I entertained them. The Honourable Mrs Humphrey Wyndham was a very good shot. Sir Derrick when he bought the estate off Colonel Astley never carried a gun out to shoot a rat in his life. There you are. But *they* wanted something to do and of course I was the keeper and I suppose it was part of my work though I didn't much like it.

Ben Thomas used to store some potatoes in the kitchen garden cabin and one Saturday there was one of his gardeners said, 'There's plenty of rats under the cabin, Evan!' 'Is there?' I said, 'All right. I'll be there in a minute.' 'I'll stop inside,' he said. 'There's some holes in the boards,' he said, 'and I'll go and put a brick over them.' 'Oh,' I said. 'All right. Thank you,

Harry.' Harry Wilkins the young man's name was. So the Colonel stood up one end of the hut and Mrs Wyndham the other side of the hut and I'd got *my* gun with me that day and the Colonel said, 'We can't see all round. You stand opposite in the ducks' nest'—a rough piece of place by some poplars. I stood by the poplars and threw a couple of ferrets down on the ground. They went under the cabin, and Mrs Wyndham, she banged away at a couple of rats and the Colonel had a shot or two as well. Harry Wilkins shouted from inside the cabin, he said, 'They ain't half making a noise under these boards!' And, with that, out comes a big old rat and he was going between this kitchen storehouse and me, a lovely shot. Bang! I shot this rat dead. And sonever I shot this rat dead—there was inch-boarding all round that house to make it strong, to make it rat-proof, but they'd burrowed down in the earth and got in underneath in the floor and then bored a hole up and got into the potato clamp inside—as I pulled the trigger and the gun went Bang, Wilkins in the shed, he shouted, 'Oooh!' He'd got leggings on, and his boots, and stockings underneath, and pantaloon breeches underneath that, and my shot killed the rat, it went through the inch-boarding, through his leggings etc., and I pulled out seven shots out of his ankle just above his boots! And I was thirty yards away! So see how simple it is for dangerous accidents to happen. I think that was the end of the ratting with Colonel Astley and the Honourable Mrs Humphrey Wyndham. That was enough . . .

But back to the days of Harry Darling when we was rabbiting in so big a way. I go out with my gun, ferret and cartridges. I come to a rabbit burrow. I have a look, see if it's 'worked', that's see if rabbits have been going in and out freshly. If they have, 'Oh, I've a rabbit in here. Fine.' So you take your ferret out of the bag and you put her in the hole and you stand back about twenty yards. Out pops your rabbit. Right, it's up to you now. Up with the gun. Bang! It takes a lot of practice to shoot a running rabbit on the ground, especially in a wood because he's popping in a bush and out and around the butt of a tree.

It's what we term as 'snap' shooting, and you've got to get used to it. Well, the old keeper taught me how to use my gun for that, and I don't mind explaining because it's important to a beginner. I was used to using a rifle in the army, and with a rifle you've got to get the tip of the foresight in the back of the U-sight on the barrel. Now, I was using the gun the same way and Harry, he'd say, 'That's not the way to use it, Evin!' He'd come up to me and he'd say, 'Now then, point that gun at that rabbit the same as if you was pointing at it for me with your finger!' He said. 'Use the gun the same, boy! Point and pull and it's yours! If you draws any person's attention to see a thing—"Look at that blackbird sat on that pole!"—' he said, 'nine times out of ten your finger is direct on that object. Use the gun the same!' So I did it. It took me about, oh I dare say, a couple of hundred rounds before I got used to it but, my word, it was a lovely lesson and I never forgot it.

So we'd go out ferreting and shooting the rabbits when they'd bolted from the ferret. I tell you, they was going faster than thirty mile an hour. A rabbit running on his own ground, he *do* run! It's different if you catch live rabbits and loose them from a bag for somebody to have some sport. But to shoot a bolted rabbit on his own ground it takes a clever man to knock down four out of five. He used to bet me a pint of beer which was sixpence in those days and we bet one another till we was tired. He'd kill fifteen rabbits one day and I'd kill eleven. I think we used to put twenty-five cartridges in our pockets each. You has one shot. He has one shot. Of course we never shot them for the market, we always snared or netted them for market for the simple reason that when you shoot a rabbit you damage them for home cooking. But to supply the Big House for boiling for dogs and that, it was all right. At the end of the one season Harry gave up the betting because we calculated it up and he only beat me by three rabbits. The last time I shot a *lot* of rabbits was in about 1921 when some scouts come and pitched their camp here at Brinsop. I had to supply them with rabbits three times a week for about a fortnight. I'd got two

74

little black cocker spaniels then, and they used to work the bushes for me. Well, it come a snow and I happened to dip the gun and, unbeknownst to me, I got snow in the barrel of the gun. It was a Belgian gun and I'd only just bought it—a double barrel. This was the last day and I was shooting the last rabbit of my quota as it come out of some briars into the ride of the wood. Bonnng! Two inches of one of the barrels exploded in my hands, and I've never bought a foreign gun since.

Of course you've got to *train* a ferret to go rabbiting; they've got to know what a rabbit *is*. If you'd fed a ferret on only bread and milk when he was young and took him out and put him in a rabbit hole, he'd just sit at the mouth of the hole and look at you. No, you've got to feed him on rabbit first and throw the rabbit to him when it's warm so he gets to know the smell. Then, whenever he gets to the mouth of a hole, he can smell rabbit and away he goes and gives a nip and you hear bump bump bump under the ground and out comes the rabbit. The next thing is to get him to come out of the hole when he's bolted all the rabbits and not to keep running back when he sees your hand wanting to pick him up. What you do is, on his first day out, you put a tiny collar on him with a little piece of string attached about two foot long, and when he comes out of the hole and goes back again you can get hold of the bit of string which you can still see and pull him out. When you've pulled him out you then pick him up and let him know it's your hands as is handling him by stroking him—you should have handled him before because a ferret is a little brute when he's savage; he's got tusks like a big dog has; you've to learn to hold him at the back of the neck in one hand so he can't turn his head and give you a nasty bite; I've seen a ferret hold a rabbit at the mouth of a hole and he wouldn't let him go, the rabbit was swinging back and forth and couldn't jump away from him. So when you pick him up off the ground with this bit of string attached, you stroke him. And you only want that collar and string on him one journey out ferreting. The next day you

75

take him he'll come running out and he'll wait to be picked up : he won't run back because he thinks it'll be a waste of time.

Say a jill is killing a rabbit in a hole. Well, you listen where the rabbit is crying underground—I've been down on my knee on a bank many a time listening—and you get your rabbiting spade and dig straight down to your jill and catch hold of the rabbit and finish it off. If it's a very deep earth and you've got a *lot* of soil to move, you use a 'liner', that's a hob ferret with a line attached. You let the line out, and every yard you've got a knot so that you know how many yards he's gone in : as he's going in you count the knots just to know how much earth you've got to move. It's a big advantage to have a line and a liner to dig out your jill and get on with more ferreting, else that jill will have a feed of that dead rabbit, curl up in its fur and go to sleep—I once had a jill underground for a fortnight; it went under a great elm tree and there was too many roots in the way of digging. And you mustn't put a liner under a tree because he may go around a root and you won't be able to pull him out. I've had that happen but as luck would have it he bit the string and released himself. If he hadn't, he'd have starved and died on the line.

As regards the trapping and the snaring of rabbits, snaring is not so cruel. Snares are made of copper wire and, if the rabbits are running when they put their heads in, it chokes them instantly. If they're jumping, they circle round and round, and you must go to them and click their necks. The jaws of a trap—I never use traps for rabbits now—used to catch them by their feet; there they were with this big lump of iron on their feet till you went to them. Under Harry Darling I'd go along the hedgerow clicking their necks to put them out of their misery. I'd kill the next one and the next one and the next one till I'd killed them all. They were all alive the one way, and when I was coming back they'd all be dead. I'd come with my stick and my knife and I'd take them out of the traps, cut a slit in one hind leg above the heel-joint, pop the other hind

76

leg through the slit, put my stick through the space between the legs and the back passage, and then, with the rabbits hanging with their heads down, sometimes twenty rabbits a side, I'd put my stick on my shoulders and carry them home.

Sir Derrick Bailey bought this estate in 1947. I was catching rabbits up to three years after he was here. Then came myxie, and it's been the easiest time of my keepering since because I haven't had to catch all those hundreds and hundreds of rabbits that devoured our crops . . . But that was after the Second World War and I was telling you about after the First. The First, as well as holding up the keepering, held up rebuilding the Big House and making general improvements to the estate. I took on all sorts of extra jobs in my spare time—and not just farmwork, either—and I've done them ever since. Not two months ago I made some stable doors out of second-hand wood for Master Tom . . . For old Mr Astley I was building walls and putting on the coping; I was planting trees, falling timber, hanging gates, putting up fences, digging foundations for a new church vestry, even cutting Major Thompson, the steward's, hair! Major Thompson died in about 1928. I'd promised to go down to cut his hair and Mrs Thompson met me on the steps by her gate. She said, 'He's just passed away, Evan!' I came away bewildered. He wasn't sixty and I liked him very well.

The young people today, they don't know what the word 'work' means. There's been young men come here recently—young men of twenty and twenty-three years of age; they've come here on a month's trial to see if they're useful. You offer them a shovel. 'Oh no! I didn't come here to do *that*!' They've never seen a shovel in their life before! Some of them would faint over it; you'd want to send for the ambulance to take them down to the hospital. No, siree! Work is out of the question. Go out through the gate at the top of the Arbour! You'd think anybody could drive a tractor through there without hitting the pillars, wouldn't you? Well, go and look at the one on the left as you go up now! The hinge is knocked clean flat in the stone-work, and the gate, you can't open him or shut him, he's just put to stand there. They couldn't care less! 'Oh, buy a new one!' they say. Turn round and ask them, 'Are you going to pay for it?' Damn likely! Master Tom have asked *me* when I've got time to go and repair it. The other day they knocked off the head of the wooden gate, the main gate leading to the entrance of the Court. Too lazy to get down to open the gate! Pushed it open with the tractor and then one wheel goes against the head of the gate and the bars—Crash, off it goes! There you are. Oh, it makes me mad. But, there, I'm getting too old now to worry about it, but I *do* worry about it because I don't like to see things broken and hanging. A few year ago when I was *real* lively and healthy and could jump any gate on the place, there wasn't a gate on the whole of this estate that wasn't perfect; I'd hung them so as they'd close on their own. You could just take off the chain, lift the latch, walk through, then all you had to do was put the chain on again, put the peg in, no trouble at all. You can't go to a gate now that isn't tied up with a bundle of string or you've got to lift him and there's no string on him at all! I made sixty easy of those wooden gates—every one on the place! *And* there's thirty-two of those pairs of iron gates—I've put in every one of *them* myself, too. All the wooden ones are smashed and broken up but only one of the iron ones is damaged, even slightly. Some drunken youths was coming down the main road from Tillington one night at seventy mile an hour and something went wrong with their car and they knocked my post and it never moved a quarter of an inch though the car turned a somersault. They're hooligans! The likes of me, we're not wanted any more; we're rubbish. All decorated up like scarecrows and flying about in cars and on motorbikes! The grocer and the butcher bought residences in the new built-up area of Credenhill. What I'm telling you now is the truth. Do you know, they've had to go and buy private property two or three mile away before they can go to sleep of a night? About twenty or thirty youths go out on the car park in front of the grocer's shop and the butcher's shop of a night! Go there and you'll see them sat on them doorsteps there, smoking cigarettes and with bottles of beer from the Cash and Carry! There they are, half drunk, sick and all the rest of it and rrrrrrrrr buh buh buh buh till eleven, twelve, one, two and three in the morning. Oh my God! They took the policeman off the beat—you only hear a policeman once a week going through the village in a motor car. What damn good is that to you?! You can't beat the old policeman on the beat. That's my view. The sight of a policeman and the children, right, they go like a fox from the hounds. I'm not boring you?

Of course, there's the *occasional* laddie. There's a young one here going to school—I think he's leaving school in about eighteen months—and I'd put him against a dozen tractor drivers! He'll come home from school at four o'clock, have a cup of tea and a sandwich and he's out on the tractor with his father and he's doing the same work as a grown man as if he was getting forty or fifty pound a week—and doing it better. Well his father is marvellous too; it's born in you. But they're the exceptions; the happy days are gone. I used to see men going to work here, 'Hi-dee hi-dee iddledy yumpety iddledy di-dee di!' and whistling, happy as sandboys! I've even seen men running to work not to be five minutes late. In the old days they respected their bosses and they worshipped them and they'd do anything for them. They were interested in their jobs. Are they interested today? No! They couldn't care damn less! Nobody cares. It's 'Bugger you, Jack! I'm all right!'

Old Mr Astley and Lady Sutton—and then Lady Sutton when Mr Astley died in 1925 and the Colonel took complete charge—they had twenty-one labourers on the place including the shepherd, the stockman, the groom, the waggoners, and the hedge-layer and ditcher. Indoors there was the butler; there was the footman; there was the butler's boy; there was the lady's companion and the lady's maid; there was the cook, the head housemaid, the underhousemaid, the kitchen maid, the scullery maid; there was the odd man as used to carry in the coke for the boilers; and there was the hall boy, the little odd boy to

79

wait on people and to clean the boots and knives and forks. Then there was the chauffeur, the electrician, the gardener, and the carpenter and, of course, the bailiff and the steward, Major Thompson—not to mention the keepering and the birdman for the aviary. I remember the butler's cottage, the chauffeur's cottage, the electrician's cottage and the gardener's cottage being built by the Big House right from the foundations. And I remember the Bothy being built for all the young men as was single—they used to sleep and have their food in this Bothy and one of the workmen's wives would go in and cater for them and another would do all the cleaning and make their beds and there was a woman who used to wash the sheets about once a fortnight when the beds were changed and take them away to her cottage in a cart pulled by a donkey. Most of the working-men was married by the time Mr Astley died so the Bothy wasn't required and it was more or less made into lumber rooms to keep oddments in. Now Mr Pritchard, a farmer bailiff who's become half-tenant of the whole estate, he lives there next to the big garage and the hackney stables. The Colonel when he come down from his flat in London would bring his valet—I think he was his batman in the army. This valet had to carry his gun-case with a pair of Purdeys in it. They were 'dog-leg' guns because the Colonel had a weak eye. With the dog-leg guns the grip of the gun come across his chest and he put the butt of the gun to his right shoulder but he shot with his left eye. . . .

But, oh, Brinsop was a place of perfection in those days! We've Herefords now for producing beef, but then we only had black Dexters for producing milk for the Big House. Everything was black—we'd black cattle, black pigs, black horses . . . And, I'm not bragging or boasting but I fenced round the whole estate all on my own—a post every nine foot—and every fence I made was of oak. They lasted sixteen and eighteen years and then I went round and I made nearly all of them again. You fall your tree at ground level in the last week in May or the first or second week in June when the sap is running up him. Then before you make your posts you take off all the big boughs and saw him in lengths and bruise the bark with the back of a heavy instrument and get your axe and give a chop through the bark about every six inches around the trunk and it falls off like pig-troughs. You put those shells of bark out to dry in the sun and then they're packed one in the other and loads go to the tanning-yards for tanning leather. The tanners used to buy tons of it out in the countryside. Peel-barking made my posts nice and hard to go in the ground. In the days of Dearman Edwards they used to pickle them in creosote too. There's some posts as was pickled still here today; I'll go up the wood and I'll show you a corner post as was pickled and he's as hard today as he was eighty years ago.

As regards planting trees, I planted ash and Douglas around the pleasure grounds and near to the Big House. Me and Ben Thomas, we planted the big cedar on the lawn. He was six foot tall when we planted him but we cut the leader out of him so as to make him spread, which he did nicely—there's two or three leaders to him now. The Astleys put tables and chairs under him and sat and had afternoon tea underneath. I've always proposed, then done what I wanted to do in the way of planting. The drive running through the Park to the Big House, Mr Dearman Edwards had it made for when his daughter, Miss Winnie Edwards, got married. She drove down to Brinsop Church that way in a carriage and pair. The Park cottagers then, opposite from the gate, put rods over the stone pillars and roses on the rods so as she could drive through an archway of roses to and from the wedding. Well, I helped to plant two lines of lime trees all along the drive for Mr Astley. Colonel Astley later had them bulldozed out. Several of them had died and the remaining ones looked unsightly and there was water lying on the gravel. The gravel's all grassed over now, there's sheep on it. About five acres of land we was covering with the avenue and the two lines of trees. Which is better—to have a good crop of grass or just watch lime trees?

Down in the centre of the Park there's still two oak trees.

81

One of Mr Astley's Australian cranes had a nest right by one of them. He took a big armchair down for me to sit in night after night to keep the dogs and the foxes away while she was sitting, and she hatched one egg out of the two. All his cranes— the Australians, the demoiselles, the Manchurians—they were in pairs but the pairs were never put together. There was a pair in one field, a pair in the Park, a pair elsewhere. Motorists used to stop car after car to watch them. The old cock bird would dance around the hen and manoeuvre up and down, open his wings out. It was a marvellous sight here. It was better than going to a zoo. And Mr Astley had all kinds of ducks on the moat. There was the Chiloe widgeon, the pintails, the garganey, the teal, the tree ducks, the mandarins. They were a picture. I'd to make boxes with no bottoms for them to lay in season. In the aviary—about ten aviaries all in one, heated with hot water-pipes in winter— there was minas, motmots, tragopans, bleeding heart doves, foreign partridge, foreign pheasants. A foreign blue type of bird escaped once and mated with some of the wild hen pheasants in the coverts. We had cross-bred pheasants the fol- lowing season—blue feathers intermingled in their original light chocolate-coloured construction. The strain lasted for years. Lady Sutton used to open the gardens for people to see the flowers and the birds. I would take over £100 at the gate in half-crowns! There was over three hundred birds, every kind you can men- tion. Mr Astley had ten of those lovely flamingos stood up with their great long spiry legs, big pink birds. You've seen them in zoos, haven't you? When they stretch open their wings they show feathers of black all underneath. He was fined in the war for feeding them with wheat—clean wheat, the best wheat which we grew on the farm. They tossed it onto their beaks with the webbing of their toes.

I've a story about the flamingos. Usually they weren't let out onto the moat till summer but it come up a nice spring one year and there was such a warm day about the end of March or the first week in April that Mr Astley said to the birdman, the little chappie as used to look after the birds, Mr

Chapman, he said, 'Let's turn the flamingos out for a couple of hours.' Mr Chapman didn't want to do it but he did. There was three or four of us helped him, some this side, some that, to make a kind of an alleyway from the little gate at the out-side of the aviary down to the moat. Of course the birds loved it. Well, it come about three o'clock in the afternoon and it went off cold, the wind started to blow, and we tried to get the flamingos back into the aviary for night protection but they went farther and farther into the water to where it got about three foot deep. Now there's an island in the centre of the moat and they was close to this island and the branches of the trees on it was hanging over so it was decided, 'Oh, they'll be all right over the night. They'll be sheltered.' So they were left till next morning. Well, lo and behold, it come fourteen degrees of frost during the night and by morning the ice on the outside of the moat was just over an inch thick. The birds, they'd all clamped together and with the heat of their bodies the ice was kept from freezing up to within six inches of their legs. A flamingo's leg is three foot six long and it isn't no thicker than a lead pencil, not a half inch. If they'd moved, the sharp ice would have broken their thin little legs.

The birdman went in and told Mr Astley about the birds in the ice and that he couldn't get across to feed them nor give them water so Mr Astley sent him to me. 'Ask Evan to come up at once!' he said. I went up. 'What's the best thing to do, my dear boy?' he said. I said, 'Well, what we want to do is to try and break a roadway through this ice and get them back into the aviary.' I got a mallet and a big wide two-inch wood chisel and big long waders, and started chopping the ice to get into the water. I did it very quietly not to disturb the birds, else they'd flutter and fall and that would be the end of Mr Astley's flamingos. The dear old gentleman, he said, 'Now you'll go very steady, won't you, my dear boy?' I said, 'Yes, if you'll just get away, sir, and let me get on with the job.' I kept my eye on the flamingos. I cut a block out. I cut another block out. I pressed each one down and slid it under the remaining ice out of the

way. Chop along there. Chop along here. Chop along here.
Slide another one under. And as I was going on in, so the ice
got thinner. The birds weren't moving a feather, only talking to
themselves: blablablabla blablablabla. I'd travelled nearly thirty
yards. I got within a yard of them and now, after I'd done all
this labour, I didn't want to frighten them with the mallet and
the chisel so I squeezed the ice down with my hand and it
broke around them and I pushed it aside to make a bigger
waterway. Then I waded round where this ice had broken off
freshly and got behind and guided the flamingos slowly back as
gentle as anything until they got that they had to lift their feet
out of the water onto the earth. By this time Mr Astley had got
about six or eight men including the steward, Major Thompson
out of the Life Guards, and they'd formed a double line for
the birds to follow between to the gate and into the aviary.
Suddenly the birds opened their wings and made for the gate
but the last one turned across to this steward and—I shall never
forget it—it rushed past him making a terrible noise and round
and back and flopped on the ice and then into the water again
where I'd been cutting and stopped there just a few yards in.
The steward, he said to Mr Astley, he said, 'I'm like a great
elephant, sir!' 'Not half so intelligent!' shouted Mr Astley—you
could hear him from here to Credenhill. I stepped down again
in the water without making a splash, got round behind the
flamingo and I said, 'Come on now!' and all the other
flamingos started to call 'Cacar cacar' and this time it ran
between the two lines of men as it should have done in the
first place. We got them into the aviary and they wasn't let
out till the first of May. And that's the end of the flamingo
story.

He was a dear old chap, Lady Sutton's husband. He wasn't
interested in the farm and he wasn't interested in shooting but
he enjoyed himself with his aviary and his ducks and his cranes.
And he must have taken to me because I was never in the wrong
with him, he never called me anything other than 'my dear boy'.
His wife—some people called her 'Mrs Astley'—I never had

much to do with. She used to stroll up round the gardens some days, always in a long dress. A fine lady she was—a six footer, big, bold looking, great large bosoms. If I met her I said, 'Good morning, my lady' and after that just talked to her normal all through my sentences. Not 'my lady this' and 'my lady that'. Not necessary. Just 'Good morning, my lady' or 'Good afternoon, my lady', whatever time of day it was. The working class on the estate, we all met once, sometimes twice, a year in the banqueting hall for a social evening and a chat with one another, and she'd come round and ask everyone how they were. And she took a great interest in the poor of the parishes around. She used to send her lady's companion, Miss Tiddiman, a month or so before Christmas to find out who was in need in Burghill, Credenhill and Tillington. Then a grocer in Hereford would make up parcels and hampers of meat and tea and sugar and sweets for the families according to their size. Captain, Colonel Astley, her son, now *he* was a young gentleman as hardly ever approached us working class. He always took notice of the bailiff and the steward. They used to give him all the information on how we acted and did our jobs. He wasn't I'll say 'with' you. I noticed it very much. When he got that the place was transferred into his name when his father died, he did *walk* the farm with the old bailiff as was here but he never used to come and have a chat with the working men. I could teach him very little. Not like Sir Derrick. Sir Derrick was 'with' you all the time. It was lovely to work for him; I miss him a lot. The Colonel, he'd just come down about once a fortnight from London and wouldn't mix. And do you know what he gave me when he left, when he sold the place for thousands and thousands and I'd helped to make it what it was for him? A five pound note!! Are they taught to be like that in their private schools? I can't understand it. If they wants a car or anything else for theirselves, that's all right. If *you* wants a broom to sweep the house, they'll say, 'Can't you find another way of doing it?' to save them spending money.

Five

One day before the Great War when I was busy here as keeper's boy to Harry Darling—it was February or March—I was up in the meadows by the road leading to Wormsley and on to Weobley, the road going through our estate, and I seen a pony and trap coming along and there was a cow tied behind and a calf with a net over it in the back and there was a young lady sat driving the pony and a crate of fowls by the side of her. I shall always remember the hens with their heads out through the battings of the crate. I was on the other side of the hedge and this young lady, she put her hand up. I said, 'Do you want me, madam?' 'Yes, please.' So I ran to the gate and went to the trap and she said, 'Could you direct me to Grange Hill?' I said, 'Certainly. I'm not on an important job,' I said. 'I'll come with you now. I'll take you up there.' 'Oh you are kind,' she said. I tucked my trapping hammer and the few traps I had in my hand in the butt of the hedge and I just walked by the side of her pony. She was a person older than me with lovely auburn hair like gold and a little round face. A little darling she was. I walked with her till we reached the stone cottage where there's a turning to go up to the hilltop. 'Do you think the pony's strong enough to go up that bank?' she said. I said, 'Yes, I think so,' and I took her up through the old rabbit warren at Wormsley where my father was once keeper, up steep grass-land, along tracks, to this farmhouse, only a small house but with plenty of outbuildings, and I helped her put the cow and the calf in one of the cowhouses. 'Oh,' she said, 'I don't know

how to repay you!' I said, 'Oh, don't you worry about that!'
I said. 'We shall be seeing one another often, I hope!' 'I hope
so, too,' she said. 'This is where I'm going to come and live,'
and we went and sat down in the kitchen and she told me her
name was Molly Rowberry and she'd come from Westhide,
close against Cowarne Court the other side of Hereford to keep
house at Grange Hill for her brother Bert Rowberry and her
half-brother Will Smith. (Molly's mother was married twice;
Molly and Bert Rowberry were the latecomers belonging to the
second marriage.) While she was telling me all this, she put
her head on the table and she sobbed. I suppose she was sad to
be leaving home. I put my arm round her and I gave her a kiss
to quieten her down and, as I did so, in walked her brother,
Bert. 'Hello!' he said. 'You're quick on the mark, ain't you?!'
I said, 'No! I've led her and her pony up the roadway!' Oh,
me and Bert, we became great friends. Will Smith he's dead
now, and Bert, as I've told you, he's laying on his bed in
hospital.

To cut a longer story short, Willie Smith, he married a girl
called Hannah George and Molly wasn't wanted any more as
housekeeper at Grange Hill. Well, being as I was working down
at Brinsop and being as I overheard that Lady Sutton wanted
a poultry maid, I went in and seen the butler, I said, 'I hear
Lady Sutton wants a poultry maid.' 'Yes,' he said, 'she do.'
'Well,' I said, 'I've got the right girl for her.' 'Who is it?' he
said. I told him and I said, 'Will you carry the message to Lady
Sutton?' 'I certainly will,' he said. 'It'll be a feather in your
cap, young fellow.' He went in and he told Lady Sutton, he said,
'There's a Miss Rowberry living with her brothers at Grange
Hill and one of them's getting married so she won't be wanted
to keep house for them and she'd like the job of poultry maid
here.' Right. Molly come down and seen Miss Tiddiman, the
lady's companion, and she stepped in as poultry maid and the
electrician's wife took her in to live with her in the electrician's
cottage.

So Molly was poultry maid for Lady Sutton and living at the

electrician's all through the war. I wrote to her sometimes while I was out in Salonica and, when I was in the Redcaps, I'd pop out here to Brinsop now and then, pop up from nowhere, and have an hour with her. Mrs Poole, the electrician's wife, used to make us a cup of tea.

Well, the time came after the war that Molly was well established with Lady Sutton as poultry maid, and I was well established under Harry Darling, the keeper, and doing all those other extra jobs—I was up to my neck in work and Molly was up to her neck in work with White Wyandottes, Sussex, Rhode Island Reds, laying-pens, incubators, and foster-mothers for the chicks—and the carpenter who was kept for the barns and galvanized work and was living at Park Cottage gave in his notice. This was in 1920 and I was still living with Harry Darling and his wife and sleeping in the bedroom above my present kitchen at Ivy Cottage. I goes to Mr Astley and I said, 'Pardon me, sir,' I said. 'I hope you won't mind me approaching you, but I hear that your carpenter's leaving.' 'Yes?' he said. 'Well,' I said, 'is there any chance of me having his half of Park Cottage?' 'What?' he said. 'Are you going to get married, my dear boy?!' He'd seen Molly and me together on Sunday mornings at church. Being as he was an ex-vicar he always went to church and everyone working on the estate had to go to church. 'Yes, sir, I am getting married,' I said. 'The army fed me up,' I said, 'bamboozled me about,' I said, 'and I want to settle down.' 'I'll go and see what Con says,' he said—'Con' was Lady Sutton—and the answer came out, 'By all means he can have the cottage.' She bumped into me one day, she said, 'Oh you bad man!' she said. 'You're taking away my poultry maid!' she said. 'I *shall* miss her!' In those days when a man married he liked to have her indoors and not be waiting for her to come home. What do a man get married *for*? For his wife to go out to work? It should never have happened and it *would* never have happened if it hadn't been for the Second World War when they made it compulsory for the opposite sex to work in the factories. That's the upset of the country today—fathers and mothers going out to work and the children left to fend for themselves, or next door to it. I don't agree with it at all.

Anyway, me and Molly was married in 1921 and it so happened that Harry Darling left soon before to be a keeper in Cirencester and, as the Colonel was virtually running the place through the bailiff and the agent for his mother and father and taking an interest in the shooting, he made me head keeper at eighteen bob a week, so I had some extra money to furnish our new little home about seven hundred yards under Merry-hill. To give us a start Lady Sutton gave Molly a cockerel and eight hens. Father gave me a flitch of bacon and two pictures. I don't know why he gave them, I'm sure. I could forgive him for getting rid of my animals but I couldn't forget. The marriage was at Westhide Church and we drove from there to Grange Hill to have our honeymoon. In those days we was allowed one week's holiday a year but we had to work overtime for that holiday: every bit of overtime that you put in, they booked all that down and during the year, instead of pay, you could have as much holiday up to one week as what you had done over-time. I'd done so much overtime that I was allowed to take ten days! In fact, we lived at Grange Hill for a month before moving in to Park Cottage—Hannah Smith, Willie's wife, had just had a baby at home and Molly had promised to help her for a while with the housework if ever she had a baby there. Aunt Jemima came and joined us in 1926, and in 1930 Mother and Father went to live in Size Brook Cottage, a black and white stone cottage in Canon Pyon. Edwin ran Nupton Hill for five or six years and then he went away to work on other farms.

Park Cottage was a double dwelling with a thatched roof. Our end had a front room and back kitchen and three bed-rooms. There was no electric light—we used torches and paraffin lamps with a big shade and a fine gauze that fitted over the burner. For a wireless we had a contraption on a table and you had to take your batteries to Hereford to have them charged. I remember I spoilt a keeper's suit. I put two batteries in the pockets after they'd been charged and the acid all run out of the pockets and ate away the bottom of the coat and a part of the breeches. For water you went with your bucket to the pump at the back door, and, also at the back, was the garden with my ferret hutches and dog kennels and laying and hatching and release pens. Up by the release pen was a bucket lavatory. Every week-end you emptied the bucket into a pit about two foot deep. I've got a bucket lavatory here at Ivy Cottage now but it's indoors.

I used to pass Park Cottage on the way to Brinsop School. It was a school itself before Brinsop School was built. The children used to hang their little frails in the covered porches at both ends. The teacher lived where my neighbour, the cow-man, was, and he had a kitchen three times the size of mine which I take was once the schoolroom. When first I was going to school, there was no road at all going past the cottage—it was just a track for horses and carts. Then huge great heaps of stones from the Clee Hills was tipped to make a road. One man laid them all himself with a pair of goggles on. Kibbled stones were then rolled in on top. Later, of course, came tarmac. I remember my first bicycle—I bought it off another boy for twelve and sixpence while I was still at school. It was what I term an old bone-shaker and I learned to ride it on the cart-ruts where the spindles rubbed the soil. The tyres were solid and it had a fixed wheel—as the back wheel went round so your pedals went round; if you was going down hill you was going like hell. When the tyres wore out I got a wagon rope and cut it in pieces and pulled them around the wheels. After I got married I bought a good machine with a free-wheel—a Raleigh. £12 I think I gave for it. I sold it for the same amount after eight or ten years because the price of bicycles went up. I've always stuck to a Raleigh. I've had two since. The one I got the year before last has a Sturmey Archer three-speed gear. I gave £65 for that.

When my daughter, Mary, was born I had a James motor-cycle. I used to take Molly for a ride on the back some Sundays and go down through Abergavenny, up over Horse and Jockey Hill and down into Oakfield Road, Pontypool, to have tea with her sister, Phoebe Morris. After tea, Molly would say, 'Are you coming for a walk?' I'd say, 'No. Go with your sister and enjoy yourself. I'm going to have a nap on the couch.' I was always as drowsy as if I'd been drugged. I used to stretch out and I was gone in a few minutes. Those valleys in South Wales, they're nothing else but coal dust; the sky seems to be hitting you all the time.

Before the James, we went on my Ladies' Ner-a-Car, a two-stroke motorcycle covered with a casing to stop the dirt going on ladies' skirts and with a platform on either side. It was too heavy for Miss Tiddiman, the lady's companion, to handle so she sold it to me very, very cheap for £26. It was fine for three or four years, then it let me down and I'd to take it to a garage to have it repaired. The following week there was an advert in the paper: 'James motorcycle 3½ h.p. for sale or would exchange for a ladies' machine'. So I wrote to the party, a Miss May of Marden, a schoolteacher, saying I'd got a Ladies' Ner-a-Car that I wouldn't mind exchanging if we came to terms. So her father and mother, they come in a car, and their daughter come on this James motorcycle, a huge great machine—and the daughter was a fine beauty too. She had a look at the Ner-a-Car and she said, 'Give me a ride on it,' she said. 'I'd love to go up some hill with it.' I said, 'Yes, certainly,' I said. 'You sit on the back, girlie.' I went with her up Ladybank, a very steep hill, and over the top and down into Credenhill. 'Oh,' she said, 'that's far enough!' she said. 'We've been up a lovely steep hill!' I said, 'Yes. And don't forget I'm on it and you're on it and *I*'m fourteen stone!' I said. 'She'll pull some weight, won't she?!' 'Yes, I think she will,' she said. Went back. I got off the machine and she had a ride on it by herself, come back, put it on the road by her parents' car. She'd leant the James up against the iron gate leading into the Park. Time was getting on so Molly come out and she said to everyone, 'Would you care for a cup of tea?' 'Oh yes, please!' said Mrs May. So in they came and I went to the drawer and got out the 'Received from Evan Rogers the sum of £26'. I said, 'Well that's how cheap I bought *my* machine,' I said. 'I think the *full* price was eighty some odd pound.' 'Yes, I quite believe that,' Mrs May said. 'Well,' she said, 'we wants to dispose of the James first,' she said. I said, 'What about a clean swap?' 'I think that'll be fair enough,' Mr May said. The bargain was made at the tea table. Goodbye. Thank you very much. Away they went.

About a month after, there they comes one Saturday afternoon, the motor car and the old Ner-a-Car as I swapped for their James, and Mr May come up the garden path: 'Where's our James?!' I said, 'Why? Is there some man about here or something?' He said, 'No! My bicycle!' I said, '*Whose* bicycle?!' 'The James motorcycle as my dauthter left here! You sold us a pig in a poke!' I went and had a look at it. They'd got the starter tied up with a piece of rope; the handle-bar was bent; and there were several things missing off it. To cut a long story short he said, 'Then you're not going to let us have our James motorcycle back?' I said, 'Certainly not!' I said, 'I'll tell you what I *will* do with you,' I said. 'You take that into a garage and have it put the same as you had it off me. Then,' I said, 'I'll be *quite* willing to make the exchange back again.' I said, 'There's some faults in *your* machine,' I said, 'but *I*'m not complaining!' 'Oh no, I'm not doing that. I want my James back!' I said, 'No! Not today, sir, thank you! And I'll defy you or any other man to take it back!' 'You will, will you?!' I said, 'Yes!' He said, 'I'll see my solicitor!' I said, 'Very good. See him! I can see mine!' Of course, we didn't have to go to court. My solicitor—and he never charged me a penny—just sent him a letter, and that was that. That Ner-a-Car was out six weeks on the road in front of my house, so you can tell what it looked like when they come for it—it went as rusty as a horseshoe! They come for it one night in the dark and took it away, and I've never heard a word from them since!

Soon after we was settled at Park Cottage I was made sexton of the church. Mr Astley, as I said, was very keen on Church.

The workers had to bring their children. If they wasn't there he'd be round next day to their mothers. 'Where was your children yesterday?' 'Oh, one of them had a bad cough.' 'No excuses. Let me see them there next Sunday!' He made a little children's choir, bought surplices for them, kept on pegs in the new vestry. You don't see many children there now. Charles Stoker was the vicar then. He'd two parishes—Wormsley and Brinsop. He held one service at Wormsley at three o'clock, and two at Brinsop—eight o'clock and eleven or else eight o'clock and six. Now there's one service a month and the vicar as is doing it have got five parishes. There's a shortage of vicars and a shortage of money to pay them. We manage; we go along without them, don't we? Take my son-in-law when I buried my second wife only two months ago. He took the burden off my shoulders. He did everything for me. Well, if one individual can do that like my daughter's husband, why the devil don't we organize and do things on our own? The ladies of our land, they've tried to intervene and become priests. What did they do with them? They turned them down, I don't know why.

I was sexton for fifty-three years. I gave up last April twelve month. I'd blown the organ, rung the bells, waited on the vicar for most of that time, and I'd even dug graves down there— they cost £15 to dig today—for 10/- till I lost my dear little Molly in 1939 and I couldn't think of being punching a grave to make a noise in the churchyard with her lying there. Forty-three graves I dug up to her death but her grave was dug for me. She's buried there in Brinsop Churchyard and my second wife, Ann, by the side of her, and there's room for me by the side of the two of them when *I* go. All I got for my work as sexton was £4 a year till Sir Derrick had it put up to £6. I've often wondered why Sir Derrick, with the money he has—and only a few year ago he re-roofed the church—why didn't he put an electric organ-blower in. He put in electric light, *and* an electric blower for the heating so the boilers wouldn't have to be stoked up with coke.

Those bells, you know, are very, very heavy—I'm eighty-one and I was still ringing them up till last April twelve month. There's three of them. You ring one with the foot and the others in each hand. You've got to strain those ropes down until you can make a sound—the bell turns over before he'll bong 'ding-dong-dell'. To be honest, I think I threw the whole job up for a while after Lady Sutton died because I wasn't getting paid for it. Ben Thomas, the head gardener, did it, but he couldn't ring the bells. And no one's rung them since I've retired. You ask anyone in the parish.

Mr Astley had the organ built in 1923. Molly used to supplement my eighteen bob as a keeper by taking in paying-guests so we lodged the organ builder. It took three months to build. We put all the chairs and everything out of the church and into the churchyard. That organ was hauled by road from London and was spread all over the church floor and there wasn't room to walk, only just on little pathways through the pipes and the keys and the bellows and the framework. There's the same little organ there today. Oh, the church was in a terrible mess when Lady Sutton and Mr Astley came. I'd to help a mechanic put up a tester with pulley-blocks right into the top of the ceiling to stop the bat-droppings. The amount of money that's been spent! Most of the windows was designed by a Mr Comper of London. He was the son of a bishop and it happened that when he was a young man in the trade of stained glass etc. his father was giving a tea-party for some children and he'd got a bowl of strawberries in his hand and he was handing them out to the children and all of a sudden he dropped dead. So you can always know Mr Comper's work because he always adds a little memento of a spray of strawberries. There's sprays of strawberries on windows in memory of William Wordsworth's wife and sister. They all used to stay at the Court years ago. William planted a cedar on the west front known as 'Wordsworth's tree', but it was blown down in 1916 in a gale.

You'll find strawberries on the War Memorial Window. There's also strawberries on the window in memory of Mr Astley and his aviary. It says, 'Hubert Delaval Astley. Died

94

May 26th 1925' and there's a picture of a motmot, a little owl, a dove, and a flamingo like the ones I drove out of the moat. But best I always love to look at the alabaster reredos to Mr Astley behind the altar. There's stags and our Saviour on the cross with the nails. And there's a cross-bill. Mr Astley had a pair of live ones in his aviary—the beaks really crossed. That bird was supposed to pull the nails out of our Saviour's hands—that's how he got his crossed bill. The whole thing is patterned after the birds in the aviary—the little kingfisher—you can tell it's a kingfisher by the short tail—a robin, doves, even a parakeet. When Mr Astley died, all the birds except for the ducks were bought by a foreigner. He came to church one Sunday; he was a beautiful singer; the echo from his voice was marvellous. We knocked the aviary down only last year. I've stored about forty of the windows in a shed.

My daughter, Mary, was married here at Brinsop Church in October, 1948. I was very pleased that she married such a fine fellow—Charles Hancox, the son of a Stretton carpenter; he's now a constructional engineer in Dorset. All around the parish everybody was pleased with them and brought their presents. After the wedding was over we had a feast in the Parish Hall at Stretton. There's a photograph of me strolling up the churchyard with Mary. It looks as if I was pulling her along. I'd a very stern face because I wanted to get in the church, see them happy together and get the thing through. Charles is thick-set, hearty and well-met and I don't think there's a husband in this world that's looked after a woman like he's looked after my daughter. On holiday at Brinsop with me and Ann, my daughter's stepmother, he even potted the babies when they was tiny to save her getting out of bed. She's remarked many a time, 'What a husband!' I've told you what he was like this January when dear old Ann died. He went and seen the undertaker, he went and done this, went and done that. I had nothing to do. It was like a dream. Even when they were here last week-end [Easter, '78], whenever dinner was over, he cleared away, washed up, wiped up, went and turned

95

the coloured telly on as I bought dear old Ann and she never lived to see. Everything's got to be just so.

And if any man wishes to have a better daughter than I've got, well, he deserves to go on wishing. We lost the first child at birth—a baby girl; she was born at Park Cottage exactly three years after Molly and me got married in 1921. The nurse called the doctor too late. Then, two years later, Mary was born. Nothing has pleased me more. My only regret of this life, the only thing that I'm sorry for in this world, is that we didn't, after, have a son. I should have liked to have passed my work on to a son. Well, yes, there's one other *small* regret: I should like to have had a couple of days up in Scotland on the grouse moors, but I've never been invited. I've never heard of any grouse in Herefordshire. They've had a few over on the Welsh Borders in the Black Mountains, but no big bags like they kill in Scotland.

Mary frightened me one Sunday when she was three or four. Between two and three o'clock the sun came out beautiful and I decided to exercise the dog. 'Me come with you, Daddy?' 'Yes, certainly. Come on, dear.' Up on my arm. I took her up under the wood on my arm and she went as blue in the face as you've seen any sky. And then she started to turn black! I was flabbergasted, I didn't know what to do, so I ran with her helter-skelter down the meadow and I shouted, 'Molly, where are you?!' My wife was up in the bedroom and she nearly fell down the stairs; she could hear by my voice I was in distress. I said, 'What's the matter with dear little Mary?!' and she just hugged her for a little bit. I thought she was going to stop breathing so I rang Dr Steed from the Big House. She just recovered on her own but we never found out what was the cause of it, and that was the only illness I remember with little Mary.

At Park Cottage I did a lot of 'showing' of the garden and the garden produce. I've got four certificates in the drawer—two 1sts and two 2nds—for the best kept and cropped cottage garden in seven parishes. As regards the produce, the judges came round once a month in the spring and summer to see you grew

96

what you exhibited. One year a competitor was showing gooseberries and he hadn't a gooseberry tree in his garden! It was all
connected with the Wyeside Show. For the last one in 1933,
before the Show went bust, I entered twenty-one lots of vegetables and came away with eighteen 1sts, 2nds and 3rds. I'd
to rent part of the field behind as my own garden wasn't large
enough. In 1928, the second time I entered, I had this Lancashire Lad gooseberry tree and I'd got gooseberries on it . . .
well, two gooseberries made one ounce so you can tell they was
lovely large gooseberries. I went home from work one evening
in the summertime and in comes little Mary, 'Oh, Daddy!
Look what *I* got!' She'd picked all my blasted gooseberries
and put them in her little apron—the few I'd left on the tree
to get larger for the show! What could I do?! I said, 'You
mustn't! You've done wrong, Mary!' I didn't touch her. My
father would have half killed us, he'd have brained us if we'd
done such a thing; we wouldn't have dared show our face to
him for a couple of days. She was only four then, but I never,
ever, put a hand on my child and she never took advantage.
When she was about ten *she* won a prize at the show with a
collection of wild flowers. I went on my bike for about three
and a half miles to get her some of the little water-rush that
grows in bogs—there's only one place in Herefordshire where
I knew it was. Just like little powder-puffs they are, on a little
green stem. She put them in a vase along with Meadowsweet
and Robin-in-the-wood and come to the showground and put
them up on the stand.

She was always a happy child, as happy as a little sandboy,
satisfied with anything, and she spent a lot of her time playing
rounders and cricket and hide-and-seek with the children in the
other cottages. On a Saturday there'd be three or four families
playing with her up by my pheasant run. Then I let them have
the hut I used to hang my rabbits up in so as when it come
wet they wouldn't be all round my wife's feet when she was
getting ready the meal. They papered that little hut, they took
vases up there and they put wild flowers in them, and they made

it all like a little kitchen. It was a sociable, peaceful countryside, the children all together, making their own sport, their own entertainments. We'd get little parties up. For instance, in the spring of the year, on a Saturday afternoon, or on a Sunday afternoon after they'd all been to church in the morning, my dear little Molly used to get three or four families and take them up among the daffodils. Up over old Nupton Hill there was five acres of all nothing but a yellow glow of wild daffodils, and she'd take them up, all the children, and have a picnic. Something to interest all the little children! But today who's interested in them?! Their families don't want them, and they don't want their families! I've heard a woman on this estate—she was sending her ten year old daughter to the village on the little bus and gave her a pound note to get odds and ends for the house and she gave her a half-crown coin to spend on sweets for herself. I wasn't above twenty yards from them. She said, 'Now hop along and don't be long!' Do you know what that child said?! At the age of ten to her mother! I was there! I heard it! She said, 'Is this all you're going to give me, you bloody old bag you?!'!! Called her that in front of *me*! I wanted to turn her petticoats over and smack her arse till she couldn't breathe.

From the age of five to eleven Mary went to Credenhill School, a Church School—Brinsop School was closed by then. She went with Ben Thomas, the gardener's children. *They're* all married now, too, bar one girl, Kathleen, who's working for her brother, Gilbert Thomas, down in Abergavenny. Gilbert's got the Flowerland Nursery, and Kathleen and his wife help run the business for him. They used to walk to Credenhill and back—about three miles there and three miles back every day! Molly took Mary on her bike to begin with. Then before even she was seven she walked with the others playing games like 'All in a Row to Tiddley Toe'. There was no traffic; they could just run along the roads, playing. Molly would be nearly always on the road somewhere to meet them coming home and join in the fun. They knew Molly as 'Roddy'. She was wonderful

98

with children. Everyone loved her. She was the perfect mother.

Mary loved playing hobbly honkers at school. 'Hobbly honker' is the nickname for the horse chestnut, a very hard nut with a brown skin. Children loves to bore a hole through and put a bit of string on and try to break one another's hobbly honkers. At Credenhill there's a big hobbly honker tree grows in the school yard. Mary brought some of the nuts home and she said, 'Daddy, plant me one of those!' I first planted him in a pot. Then I planted him in the garden and then after about six years he got too large in the garden so I planted him up the Rowalls, the field above the garden. That tree is over fifty years old now. He's forty foot high and he's got two trunks to him and he had hobbly honkers to him last year.

Many a time I've watched an old vixen out training her cubs when they was about nine weeks old. I've had my field-glasses on her only about a hundred or two hundred yards away and she's never noticed me. I've seen her go out to a rabbit burrow and sit in the grass with her little cubs sat by her and perhaps she'd be licking one or two of them while she waited for the little tiny baby rabbits to come and sit at the mouth of the rabbit hole when the sun came out. All of a sudden she'd give a spring and she generally knocked one dead and caught it in her mouth and then the little cubs would run after her out on the meadow and she'd throw it up in the air and you'd see them all tugging away at it. A young rabbit is very tender—one would have a leg; another would have a leg; another would have a shoulder; and they'd be sat around in the grass eating and then they'd all come back to the burrow looking for more. When Mary was about five I took home a baby vixen for her as a pet. This little vixen must have been quite a month old because she could just see—cubs can't when they're born; they're like puppies in that respect. We fed her indoors on bread and milk, and she used to sleep in a little cubby-hole under the stairs. Mary and her friends loved playing in the orchard with her. Then, after about three year, she got very snappy and I was afraid they might get bit, not to mention the fact she got in the fowl pen one night and devoured some of my fowls and killed two bantams. A well-sinker from Bath was lodging with us—he was helping to sink a well and put a windmill up to get more water to supply the Big House—and he gave Mary a few shillings for her as she was getting to be such a nuisance and he took her away as a pet for himself. I was sorry she had to go really, because she was serving a very good purpose. When she was in season—that's when the dog foxes are running after her, in March and April as a rule—I used to take her up of a moonlight night to the pen where I hatched my pheasant chicks and tie her inside at the top corner and sit down by the side of the pen on a chair from the kitchen with a green bough or two over me and my gun at the ready, facing my wood, Merryhill. She'd start to screech Heeyoooh! and the old dog fox, he'd answer; you'd hear him about half a mile away, a faint ko ko ko, and then a loud Ko Ko Ko, and when he was coming real close I'd pick up my gun and put it on my lap. I shot three dog foxes one night coming to lie on my little daughter's vixen bitch. The moment they showed their white breast coming down the hedgerow—Bang!

Mary was always interested in nursing. When she was only two foot tall I gave her a little nigger boy with a china face and a cardboard body—I think she's still got that doll—and one day he'd have a bandage round his wrist, another day he'd got a bad arm, another day she'd sneak a bit of plaster from her mum and stick it on his cheek or she'd wrap a bandage right round his face and say, 'He's got toothache today.' She was *always* wanting nursing so Molly and me, we scraped together what I'd saved out of my eighteen bob a week and tips and selling skins and so on, as well as what Molly made from taking in visitors, and we sent her for extra schooling to the Blue Coat School in Hereford. Originally it was part of Christ's Hospital Trust set up for underprivileged children but by then it was taken over by the State. To begin with we'd to pay for her to stay with a family in Hereford because the school was only for town children. She come back home again after a year when she was established but it was still a lot of money for us with the books and uniform and the sixpence a day in fares. To make a longer story shorter, she ended up doing a course at the County Hospital in Hereford and qualified as a State Registered Nurse when she was twenty-one. She was a Silver Medallist! She stayed on as a staff nurse for a year and then she become a midwife and went on at that till her first baby was born, and when her second child was ten, I think, she went back to nursing as a midwife and she's been doing it ever since. She looks lovely in a uniform—she and the uniform seem to tone together. Her son who's twenty-one, I think, is studying Theology at Cambridge, and her daughter, who's twenty-three, she'll be a fully-fledged doctor in June and she's marrying a doctor in July—there's some things she can't stand, though: tobacco smoke affects her chest and, if a dog comes into the house, the hairs on its coat make her wheeze.

Mary and my two grandchildren—I'm so proud of them! The thing is, where did they get the brains? It's in the blood-stream, isn't it? Molly was very clever, and Molly and me, we both had a share in Mary—no mistake about that! When she was small she was as interested in my work as her mother was. She's been out with me in wet weather when I've been shooting rabbits until the tops of her little Wellingtons was full of snow—I've had to pull them off her feet and shake the snow out and put them back on again. When she was older, she was more with her mother. Her mother was always teaching her things—how to cook a good dinner, how to make a bed. It would have been different if I'd had a son no doubt, because I should have took more interest in a son than in a daughter, and him in me. I had my duty to do weekday and Sunday. That's a keeper's job; he's never idle all the year round. Well, that's how it happened: that was my situation. I was very busy all through Mary's life, but she's always loved me just the same; she's been marvellous.

Six

Colonel Astley gave me a couple of years to get things going as
head keeper so I suppose my first shoot was in 1923. For him
and Sir Derrick I've never reared more than three hundred
pheasants for the season. In Colonel Astley's time I depended
for the eggs entirely on what I term as 'danger' nests. A sheep
dog takes a hen off a nest—well, I must save that brood of eggs;
there's twelve chicks extra to be shot at. Or birds go and lay
by the hedgerows on the roads running through the estate
because they like to eat the grit and a motor-car knocks them
spinning so I goes up the roads about three times a week and
collects *their* eggs too. Very seldom you'll find a clutch of eggs
that aren't fertile in the wild so I takes them home and puts
them on sawdust in boxes. Then in April I takes them to the sitting boxes to my broody hens and bantams, and when they're
hatched I put them out in coops and pens on the meadows for
six weeks till the end of May, then to a release pen with dummy
perches to teach them how to roost—that's till the end of June.
Then I carry them in hampers to the coverts so they'll be ready
to be shot in ten or twelve weeks' time. I've trembled many a
time at the thought of all the things as had to be done, but
by perseverance I've done well. It could take almost a day just
to get round the coverts, feeding from my feeding-bag with
sweepings from the granary. Best of all pheasants like corn that
is just spurting. If there was ever a leakage in the roof and the
water affected a patch of corn, Colonel Astley and Sir Derrick

used to say, 'Go and help yourself to that dunce stuff!' and I could let my birds have it in some style. You feed the wild birds, too. Well, if you didn't, you wouldn't have one on the place; the next estate would be feeding and entice every bird away from you. How I loves walking round the cornfields in June and to hear the chicks as has hatched in the wild chirping and their mothers calling them! That's like *music* to me! But God help you if there's foxcubs in the corn. They'll rob you of every chick, kill them all in a couple of nights. You've got to get men together and walk a field out with a couple of guns ahead and shoot them; otherwise the sport is finished for that season. As I say, you're on your toes all the year round. Never a dull moment.

Anyway, my job for that couple of years was to improve the shoot by rearing and by conserving the wild and my reared game. I did it very nicely, thank God, because, the first little drive we had, we killed ninety-nine birds and Colonel Astley gave me a box of a hundred penny packets of five Woodbines for my trouble.

You puts your marks up—cards on sticks—for the guns the day before the shoot, sometimes earlier—5,4,3,2,1, fifty yards apart; then, if it's a big covert divided into sections, 1,2,3,4,5, at the next position so that the gun as was stood in the bottom of the covert at the first drive is up at the top at the second. I've never seen a gentleman dissatisfied yet so long as he has one high bird in a day's shoot; there's no sportsman as don't like a nice high bird; if he can fetch a high flying bird down in his day's shooting he's just made for the day. Then you've to arrange for the beaters with their dogs and sticks to meet you at a certain place—as many as fourteen schoolboys and men paid at the farm labourers' rate (the schoolboys at half). Colonel Astley used to say as he walked through the meadow gate with the guns, or as we all went along in the game-cart driven by a tractor, 'Marks up, Rogers?' 'Yes, sir. All ready for you. You'll see 1,2,3,4,5.' 'Thank you. Carry on, Rogers.' Then away I'd go with the beaters right to the end of the wood and the guns'd go up to their positions. Then I'd call, 'Right away, beaters!' and the shoot began.

The more noise the beaters make the better. They clap their hands and shout 'Oyoyoyoyoyoyoy!', and 'Hi! Get in there! Good boy! Seek!' to their dogs. Then, if I can hear the guns having a lot of shooting, I shout, 'Hold hard down the line!'—they're flushing the birds too fast and the guns can't contend with the birds flying over. If you put up twenty to thirty birds at a time, you're going to drive all that you've got in your covert in a few minutes and the guns are stood still then with nothing to shoot at; you must rise the pheasants steady, give the guns a chance to load if they haven't got loaders. Then I pick up the birds that's knocked down and put them in the trailer, and the guns go on and me and the beaters go along the back side of the covert and bring the birds in the next patch back over them again. Pick up all the game. Perhaps one gun, he'll only have one shot during that drive. Perhaps another will have sixteen. Another will have three. I put them all together, put them on the game-cart. The main thing when the beaters are driving is to keep in line, about fourteen yards apart like beans in a row. If one goes on and one stops back, if one man is here and one man there, you don't know where the devil you are, and any amount of birds will be left between, the birds will squat in the bushes and they'll let you pass. You must keep in line and keep thrashing the bushes with your big sticks and, as they rise, just clap, and they go straight over the trees, straight over the guns who can enjoy themselves.

Whenever the last drive of the morning is over and I've collected all the birds out of the wood, I get on the gamecart and I'm down to the Big House so that by the time the guns and the beaters have walked down I've put all the game out in rows, coupled—a cock and a hen, a cock and a hen, a cock and a hen, a couple of hares, woodcock, wood-pigeon, anything what they've shot that morning. And as the guns goes in to lunch they'll shout, 'What's the bag, keeper?' There it is, all lined out for them to see on the floor in front of the Big House. In the Astleys' time the guns then went through the courtyard in to the Gentry's Kitchen, and the rest of us went in to the Servants' Hall, where the indoor servants had their breakfast, dinner and tea, and we sat down to the table with our knives and forks and had a jolly good meal with pudding after it and the men had cider or beer, whichever they wanted, and the boys a bottle of pop with a glass marble in the top. 'Oh, a bottle of pop for me, please!' and they pressed the marble and it all fizzed up. But only the guns have been given a meal since Sir Derrick's been here.

Right. At a certain time we have to be all stood outside ready for when the guns come out, load up into the gamecart, and off up the wood again or another wood. Then, with what we shoot in the afternoon, I do the same again—a continuation of the line, the more the merrier. Total of so many: total ninety-nine: ninety-nine head—thirty-three brace of pheasants, six hares, one woodcock, thirteen pigeons, and so forth, all the whole bag. The guns will have a little chat. Then Sir Derrick will come up to me and he'll say, 'Put a brace of birds in each car, Evan, please!' Perhaps there's eight guns or five—it depends on how many guns he's invited. I put a cock and a hen in each car. You always pick the best, never a bird that is half blown to pieces with the shot. The guns are generally changing out of Wellingtons, putting their low shoes on to go in the house; perhaps their Wellingtons are mud all over, and they're throwing them in the boot. Well, while they're doing that, I'm taking the birds round and opening the car doors and putting their game on the side seats for when they drive home. 'Brace of birds, sir, with Sir Derrick's compliments.' 'Thank you, Rogers. And thank you for the nice day's sport. Here you are!'—a pound, or two pound, often a five pound note. The beaters now get thrown a rabbit each if they're lucky. When Colonel Astley was here I used to give the beaters a pheasant too. I suggested it and he said, 'Carry on, Evan, if you think it'll do good.' 'Well,' I said, 'it's bound to. There'll be no poaching with the men as works for you if you just give them that

105

little appreciation for coming and putting in the energy they do,' I said, 'beating bushes all day long. It's a strenuous job,' I said, 'up hill and down dale.'

None of the invited guns gets more than a brace. There's no argument about it. They just come for the day's sport. A man who shoots only one bird is therefore quite happy at night when he gets the same as the others who may have shot more. The rest of the birds I hang in the safe and at Christmas time a brace is sent to one friend, a brace to another. The rest are kept for the house. The safe is a little hut kept out of doors with a padlock on it. It's covered with perforated zinc like a very fine meat sieve. Flies can't get in, not even those little black flies, half the size of a meat fly, that lay the maggot egg; they'll lay their eggs only on dead birds and dead animals and without the zinc you'd have a frameful of rotten maggoty birds.

Sir Derrick only gave me two brace of pheasants in all in thirty-three years and Colonel Astley one hen bird before him. Once, I took a wild duck home. We was wild duck shooting one day up at Harlands Pool. We killed about nine or ten brace and I had a little water spaniel which retrieved them off the water to save going in with waders. When I went up next day to feed on the island of this pool I picked this duck up that had been washed to the side and must have fallen down dead after circling round and round in the air a long time on wing. I examined it and found a couple of pellets so I was quite happy it hadn't died from any disease and brought it home to Ivy Cottage and Ann, my second wife, cooked it. And, I don't know, I *think* they do, I think duck smell very strong when they're cooked. Well, this one did. Whether it was Ann's gravy or what it was, the steam was rising and at the same time as she dished this duck up Lady Bailey come to the back door and opened the door and she said, 'Oh, what a lovely perfume!' I said, 'Yes. We're having wild duck today, my lady,' I said, 'one I picked up dead on the water,' I said. 'There's the remains of it there on the dish, look, and I hope I shall enjoy it.' She said, 'I hope you do!' I expect she told Sir Derrick, but I didn't care whether she did or not because he wouldn't have had it if I hadn't have had it.

I reared ninety duck one year and put them on the island. But there wasn't the sport with them. A tame duck isn't a wild duck; they get that used to your feeding them daily, they won't trouble to fly. You can clap your hands and shout, and there you are, all you can hear is *keh* keh keh keh keh, *keh* keh keh keh keh. When it come shooting day I put two or three bales of straw on a punt and rowed across to the island, touched a match to them, clapped my hands, done everything to get them on the wing, and only about a third of them rose and then they'd only fly low! Give me the real wild duck that have got nothing to do with the human being, and they're up and away and it takes a good shot to knock them off. And, by the way, No. 4 shot you always use for killing duck because if you use a No. 5 which is smaller, if a duck is more than thirty-five yards away, the shot won't penetrate the feathers. Under the top line of feathers the duck have got a line of down, a downy thick, fine feather underneath, and the shot won't penetrate into the heart or anything, and the duck still carries on. But No. 4 shot, they sting them and go straight in. One little pellet I've seen knock a duck down even if it only caught him in the eye. It's the size of a sweet-pea seed, a larger shot of lead.

We usually have about three duck shoots in the season. It depends on how many wild duck come in. You see, what happens is this: other large estates have got pools and their keepers is doing the same as me. Well, if they have a shoot and put up their duck, they'll come to the next estate and fly round and round and when they see duck on our water they'll congregate and we'll have duck from somewhere else and I can feed them to induce them to stay. Then I say, 'Oh nice lot of duck yesterday morning, sir! What about a duck shoot?' 'There's more come in?' 'Yes, sir.' 'Right. We'll have a morning flight.' You pick a morning. Five o'clock you get up. If you haven't fed them they go out overnight onto the stubblefields of oats, barley and wheat in droves, thirty and forty at a time, and you shoot them from your hides beside the pool in the morning as they're coming back again. You must put the guns in hides all the one side of the pool. Then there's no accidents. Talking about accidents, just after I left school I went to Wormsley to Squire Knight's as a beater for a shoot in Cock's Park Wood— we used to get a shilling a day and a rabbit for beating as children. Squire Knight was walking with his headkeeper about ten yards in front of him and somebody trod on a bush and up went a cock pheasant up through a huge great ash tree. Squire Knight, he'd got his gun loaded. Up with the gun. Bang! The head keeper shouted, 'Oooh!' and seven shots had to be pulled out of his cheek and his ear and his lips. As the lead pellets hit the hard wood bough there was a rebound, and we watched this old keeper—the one who replaced Father; his name was Charlton—holding a handkerchief and rubbing the little specks of blood all morning. But Squire Knight killed the cock pheasant—Charlton's dog retrieved it to him! *I*'ve never so far as a keeper had any accidents with a gun to myself or to any-body else. The main thing you've to watch is gates and getting over stiles. I *always* opens gates for the guns to go through or send a beater forward if I'm not able to do it myself. And, at a stile, I always get over first and I say, 'Thank you, sir' to the first gun and catch his gun so he can put his two free hands on the top rail to get over comfortable. Then I takes the next gun— 'Thank you sir'—and the next. When they come to a gate or a fence they should always have put their guns safe with that little catch for the thumb, but you can't be sure. An accident is one of the greatest things as you've got to avoid.

Several years after I was here on my own as head keeper, an uncle of Colonel Astley's—the Colonel was still only a Cap-tain then—he come down shooting one day and he said to the Colonel, he said, 'I'll organize the driving,' he said. 'It's beautiful up that Vallet's Wood.' So up we goes. The Colonel said, 'My uncle's going to take the guns, Evan.' I said, 'The marks is at the other ends of the drives.' We drove till lunchtime. I dare say we put up over a hundred birds and we come in with a brace and a half, three pheasants. I was that fed up I said to Colonel Astley, I said, 'Sir?' He said, 'Yes? You looks worried, Evan.' I said, 'I'm not worried, I'm disgusted!' I said, 'For your uncle to come here when he don't know the land and put the guns,' I said, 'in ridiculous places like he did . . .!' This uncle of his had put the guns the wrong end of the wood. The beaters was rising the birds and they was curling in the air and he was shouting, 'Back over! Cock back over! Hen back!' The birds wasn't going over the guns, they was going back over the beaters! The birds have to be driven the right way, the way they want to go, the way they always go. Pheasants always fly the same way every time you rise them. When you're walking single-handed through a wood, a bird will get up and if he intends to go one way he'll go that way, you can't turn him; and you'll put him up tomorrow and he'll go the same way. The strange thing about it is, you can rear two or three hundred chicks and the ground is all new to them, they've never seen the estate before, and you'll put them in the wood and they'll fly the same way as their predecessors. You ask any keeper on any estate. You've got to be used to the place and see which way your pheasants go for the first couple of seasons: you only have to observe them and you'll know they'll go the same way every time. Now partridge is different. You can drive partridge any way and they'll always fly from you, never back over you. I've never had a partridge come back over me in my life.

You never find partridge in the woods: they never go to roost: they're out on the land and in the root crops—mangels, potatoes, swedes, turnips, kale, rape, mustard, whatever's planted on the estate. You line out your beaters in a single line up in the crops —two beaters and a gun, two beaters and a gun; or, according to how many guns you've got, you divide them equally. The guns have a dog each and the dog goes ahead and works in the roots in front. You don't do no loud shouting in driving partridge because if you did you'd drive all the coveys out of reach; they'd make away to another patch of roots and you could walk your legs off and you'd never get near one of them. For the same reason, your dogs mustn't get out of distance, out of the reach of the gunfire. A little puppy, in particular, if you let him go after a bird that has dropped in front, he won't trouble about that dead one, he'll go on hunting for another bird and put other birds up. No, you must walk on past where that bird dropped and put your hand up—'Halt everybody! Hold hard!' —and the line stops, beaters, guns and all. Then you take your puppy back over the ground that you've already trodden and put him to seek for where the dead bird dropped. I was only a young keeper when an old gentleman gave me that advice, and I took notice of what every old gentleman used to tell me in those days because we had no books to go by, we had to go by experience, what we experienced ourselves, for our livelihood, and if you made a slip you had it from your master—and hot, too. This old gentleman, he said, 'Don't "send" your puppy, Rogers,' he said. 'You may spoil it.' I said, 'Thank you, sir,' and so whenever I passed a dead bird I marked the area with a white handkerchief on the root leaves and then, about ten foot on, I halted all the guns and beaters and took the puppy back.

Gun dogs can be labrador retrievers or spaniels, dogs or bitches. Dogs are slower workers than what bitches are; I'd sooner train a dog. A bitch is that quick you can't always watch her; she's much more on the alert; she's here, there, and everywhere and you've got to keep your eyes skinned to see what she's doing. And, as regards the beating for pheasants, a labrador isn't much good in these woods. He can't get through the briars and he can't get under the bushes. Best of all is a good strong springer spaniel. The cocker spaniels have got too long lobes with a lot of hair on so, whenever they go in a bush, Aaaghgh!, they can't pull their ears out, let alone go through. There's a lot of sporting gentlemen never uses a retriever except when he goes out for a day's shooting to sit by his side and retrieve the birds that he falls, so some retrievers have never been inside a covert yet!

I've always been involved with training sporting dogs—my father trained them at Nupton Hill for the local gentry. At Park Cottage when I started as head keeper I bred my own cocker spaniels. One was called Sue. When I've had dogs, I always gives them a short name like Sam, Shot, Rob, Bob, Sue. 'Penelope, come here!'—it would take her a month to learn! A short name sounds definite and recognizable; it's easier for me to enounce and for the dog to understand.

I've only got one dog now—Sam, a black labrador retriever. I gave away my other one (a black retriever, too, and also called Sam); I couldn't afford to feed the both of them on my Old Age Pension. I feed him once a day with a tin of dog meat (Chappie) and about half a pint of milk at the bottom of a tray of Houndmeal biscuits. At the week-end I give him a large leg-bone of sheep if I can get one. When I was keeper's boy for Lapage and Bromage I'd to look after three labradors and they got a bowl of fresh water at nights and one meat biscuit and a half, four inches by five and an inch thick, and they were as healthy as crickets, never had no disease—no distemper, no nothing. Animals can be overfed, you see. Many a time I've eaten a dog biscuit myself. I believe what's good for a dog is good for me. I feed Sam just before it gets dark. In the winter-time that's half past four and five o'clock. Tonight [3rd April, 1978] he had his supper at half past seven after I'd given him a ten minutes' run so as he made himself comfortable in both jobs. If dogs are fed properly at a particular time, they're not hungry till the same time the next day. But I've seen dogs, not mine, thank God, tear a bird to pieces in the bushes because they were hungry and not getting proper attention. I do everything for the dog myself. I don't let anybody else even put out his bowl of water. There's an old saying and it's a true one: 'You never have satisfaction unless you do a job yourself'. Perhaps you might send a person to feed your dog that is *afraid* of dogs. And he may *throw* the food into the kennel—well, the dog isn't going to eat his food when it's thrown down in the dirt. If Sam gets very very wet or gets mud all over him I have him in front of the fire and rub him down with the house towel I use to wash my hands with. It's a sad job to put a dog in a kennel of a frosty night and he's wet through.

It's wonderful how a retriever will get hold of a big bone the size of my wrist and hold it for a pastime in his paws and granch away at it and then get his tongue down the centre and keep licking to get all the marrow out. After he's finished he'll save it for another day. Sam pushes his under his straw. Some dogs, they'll dig a hole and bury it and in a week's time they can uncover it and that bone, they can chew it up just like a biscuit—the nitrogen in the earth has taken all the hardness and strength out of it. I'll tell you a story about that. I was short of partridges one year—it was a bad season—and Lady Sutton she loved partridges; in season she *would* have her brace of partridge a week—that was her delicacy. Well, you can bury a tough old cockerel out of the yard, leave him in the ground for three or four days and when you pick him out, the feathers will nearly drop off him; instead of boiling him you can roast him like a twelve weeks' old chicken, he's that tender. So that's what I did one week with a brace of old partridge for Lady Sutton. The next Sunday after I'd supplied her at the Big House was Harvest Thanksgiving at our little church. She came up to me out of her seat. 'Oh, Rogers!' she said. 'Those partridges was *lovely*!' she said. 'They *melted* in my mouth. *Do* get me some more!' I had to kill every blasted old partridge on the estate just to supply her fancies! I wished I'd never done it because if they'd been tough she wouldn't have wanted any more. That's the end of my story about burying; that's a little hint for you when you want to go cooking and make a tough piece of meat tender. Bury it under the ground away from the oxygen of the air, and the nitrogen in the earth sucks every bit of strength out of the bones, flesh, and all. Roast it after, and *it*'s so tender it will nearly drop off your fork.

Dogs were never for indoors except when they gets very old. I'm speaking of labradors, not spaniels—they're a different matter altogether; they wants a very warm house to stay in in cold weather. *We*'re a lot healthier out in the fresh air, aren't we? It's up to human beings to exert their bodies to fight against the cold. I love the frost, hard frosty weather; I love it. I don't often wear a coat, I'm generally in my shirt sleeves, but I remember once, when I had my big old army coat on and I was hidden in the woods waiting for poachers, everything was very quiet and suddenly an old badger on the other side of a tree screamed Haaaaaaagh! and my blood curdled.

Yes, I've killed many a badger. If an old badger in the spring when the birds start to lay, if he goes down a hedgerow in the countryside from the woods and he finds a nest of eggs, whenever he tastes those eggs, he'll search that hedge and another hedge and, if you've got two or three badgers doing that, you won't have an egg left on the place. You can always tell if a badger have sucked the eggs because you just get a crumpled-up lot of shells. They can't suck them properly, I don't know why; they seem to chobble them up and it's as if they spit the shells out in blobs. To trap them, snaring is the best because it chokes them straight away. I've shot many a one just at dusk when they come out of their earths, but they hibernate all the winter, they curl up like a squirrel in their nests and go to sleep. They're silver grey in colour, similar to an elk hound. That's a silver-coated dog all over, but the badger's got three white streaks—he's got a white streak straight up over his forehead and he's got two white streaks, one on each side of his cheeks. Once a badger grips anything with his jaw . . . I've put a stick in a badger's mouth—a stick three inches thick which is thicker than my wrist—and I've kept turning it and turning it and turning it just to see how long he would hold it. Believe me, I've turned that stick until it's severed, and he's never let go. Oh, they're vicious animals, very vicious. And alert. They're as alert as a fox, and the fox is alert in every way—in hearing, sight . . . when you show yourself and a fox is in the vicinity of the woodland or anywhere, he's got you spotted and he's away on his little trotters. My daughter, she bought me a book about twelve month ago by a man who had reared badgers since he was a baby. I scolded her, I said, 'It's a real insult you giving me a book about badgers!' I said to my daughter, 'Fancy you giving me a book like that when I've dug them out and I've even had one in a cage for nine months till I give it to someone who wanted it!' I read some of the paragraphs but it was stale to me. A month later she gave me a pencil sketch of one, a very good drawing. I know it's good because I've been a man as have studied beasts—and birds and trees—all my life. I can tell if a chicken has been killed by a badger or a fox—a badger always draws out the entrails and a fox always takes the head, he doesn't trouble about the body, because he's very fond of brains. (But a fox won't take the head off a rabbit. I don't know why.) Then when I see a dead rabbit lying about I can tell if a stoat have killed it because a stoat always sucks the blood out of a rabbit on the jugular vein at the back of the head between the two ears. I can tell the difference between the tracks of a badger and a fox—a badger have got six toes all in line and a big pad behind, and a fox have only three in front (and two further back) with the centre one forward like the centre finger on your hand. A stag always runs with the points of his hoof open and a hind, she runs with the two points tight together into a very sharp V. I don't know bird tracks so well but I can always track my pheasants all right because they're more like a fowl and, as you never get fowls in the wood, when you see a fair-sized poultry mark you know it's a pheasant. Partridge are much smaller, but you've got a job to tell the difference between a plover, a woodpigeon and a partridge because they've all the same sized feet. The simplest time to find a fox's track is after it's snowed. Go out early in the morning and you'll soon track a fox because when that fox runs he runs with his four feet in a dead line: a dog runs with his feet apart where you only get a direct line with a fox. And with a fox you'll just see little touches where the snow has been disturbed by him dropping his brush. I can even tell you where a fox have crossed the pathway by the smell of him—it all amounts to experience. And I can make fox—and other animal—calls. Ko Ko Ko—that's an old dog fox. Hee-yeww Hee-yeww—that's a vixen. An old badger goes [the author snorted three times]. The jay—I'll go Jehk Jehk Jehk Jehk and they'll come flying around me in the woods. As

114

for the woods, there's not a tree growing in Herefordshire I don't know the name of, and I've been on this earth long enough to know the locations birds like best and where and when they build their nests. The carrion crow is the first bird to lay in the spring—the same as a goose for the farmer. They build in elm trees as a rule—up nearly to the top of the tree if it's fine. If it's going to keep fine they'll lay their eggs in that top nest. But if the weather's going to change and be wet, they'll start re-building half way down. Another thing I know is where to go and find ripe fruit—the hazel nut, the chestnut, the walnut and the bannut. You knock the bannuts off the tree with a packing pole and pick them up. They've a green skin on them which is very tender. Well, you strike that with a four-pronged tablefork and you drill little holes all round and you put the nuts in a jar and pour vinegar and spices on them, and the vinegar enters and they're lovely with bread and cheese; they're nicer to me to eat than pickled shallots. We old country joskins have learned a thing or two! Did you know that the simplest way to catch weasels is in mole runs? Did anyone else ever tell you how to make a dog's coat come up like shining silk? All you've got to do is pour some tea in a half a basin of milk two or three different times and let him drink it. . . .

I've got an iron pen for Sam—six foot six high and about twenty yards square—and a kennel in it with plenty of straw so he's got a warm bed and can exercise. Then, nearly every Saturday afternoon, I brings a bale of straw up from the farm and I scrape out and sweep out his kennel and throw away the dusty straw he's been laying on for a week and throw the fresh straw in. He's got to have somewhere under control to exercise. You see, with a sporting dog, you're only using him three to four months partridge shooting and pheasant shooting, then he's got to stop work. Well, if you haven't got a dog under control during the off-season when the pheasants are laying in the hedgerows and all the rest of it, if you have him out with you and there's a hen pheasant sitting in a fence, right, he goes in and he flushes her off, and there's feathers all over the place and

115

twelve or fourteen pheasants gone. When you can take your dog out for a walk without a lead and stop him hunting after he's been hunting all the winter, you're a very clever man; a retriever is a retriever and he'll use his nose and go for partridge, everything, everything in the line of game, even down to a woodcock or a snipe. And then, if you're going through a flock of sheep, the sheep will start to run away and he'll give chase. I've seen a dog catch hold of a sheep, a full-grown ewe with little lambs with her, catch hold of her by the neck and throw her upside down and catch hold of the little lambs and all. And if a ewe is chased when close to lambing and she's having twins, they get tangled up and come out backwards (sic). Well, there you are chasing around after the dog, and God help you if the farmer sees you because you've got to pay the penalty.

Training a dog is like training children. First you've got to find out the temperament of the dog and the dog has got to find out yours. I may be a severe trainer but I've never used a stick in my life. If I can't teach a dog by kindness I can never continue with him, I buy another. If you thrash a dog for a wrong action you can put down your stick and get rid of him because he'll never do a thing for you. I've seen dogs run home before they'll put up with the nonsense of their owner. Scold, yes. Change your voice so that he'll know you're in a temper. 'Come here! What are you doing?! What do you mean?! No! Naughty!'—just scold him like that and he'll crouch from you. You can even train him in the house to begin with. To make him sit and stay, you go out through the door and, if he attempts to follow, you say, 'Now what did I tell you?! Go back! *Sit* there, now *sit!*' go out again and if he haven't moved, go back. 'Good dog!' and a pat and out with a little bit of chocolate from your waistcoat pocket. Obedience is the thing, and whenever he does right you must show him and he'll never forget.

Next, when he's eight to ten weeks, the younger the better, you teach him to sit and stay and come to you out of doors.

You tell him to sit and you walk around him quietly and as you walk around him you show him the flat of your hand and that means 'Stay put!' and you get wider and wider until he's a hundred yards from you—the flat of your hand shines in any weather; you could see my hand go up if I was *two* hundred yards from you. Then you whistle or you say 'Come on, then!' and you wave the flat of your hand towards yourself and he should come to you, immediately. 'Good boy!' Chocolate. He don't want telling twice! He'll sit for hours until you signal for him to come to you and then he'll come at a gallop. After that your biggest problem is to make them keep to heel when you say, 'Heel!' Retrievers, and worse so with spaniels, they *will* try to lead on, taking no notice of you and wagging their tails and smelling. What I do is, I carries a rolled up little book in my hare pocket and picks a narrow pathway in the woods where there's briars and I say, 'Come to heel!' and he'll try to pass me after to get by and so I tap him on the end of the nose. Do that a few times and he'll stay behind you even when you come to a wide ride.

Next he must be trained not to eat or kill. If he's caught a live or a dead rabbit or a wounded bird and I blows my whistle, that means he's to come with it and if he doesn't come I go up to him and scold him. I say, 'Come on! Give!' and he must pick whatever it is up and stand with it in front of me and drop it in my hand under his jaw. And if he ever kills a live bird after you've said, 'No! Leave! Leave it!', well, you can dispose of that dog and let someone have him for just a house-dog and a pet. But even some good puppies *are* what is termed as 'hard mouthed' (spaniels are more apt to be this than retrievers), that is, they'll catch hold of an animal and they'll go granching at it—biting it and breaking it up—before they bring it to you. You've got to stop that and I've found a way out how to do it. What I do is, I get a little block of wood and I drive in little wire nails all round it and then I get a pliers and take all the heads of the nails off. Then I get a rabbit and skin it and squeeze the skin on the block while it's freshly dry and it sticks to the wood and makes it look like a little rabbit. If it don't dry quick enough for your liking you can pop it in the oven and bake it. Well then, you throw this little block of wood into your bushes. 'In! Fetch! Go on! Seek! Dead!' Your dog will see it go and he'll go in and he'll go Ahhyaaaaahhh! and open his mouth. 'Come on! Bring it along there!'—*make* him bring it! He'll pick it up gently and he'll give it to you with his mouth nearly half open; he doesn't like to refuse because he knows that little bit of chocolate is in your waistcoat pocket. Then when you go out with a gun and shoot a rabbit, he'll bring it gently, never damage it, and it'll be the same with a pheasant, and look how nice it is to have a bird for cooking that's not been mauled. That's the art in training a hard-mouthed dog.

'One man, one dog' is the secret of getting a dog to know you perfectly; you must be honest with the dog for the dog to be honest with you. I made a mistake with Sam, this very dog I've got today. I've had gentlemen come here, they've had permission from Sir Derrick to come here for a day's shooting. Well, I've been that busy I haven't had time to go with them. 'Have you got a dog, sir?' 'No, I haven't.' 'You'd better take mine, then.' When he was a puppy I let him go with other guns. And what happened last season? The first shoot we went out and killed forty birds, before lunch. I met the five or six guns down at the Big House to walk with them. We went to the covert and Sam was off with another gentleman at the far end of the line working for him like a Christian. This gentleman had been out here shooting, you see. I'd let him have him and the dog knew him, he'd do anything for him. I shouted, 'Sam! What are you doing up there?!' and he come down to me at a gallop and he worked for me with the bottom gun. The gun knocked down a cock which fell on the opposite side of Round Oak bank and was a runner. Over the wire netting fence went Sam, ran the cock down the meadow, come back and jumped the fence with the bird in his mouth. The gun said, 'I'll give you forty guineas for that dog!' I said, 'You won't sir! Nor another forty with it!'

I was with a gamekeeper a few months ago half a mile across the top of Credenhill Park and he'd lost his cigarette lighter. He said to me, he said, 'I hunted this ride back and forth, back and forth yesterday,' he said, 'and I can't find my lighter.' I said, 'Give your dog this lighter of mine to smell, then, and tell him to go and seek.' He said, 'That won't do it!' I said, 'Come on, let's try it!' The dog was a golden retriever, the same breed as Sam, and the keeper knows his stuff, he knows nearly, well, *I* knows nearly as much as him! Well, anyway, he called his dog, let him smell my lighter. 'Go on! Seek!' he said, and the dog went back along that ride and—do you believe me?—that dog wasn't twenty minutes and he come and give his boss his cigarette lighter! Same with Sam. I can give him my cap to smell and hide it in a wood without him seeing me do it and I can go a hundred yards from that cap an hour later and point to my head and say, 'Seek, boy!' and he'll find it no matter where it is, how thick the bracken is or the briars. Or you can throw it into the butt of a hedge out of sight and just say, 'I lost. Dead!' and in he goes and all of a sudden you'll hear a rush. 'Come on! Bring it on, then!' Of course, a keeper has got more advantage for training a dog as he should be trained than just a workman, as you might say, who must work all week and has only got a week-end or a Saturday, perhaps, out with his gun.

There's several things that's puzzled me in life. With a retriever or a spaniel you can stroke a ball or anything with a little drop of aniseed and you can throw it in the densest forest, it doesn't matter where it goes or where it is, you'll have your dog pull it out because he's dead on finding it and can pick up the scent. Now then, a greyhound can't pick up scent at all; he can only travel by sight. If a hare goes through a hedge and, we'll say, the greyhound is running a hundred yards behind at forty miles an hour, if the hare goes left or right when it gets through the hedge, the greyhound, when *he* gets through, is lost. Why is it as one dog can pick up scent and another can't? And why is it, when you buy one of these silent whistles and all you

119

hear when you're blowing is just a rush of wind, only a kind of hiss, a dog will come back quicker than if you whistle with your mouth ordinary? It's marvellous when you come to study these things. When I lived at Park Cottage there was a shepherd here and he had a lovely old sheep dog. I was busy rabbiting in the winter and I was going down one day out of the fields about ten o'clock in the morning after I'd been round my snares and I'd got about thirty rabbits on my shoulders on my long stick and I put them down for a rest near the cowhouse. At the same time, this dog belonging to the shepherd went to the cowhouse door and the cowman that did the milking, he got a brick and he threw it at the dog because he wouldn't allow a cat nor a dog or anything to go in there. Admitted he did keep the place spotless. Major Thompson, the big noise, he used to go in and inspect it just to keep him happy and give him praise—he'd do all the more then; he even put in glass windows with bars to stop the cows' horns from breaking them. Well, as I went to pick up my stick of rabbits, I was the only man that that dog seen when he turned from the cowhouse door after being hit with the brick. The shepherd that owned that dog lived in the cottage at the top of the Arbour and—do you know?—I couldn't get up of a morning at Park Cottage over half a mile away and go up to the top of my garden and ten steps into the meadow without Boowoowoowoowoo! That dog would give the signal whenever I left home. How did that dog know? As long as that shepherd stopped here—it was about three years— everybody knew when I was out in the morning. He'd go on for half an hour sometimes, he'd bark continuously till I got inside a wood. Then he'd stop. I could never understand it. And take Sam—there's only one person he barks at and that's the Corona man on the van selling lemonade and orange squash to the Big House on a Tuesday. Whenever his van turns down half a mile away at the drive of the Big House, that dog starts to bark and he'll bark all the time—it doesn't matter if he's calling at Ivy Cottage or not—until the van is down nearly into Tillington. It can't be the man because they change men. They wear a green slop but he can't see it half a mile away, can he? Yet he takes not the slightest notice of anyone or anything else.

Just a few things more about dogs and puppies. Some parents *will* buy their children puppies without thinking. They go into a pet shop for some canary seed or finch seed or something and they've got their children with them. 'Oh Daddy, may we have that little puppy?' Well, the puppy grows up to be a damn Great Dane nearly, and perhaps they're living in a flat. Well, what room or exercise can that dog have? What comfort can he have going out on a lead? So whenever he gets to this huge size and they've got no room for him and the child don't fancy him now because he can't pull and tug him about, they just open the door and say, 'Get out of it!' Or they take him in the car and drop him in the countryside. That's what *we* put up with—dogs running through the coverts and disturbing the game and all the rest of it! That's what's happening daily. You know, it's a queer old world we live in. I've picked up several dogs and put them in kennels and reported it to the police, but no one wants to own them; you never hear who's discarded them because they've come for miles to get *rid* of them.

Another problem is holidays. I don't say it's cruel to leave a dog with someone else, but strangers, even if they're used to dogs, they never look after them like you do, not if you love your animal as you should. I've never sent mine to a Home because they're overcrowded there, especially when it's holiday time. People rushes with their car and takes the dog in. 'Here you are! Look after it!' Two or three guineas a week. Right. But the dog comes back thin. Dogs pine, you see, and that's more harm to a dog than not being fed. Whenever I've gone on holiday I've always taken my dogs with me—a spaniel and a retriever or a retriever or whatever I've had at the time. I take them to Poole and down to the shore and throw the ball in the ocean and they retrieve it and enjoy theirselves and, not only that, they have a good wash in the salt water and they come back refreshed the same as me. I once went for longer than a day with Molly to Pontypool so because of my black cocker spaniel we had to go by train. We had our baggage, and I couldn't very well take that and a dog, and the wife sat behind me, on the motorcycle. I *should* have had a spill, shouldn't I?!

Seven

As a young head-keeper I was out of bed like a shot at five. Downstairs. Make the pot of tea, take a cup up to Molly, come back, have a cup myself and off out to see to the pheasants, or something, in the garden till breakfast time. Always come in at nine o'clock for a good breakfast—fried bacon and a couple of fried eggs—and then I was right for the day, away I'd go till dinner between one and two or else I'd say, 'I won't be home to dinner, dear, so don't worry' and she'd put it in the oven and I might have it with Mary when she came back from school and Molly would just have a cup of tea and a biscuit at midday. I'd often stay out in the dinner hour to see who was doing so and so and so and so: setting snares unbeknownst to me or doing something else that he shouldn't do. I've caught many a one through being out in that dinner hour—workmen on the estate, but I'll mention no names. Leaving at nine, if I patrolled around one covert, the one wood that included the Red Bar, the Vallet's, Round Oak and Badnage, and never done another thing, it'd be ten past one by the time I got back. In the Merryhill covert, the one that was close at hand, there used to be a hazel-wood patch where I disposed of my vermin. Colonel Astley, he would have me to hang up all which I had caught every day on eighteen foot water-pipes running from one hazel tree to another. They was easy to string a wire to; all my broken rabbit wires, I used to put a bundle down by one hazel tree, and when I took up five or six head of vermin—carrion crows, magpies, jays, stoats,

123

weasels, rats—I'd just screw the wire round the animal's neck and then lap the wire round the pole and give it a twist. Colonel Astley, every time he come down from London, he'd say, 'I must go and have a look at the poles' and he'd go up and he'd count, just to see how many vermin I'd shot and trapped and poisoned during his absence. At one time I had over a couple of thousand vermin on the poles easy. They'd last for two or three years and then keep dropping off, and where there was a vacancy I put fresh ones. As regards poisoning, I used to use strychnine till I got the wind up. There was always a lot of people in those days walking your woods over the week-ends, and one day I come across a couple with a little boy and he'd picked up one of my rabbits that I'd dosed for carrion crows—they love a rabbit, especially in the eye. I knew it was my rabbit because I'd split his ear with my thumb and finger as a warning. I've never poisoned anything since except with Warfarin for killing rats which was allowed by the Government and now they've even stopped that, which is a grand thing because safety of dogs' and people's lives comes first. Three years after I met that little boy, the farmer at The White House Farm adjoining our estate, he was turning clover one day with a horse and side-rake and his two dogs went into my covert. While we was talking one of them come out, and we thought he'd been chasing a rabbit, he come out panting, sort of uha uha uha, and all of a sudden he dropped down dead under the horse-rake. The other dog come out. He done the same. I couldn't understand it. Then I realised—some dead bones which had been poisoned three years before had dropped off one of my poles and those dogs had picked them up because they wasn't so handsomely fed at the farmhouse. In my estimation a farmer's dogs, they never *are* fed properly; they're let do a lot of scavenging for their own living. Anyway, now I don't even belly a rabbit and poison it and hang it up a tree to kill a magpie or a jay. I just put a charge of shot into their nests just after dark in the month of the year I know they're laying and I blow the whole thing out and kill the young ones or smash the clutch of eggs, the humane way. I've come to the conclusion you don't know how long poison's going to last. It's very, very dangerous.

Crows and magpies and jays are the keeper's worst enemies—they all suck your eggs. I'm not so *dead* against the jay. I try to have a pair in each covert for the simple reason they always give the alarm—jack jack jack—if a dog or a fox or a human being is walking around there. The crow builds his nest in early April. I always finds the nest before the leaf comes out because it's a good hide for a bird's nest whenever the leaf is out on the tree and a lot of them gets away with it if you're neglecting your job. You could pass that nest a dozen times before she starts to sit so I mark the tree with a little dot of white paint when I'm walking along the rides, then, in future, I just looks to the paint and it saves me straining my neck looking up. In the afternoon, when you know they're sitting, you'll just see their tail on the nest and . . . oh, I've done a wonderful job here—I destroy about twenty crow's nests every season. You see, once a crow finds a pheasant's nest he'll be up on a tree and he'll watch that hen come off the nest and he'll dive straight down and run in on the nest, out with the egg, and he'll fly up on a bank and suck it. You can go up on the banks on the meadows and pick up shells galore. It makes your heart ache—but you're neglecting your job if you gets it as bad as that. Magpies are generally in the blackthorn tree. You aim at the bottom of the nest, get dead under it if you possibly can. A charge of SG up through the nest will blow the eggs, bird and all—it's instant death for them. You've done your duty.

It's a full time job being a keeper. You can keep on and on and on and on. There's the right thing to do month after month—the best time to kill the vermin, the month to blow out the crows, the time for this and the time for that. You lose a week out and you'll never pick that week up again and then you're not a keeper. Rats, of course, breed all the year round—and so do squirrels; I've killed young squirrels at Christmas, baby ones in their nest. You're with your traps all day, resetting and covering them. You've to watch for the stoat in

E 125

the cornfields—the stoat is the worst thing you can have in a cornfield when the partridge and pheasant chicks are all in there running about in the corn. They'll kill the whole issue like a fox when he goes to a henhouse. You're often carrying forty traps on your shoulder. I use a dry hazel stick as a rule. I like one with a little curve that will fit my shoulder, and it's got to be natural—you don't have it slick because you want the knots to stop the chains sliding off. You have about ten or fifteen traps on the front of you and about fifteen or twenty behind so it's got to be the size of your wrist to carry the load on both ends or else it'll crack. The stoats, the weasels, the rats, you've got to trap them all if you're to have your partridge for the 1st of September and your pheasants for the 1st of October.

The Colonel left it to me as regards the rearing. I found that if you kept down the vermin and you'd a good stock of laying birds there was no need to rear some years at all. The main thing I've noticed during my sixty-eight years of service is if the month of June is dry you'll have a good season. Once in every seven years you'll have a bumper lot of pheasants, even if you've never reared a chick, because it's been a nice June; you've killed your vermin and the little birds grow up and everything's lovely—a good shoot; you rear the next season just to bring in fresh blood. But most Junes we get downpours of rain, and a chick have only to be out three minutes in a thunderstorm and he's gone. Pheasants and partridge, they're very tender things when they're born—three dabs of rain can kill them. Every bird counts when you're out in the shooting field. I save every possible one. If I've got a spare 'danger nest' egg that's not being sat on, I even go around and if I spot a nest that needs making up, in with the egg so that the wild pheasant will hatch off a bigger brood! But you've got to put up with the weather—that's a thing that the human being can't alter. If it's been a bad season you'll see reports in the paper: 'WHAT A BAD SEASON ON THE GAME,' 'OVER A THIRD OF THE GAME LOST WITH THE WEATHER'.

As I've said, the hounds don't kill a fox very often—once

126

in seven years perhaps—so I used to have to snare them or shoot them. Before Sir Derrick came here and when I was keeper for Colonel Astley, whenever the North Hereford Hounds met in this parish or just over the hill in Canon Pyon, they always sent me a card to stop my earths. You got five shillings for a card, but if a fox went to ground you lost your five shillings. You'd stop as many as forty holes in one stoppage—an earth here in this wood and another earth in another. What I used to do, I used to roll up balls of wire netting and when I was walking up the wood empty-handed I'd take one and leave it by a foxhole. When it come earth-stopping day, all I done after was take a pike and stick it in the wire netting and ram it down the hole—no fox can scratch that out, you see, and it saved digging. You always stop a hole in daytime and always on a fine day when the sun's out because the foxes always lay out on the sunny side of your covert, basking in the sun. At the end of the season all the keepers from around Herefordshire on the area of the North Hereford Hunt had a beanfeast at The Black Swan in Leominster—we had a good dinner and a singsong and each one of us in turn would go in at about three o'clock and draw his pay from the Secretary. It amounted to about twenty-five or thirty shillings a year.

Standard working hours was seven till five, Monday to Friday, and seven till one on Saturday. Anything more was overtime—single except for Saturday afternoon and Sunday which was double, though, as I've told you, we was given it in days' holiday, not in pay. After my cooked or cold tea in the evening I'd to feed my dogs and bed them down and shut the bantams in the fowlhouse. In the summer I'd spend a lot of time in the garden. In the wintertime I'd oil my traps and make my snares and sew my nets by lamplight. I'd always a cup of cocoa and a biscuit before bed, but never a heavy supper as it kept me awake. I *liked* to be in bed by ten but when I *went* to bed was often after midnight and would depend on whether I was rabbiting. During the night I had to be always on the alert to hear if a poacher tripped over my alarm-guns. In the chicks' rearing season when I'd got my birds in coops out on the meadow, for that six weeks I'd forsake the wife and sleep in the back bedroom with the window open. Even if an owl lit on a coop, the old hen would Kaaak Kaaak Kaaak . . . Right. Off with my pyjamas, on with my breeches, and down the stairs at the double, the gun under my arm. Or perhaps it was a dog, perhaps it was a badger, turning the coops over. I had a drove of bullocks through all the coops one night, chased by a dog. You ought to have seen the mess next morning! As luck would have it, the old mother hens, they'd collected all the chicks that had dispersed save for the few that the bullocks had squashed in the ground with their hoofs when they was galloping.

The time I went to bed also depended on my duties as a Special Constable. Mr Wainwright, an old magistrate who lived at King's Pyon House, he swore me in with about eighteen others in about 1920. There was ructions somewhere, some disturbance, but we was never called to it, it quelled down. Then in 1926 when the Big Strike of the miners was on in Wales—perhaps you've read about it, perhaps you haven't—I'd to go through the same formality again. I suppose they lost all records of the first investment—it *would* happen out in a country place like this! This time they gave me a suit of blue and a flat-topped hat, and I stayed with that uniform till 1962 when I was sixty-five. 568 was my number and I've still got the 5 and the 6 and the 8 up in the drawer and they're as bright as the saucepan on my Rayburn. We never had to go to Wales in the end. I think the miners as was out of work went to some relief office and was given a few shillings each which calmed everyone down.

For every General Election while I was in the Force I had to go to the school at Mansell Lacy village for the people voting. I'd be there seven o'clock in the morning till the ballot boxes closed at about nine-thirty at night when I locked up the ballot boxes with all the voting papers and handed the key to an official from somewhere who come and took them to the

128

Shire Hall, Hereford. I also had to, you know, keep the peace. If there was any arguments or anything I'd to say, 'That's enough! Come on! Out of it! No place for arguments!'

One night I was on duty down on the main road at Credenhill, walking with my bike, and, oh at about half past twelve, quarter to one, I heard pitter patter, pitter patter, coming up the road from Hereford. Out with my red torch. Bag dark. Didn't know who it was till I seen the face. It was a little girl, about sixteen. She was carrying a great case and she was swinging it from one arm to the other. I said, 'Hallo, missy!' I said. 'Whatever are you doing this time of night?!' She sobbed, 'I missed the last bus!' I said, 'Where are you going?' She said, 'Almeley.' She'd walked all the way from the station in Hereford, five and a half miles, and she'd another four and a half to go. I said, 'I'll get you a lift if a car's going in your direction. Give me your case!' and I put it on my handlebars and I pushed it all the way from Credenhill to Brinsop Turn, about a mile and a half. We stayed there I should say a good half hour and then I said, 'Well, there's only one thing for it, girl,' I said. 'You come home with me, now. I'm going to take charge of you.' I said, 'You're not going at your age,' I said, 'up this road by yourself with that damn great case,' I said. 'You'll faint before you get home.' The case was about fifty-six pound, and she was about beat when I first seen her. So we started off up the road to Park Cottage. Got up the road about a hundred yards and I seen a car coming down Credenhill Bank! I said, 'Here! Hold this bike! I'll go down and stop this car!' So I pulled my torch out of my pocket, stood on the road and, as the car come up, so I waved my torch. It was a lady driver. I said, 'Pardon me stopping you, madam,' I said, 'but where might you be going this time of night?' 'Oh,' she said, 'I'm going to Almeley.' I said, 'Good show! Do you mind taking a little girl?' I said. 'I've just walked with her from Credenhill with a case. She lost the bus and she's going to Almeley,' I said. 'I'll go and fetch her. She's just up the road. She's holding my bicycle—case and all!' I said, 'When I seen your car coming, I

doubled back,' I said, 'to get her a lift.' I went back. I said,
'Come on! I've got you a lift!' She said, 'You don't mean it!'
I said, 'I *do* mean it! Come on!' I got her hand in my one hand
and her case in the other and banged the case in this lady's boot
and, before she got in the car, she swung her two arms around
my neck and gave me a kiss and said, 'Thank you, constable!
Thank you very, *very* much!' I said, 'Good night! God bless
you!' and away they went. And I don't know from that day to
this the girl's name nor nothing. *That*'s the sort of thing I loved
doing as a Special and that was one of the biggest thrills I had.
That's what I joined for—to help others. I shall always feel
that little girl swinging her arms around my neck, a stranger
to me. She was just beat . . .

Now, before and after his father died, Colonel Astley was living
what we termed in those days as 'a high life', and at the end
of the 1920's Madeleine Carroll was a big noise in films; people
was crazy about her. I don't know who her parents was, only
her name. I never troubled to go into details—where she was
born or anything. I do know she later appeared in 'The Thirty-
Nine Steps' with Robert Donat but I didn't see it—I've only
been to the pictures once in my life when I went with Molly just
after the First World War, and I don't remember the name of
the film. But I'll always remember the first week-end that the
Colonel brought Madeleine Carroll down from London to
Brinsop Court to see his mother, Lady Sutton. They got in to
Hereford Station about half past twelve and they went to some
hotel and had a meal, and Molly was in town at the time doing
some shopping—she always went to town on a Saturday because
we was paid here on a Friday—and they'd got a big loudspeaker in Eign Street and someone shouted through this loudspeaker, 'Madeleine Carroll's just coming from lunch! She's
now going to have her hair cut!' All the traffic was stopped
in Eign Street and Molly said you couldn't pass down, everybody was rubbing one against the other from the barber's shop
up one end of the street down to the other end of the street
waiting for Madeleine Carroll to come from this hotel and

walk up the street to have her hair done before she come to
Brinsop to see Lady Sutton who'd sent Lyons, the chauffeur,
to meet the train with one of the Daimlers.

Well, that was the first on-coming of Madeleine Carroll to
Brinsop. We heard a lot of rumours about whether Lady Sutton
liked her or not, but I don't think they got on very well together.
She and Colonel Astley—he was only a Captain then—used to
walk all round the estate up in the woods on a Sunday afternoon. I ran into them when I was taking the dogs for a walk
and just had a chat to the both of them and walked on about
my business and they went on about their love-making and
courtship, I suppose. She was a very sociable, nice young lady.
The first time we met she said, 'I've heard all about you, Rogers,'
she said. 'Very nice to meet you.' Other times when I was out
shooting with the Colonel and the other guns, when we come
to a wire fence I had the privilege of taking my jacket off and
putting it over the barbed wire and then picking her up and
lifting her over so she wouldn't scratch her legs. She was nothing to lift—between eight and nine stone, ten perhaps. I was
strong when I was a young man. I was fourteen stone two; I
could chuck a bull by its tail over a fence! Now I'm down to
just over ten; I'm just skin and grief. A very pretty young lady
she was with light yellow hair, but whether it was dyed or not
I don't know. I was five foot eleven and three quarters so she'd
be about five foot eight to be precise. She always wore skirts
but I was far too shy to notice! That was in the good old
days!

They were married in 1930 or '31—about nine or ten months
after that first visit. She was in the middle of making another
film, and from then on until they divorced during the Second
World War or just before they only had breaks here at week-
ends. Colonel Astley wasn't a one to speak much with his
workers but we once had a heart to heart. He said, 'I'll put it
to you, Evan,' he said. 'My wife was making films and I seen
her with another man,' he said, 'in a bath! Would you,' he
said, 'like to see your wife hid in a bath along with another

man?!' 'No,' I said. 'I'd shoot the bastard!' When he married her he didn't know film stars would go as far as that. I'll say this, though : after they had the divorce and before the Colonel sold the estate and got married again to Joan Bright, a relation of a Hereford auctioneer—very nice, just a normal country lady you might say—she came three or four times to Park Cottage to see how Evan Rogers was getting on. To my knowledge, she's still alive, in a residence on Lake Como.

As regards the ducks on Brinsop moat I'd made duck-boxes all round and when it came to laying I put the names of the ducks on the roofs in chalk so that Miss Tiddiman could see which duck-eggs she had when she was going around collecting for Lady Sutton. Lady Sutton, she got Miss Tiddiman to put their eggs under bantams and when they hatched they were put out in the paddock in little pens with coops and sunken baths to swim in—you know, the ordinary baths of galvanized for humans. I made the pens and got the coops myself and I had to sink the baths down level and turf them so as the little ducks wouldn't trip over. Lady Sutton used to sit in an armchair and watch all these little ducks feeding in different pens—there was about a dozen pens altogether. Well, to cut a long story a little shorter, all went well until one day Miss Tiddiman went and told her ladyship that she'd found that there wasn't an egg left in the nesting-box of a very special pair of ducks and that some-body must have taken them. Lady Sutton sent straight up to me and I had to go on night duty to see who was coming to pinch eggs. Next morning, Miss Tiddiman come to me. I'd caught no one. She said, 'You'd better go home and get some sleep, Rogers.' I said, 'Yes, I think I shall.' In the afternoon I went round all the boxes and I found one that Miss Tiddiman had overlooked because it was camouflaged by a bit of shrub-bery. It was full of leaves so I tipped it up. There was a hedge-hog inside with three baby young ones. I thought, 'Hallo! I've got the culprit now!' Out with the mother first; opened her up out of her ball and stamped my heel on her head; did the same with her three little ones, about a fortnight or three weeks old.

I put them in my keeper's bag and I went and I said to the butler, I said, 'Tell Miss Tiddiman I got the culprit as been pinching the eggs!' I said. 'No more nightwork for me, thank God, looking for people pinching duck-eggs!'

The following week-end, Lyons, the chauffeur, he went into town and met Colonel Astley and Madeleine Carroll, and, son-ever they got out of the car at the front door, I watched them walk between the moats and straight to this blessed duck-box where I'd killed the hedgehogs. Then I went out of sight. About an hour later, Colonel Astley come up to me. 'What do you mean?!!' he said. He was furious. I said, 'What's the matter, sir?' He said, 'You destroyed my hedgehogs!' '*Your* hedge-hogs?!' I said. 'Damn things was wild!' I said. 'Blinking egg-suckers!' 'They don't eat eggs!' he said. I said, 'You tell that to your grandmother!' 'I've a damn good mind to give you a minute's notice!' he said. 'Oh!' I said. 'Go on! Give it, then, sir, if you feel like it!' I said, 'I can soon get a job tomorrow—and better paid to the eighteen bob what I'm paid here!' He said, 'I'm going to write up about this!' I said, 'You write wherever you like! If they tell you,' I said, 'that hedgehogs don't suck eggs,' I said, 'they don't know what they're talking about!' He didn't wait to write; he phoned someone. He come back out. He said, 'Give us your hand, Evan!' he said. 'I apologize to you, boy,' he said. 'You know what you're talking about!' And when next I went to receive my pay I had seven and six a week rise, and my wages from then on, they kept rising every time the agricultural worker had a rise, and after about three year it come to fifty shillings a week and then it come to £3—a couple of shillings more than the agricultural worker every time. And Sir Derrick gave me extra, too, when he came in 1947. I finished up in 1967 when I was seventy, with tax and so on taken out, with £24 a fortnight, £12 a week. So really the hedgehogs did me a good turn! I'll always remember how furious Colonel Astley was, but of course he didn't understand country life, you see, and he never had the ex-perience of what animals live on or anything. Now, when I was

133

a boy at home, my father always loved a hedgehog in the garden. He put wire netting all round, put the hedgehog in and that hedgehog cleared up all the slugs, he wouldn't touch the green stuff. I had a hedgehog for years and I used to pinch Mother's eggs, beat them in with a drop of milk and love to see him lapping it up.

About the time Colonel Astley married Madeleine Carroll— my daughter, Mary, had already started at Credenhill School— I came downstairs a little late one Sunday morning in April before going to Holy Communion and, I suppose, I put a little bit too much paper on the fire before I lit it. I don't really know what happened but I heard a roar and the chimney caught fire and I went outside in my slippers and looked up and the sparks was going down over the thatch. I run into the shed, collared my bicycle and, still in my slippers, I went to the Big House, rung the fire brigade and it arrived about ten minutes after I got back. My wife had got little Mary and Aunt Jemima up the top of the garden and I can see Mary's dear little face now with her mouth half open as the whole place went crash and the roof came tumbling down. When I first ventured in, everything was saturated with water and still steaming. Almost all our belongings was charred or in ashes. I lost nearly everything bar my trousers, shirt, socks and slippers; I lost three game-keeper's suits, two guns—even the jam that the wife had made was all full of ashes in the scullery. Our old iron bedstead with brass knobs on was hanging through the bedroom floor and touching the floor in the kitchen. But, extraordinary thing, the stairs was still intact. I started to go up. My wife, she shouted at me, 'Don't go up there! The steps will fall down!' But I did go up and I hunted and I found a Victorian five shilling piece that had fallen from a burnt-out drawer of Molly's little wooden dressing-table with the mirror at the back right between the skirting board and the brickwork of the bedroom. I just noticed the top of it, shiny black, so I caught hold of it with my thumb and finger and pulled it out, and the part which was down below was bright as an ordinary silver coin, and I've still

134

got it upstairs here in the drawer as a memento; I was offered £14 about eight years ago for it but I still have it to show anyone. I hunted on, and I found a little gold locket as I gave the wife when I married her with a little photograph of me in it. But it wasn't worth saving; it had melted and the little chain had stuck one link in another; it was just a solid lump of charred gold. It was all heart-breaking; I shall never forget it. The stockman and the shepherd were living in the other half of the cottage at the time and they lost all their possessions the same as we did. Lady Sutton, she rented us all a big house which was empty up at Mansell by the church. It was owned by Major Devonport and there was plenty of room for everybody—there was about eight bedrooms to it; it was a huge great place with servants' quarters and tenants' quarters; I'd to ride three miles there and three miles back every day while we was there. Eight to nine months we were up at Mansell while Lady Sutton had a tiled roof put on and new flooring put right through the house. Then we all came back and carried on as usual. Molly's brother, Fred, he brought me a trap-load of furniture from Little Birch —a chest of drawers, a table, a couple of chairs and odds and ends like saucepans. Poor old Fred. *He*'s dead now, too. He was a dear, good boy.

The only trees I planted for the Colonel was seven acres of larch up a patch of bracken and elder bushes and birch we call Canowly. You couldn't cultivate it, and it's just like a globe; it goes up seventy-five degrees, steep. I felled the birch and pulled the roots out and planted my trees six foot apart, thinned them and sold thousands of poles. When what was left grew into timber, Sir Derrick sold them. Well, while I was planting these seven acres of larch—it was the year before the fire—I had a man coming with me to dig the holes and, come dinner hour, we seen a little stoat coming out of Merryhill Wood; she was jumping along across the meadow like a little pony with a little rabbit jumping up and down on her back, and she dived down a rabbit hole right where this man had been digging. So I said to Bill—Bill Round his name was—I said, 'Do you know

that stoat's got young ones in here?!' 'Ugh! Stinking things!'
he said, 'Don't bother about them!' I said, 'Well, I'd like to
destroy them, dig them out.' After I'd had my lunch I got
my spade and I dug that run from end to end. Think I could
find them stoats? No, though I followed every inch for ten
yards, digging eighteen inches deep. But there were these green
tumps of grass, old mole tumps, either side of where I'd been
digging. At knocking-off time, I said to old Bill, 'Do you know?
I think them stoats must be in under one of them tumps,' I
said, 'and I missed a branch-hole!' So I got my spade and I *had*
missed a branch-hole! There was a little hole leading off this
hole as I'd followed in the lunch-hour into one of the tumps.
Well, I just cut it off level with the other soil and, when I lifted
the crest of earth and grass off like the top of a loaf of bread,
I found over a barrowful of oak leaves. This stoat, she'd carried
them all the way from that covert over two hundred yards away!
I got to the centre, the little centre nest. There was horse-hair
there, there was sheep's wool; and in the middle of the nest
there was five little stoats and they was that young they couldn't
see, they hadn't opened their eyes. I picked up the nest and put
it in my Tommy bag and took it home and put it in a little
cardboard box indoors. Going round my vermin traps I always
had plenty of little baby rabbits and I took out their livers and
every time I went home to a meal I laid the five little stoats
on the table and they used to suck at this liver, and that's how
I saved them. I reared those five little stoats till they was nine
months old and then I put them in a ferret hutch in the garden.
I could put one hand on one side of the ferret hutch and one
on the other, and they'd run ring-a-ring-a-rosies up one arm,
round my neck, down the other arm and round the cage. The
news got around! I'd carloads on a Sunday in front of Park
Cottage come to see the stoats in action in the pheasant pen
where I kept my ferret hutches! Two shillings, a shilling, half
a crown they was giving to little Mary! 'Look, Mummy! Look
what I've got!' It was a money-making concern! I was kept
busy on a week-end opening and shutting the hutch!

My intentions for those stoats, what I was going to do, was to put one jill stoat along with one hob ferret and a jill ferret along with a hob stoat, and I was going to interbreed them. But after the fire I was that short of cash with the extra expense of buying this and buying that, that I sold them. I was taking then a monthly journal called 'The Gamekeeper'. I've never taken it for years now because it's the same old routine in it every year, month for month, and it's so stale to me; there's one or two little new items as encourage me, but not much. Well, I was short of cash and in that journal there was a seafaring officer, he was advertising: 'Wanted live stoats. Must be very young.' I said to my dear little wife, I said, 'Here we are, Molly! Here's a chance for me to make a shilling or two!' She said, 'What are you going to do?' I said, 'There's a gentleman here wants some stoats,' I said. 'I'm going to write to him.' So I wrote away to Devonport. I said, 'Seeing your advert in "The Gamekeeper" I have five young stoats to sell. They're quite tame. I or anyone else can handle them nicely with the naked hand. I was intending to re-cross them with ferrets to make the ferrets more active because a ferret's very slow at work.' He wrote back and he said, 'I would very much like to have them. What is your price?' So I said to dear old Molly, I said, 'We're short of cash,' I said. 'Let's say £5.' She said, 'He'll never give you that!! He'll never give you that!!' But I wrote, 'I'll accept £5,' I said, 'I am rather short of cash as I've just lost my home by fire'—it was more of a begging letter than giving a price! Anyway, I had a letter back: 'Please send stoats on the train. I shall be delighted to have them if they're up to your standard.' He sent the labels and everything. So I made a box and put them in with a little rabbit for them to eat, and next morning I seen they went on the eight o'clock train at Credenhill. A couple of days later, here comes a registered letter: 'Thanks very, very much. I'm that delighted I'm sending you an extra pound.' What he done with them or where he took them I couldn't tell you, but that was the biggest gift ever I had when I was in want.

Extra money was very, very useful—it all helps, as the man said to the stream running to the ocean. I worked here for around twenty-eight bob a week for a spell of twenty years! I can't believe that I did it, that I managed with that small amount of money! And I bought all my own equipment—everything that I've used since I've been at Brinsop Court has not cost my employers one cent; I've got them out of my wages. I'm not bragging or boasting but I've always been thrifty and I've always paid my way. I hope I'm not boring you stiff with my chatter but it's been my life. Of course, for my two cottages I've never had no rent or rates to pay. Then there's been the tips and the money from the earth-stopping, and the half a crown a tail that the Forestry gave you for squirrels between the wars. And I used to send big parcels of feathers—jays' wings and magpies' wings —to Horace Friend and Co., Wisbech, Cambridge, and always got £2 or £3 back. I didn't shoot protected birds like hawks or buzzards, though, or else I should have been behind the bars. I also sold fox- and stoat- and rat- and mole-skins to Augustus Edwards, the furrier in Hereford—oh, I made quite a nice bit out of skins. You do know what a mole is, don't you? They've only got feet, they haven't got legs and they tunnel under the ground and they push up a big heap of earth here and a heap of earth there—in the mowing grass especially. I caught them with steel mole-traps sold by the ironmongers. You put them down in the runs, down in the soil. They've got four prongs and a spring. The moles come along and release the spring and the prongs squeeze them just behind the front legs right on the heart and they're killed instantly; it doesn't matter which way the moles come, you'll catch them. One season I caught as many as three hundred. You skin your moles and throw the innards in the butt of the hedge. Then you nail your skins—we call them pelts—to a board to stretch them out to four inches wide, five inches long, and dry them till they're real stiff. You put one nail in the nose; you put one nail in the fore-foot hole and another in the other fore-foot hole and two more nails in the other feet—five nails in each skin. You must not puncture the

138

skin with the nails. The first quality pelts I got sixpence for; the passable ones with black patches on them, I got threepence for those; and the throw-outs I got a penny for. I'd tie a bit of string round them and take them in to Augustus Edwards' on a Saturday afternoon on the bus—they'd sort them out into the grades. Then they'd cure them to make the skin pliable and then manufacture them into ladies' coats. It takes about seven hundred to make a coat for a lady. They were very expensive to buy—up to about thirty or forty guineas in those days.

The agent, H. K. Foster, he asked me one year, he said, 'Will you be kind enough in your spare time,' he said, 'to go in the meadows they've put up for mowing grass,' he said, 'and catch the moles? The bailiff is complaining about buying so many cutting-knives for the mowing-machine,' he said. 'All the stones in the mole-tumps are blunting the knives and an extra man is having to be sent on the fields sharpening extra knives all the time to keep the machine going.' The Colonel, he came to me one day after, he said, 'What do you do with these skins, Evan?' he said. 'I hear you've been selling them.' I said, 'Of course I sell them!' I said. 'It's my perquisite, sir,' I said, 'for a little bit of tobacco.' 'Oh!' he said. 'Do you get some good skins among them?' I said, 'Yes, some very nice ones.' 'What do you make on them?' I told him: sixpence and threepence and a penny. So he said, 'Could you get *me* some?' I said, 'I don't see why not,' and I got him one hundred skins, picking him the very best that I had. He had a lovely waistcoat made of them. About twelve months after I give them to him, I saw him in this waistcoat and I said, 'Oh, I see you've got a nice waistcoat out of those moles!' 'Damn it!' he said. 'I never paid you for them,' he said. 'How much did you say they was?' I said, 'Well, *I* was getting sixpence each for that class.' 'Right,' he said, and he sent the butler one day to me with a five pound note, so that was a shilling each. I also gave enough to the vicar—the Reverend Charles Stoker—to have a waistcoat made. He wore it every Sunday.

Eight

My father died at Size Brook Cottage, Canon Pyon, in 1937. He was eighty-nine. We buried him over at Weobley. My sister, Mabel, took Mother back with her to Birmingham as we hadn't got the facilities, but *she* died—she was seventy-eight—twelve days after Father and had to be brought back again to Weobley for burial too. At Father's funeral I felt nothing. With Mother —ah, that was up another street. And as for dear old Molly . . . Dear little soul! I hate to talk about it. She died of cancer in 1939, a year before the death of Lady Sutton, when Mary was only fifteen and a half and still at the Blue Coat School in Hereford. The first thing that was noticeable, one night she was undressing and she said, 'Evan,' she said, 'I've got a little lump on my breast.' I said, 'What do it feel like?' 'A little wal-nut,' she said, 'or a hazel nut. Come and feel it.' So I went round the other side of the bed, I got hold of her breast and you could feel a hard kernel.

At the same time, my dear old Aunt Jemima was starting to go blind. . . . And now I've just had the elapse of my second wife. I've been through the mill, boy!

And so has Mary. She had to leave school to help me out. We tried some housekeepers but they were no good, so she stayed with me for a year before leaving home and doing children's nursing and then an entrance exam for her three years' State Registration Course as a general nurse. The last woman I had was a Mrs Green. She always sat there reading a novel. And I was keeping her and paying her 7/6d a week!

I'd go out of a night and listen if all the woods was quiet and no shooting, and I'd come in and she'd be sat reading a novel in the other room. I'd go and lock the door and say, 'Well, aren't you going to bed tonight, Mrs Green?' 'I'll be up in a minute!' 'All right. Don't be long now putting that light out!' After I'd gone and got into bed I'd hear the door going click —she'd unlocked the blasted door after I'd locked it—and there it was blowing open in the morning when I come down! She was doing it time out of number. It used to drive me up the wall. And that's only one little item. I had to swill the teapot out and make the tea because she hadn't done it. Then she'd make a second lot after I'd already made some. Well, that was no good to me; that wasn't a housekeeper. She wouldn't listen to me; she'd be reading her novel. I asked her to leave.

One Sunday after I come back from church I said to blind Aunt Jemima and to Mary, I said, 'I'm going down to town to see the Hughes family and how Edith's getting on.' Edith was my brother Bob's widow and had come back from Northampton and remarried. So I cycled to Hereford, went down to Hampton Street. Ann, Edith's sister—a cook she was—was home from London and she greeted me: 'Whatever brings you in here?!' 'Well,' I said, 'I'm looking for a housekeeper.' She said, 'You don't mean that, Evan!' I said, 'I certainly do! The old aunt,' I said, 'isn't capable of seeing things to clean or wash up or anything. Me and Mary have got it all to do.' Ann went and had a chat with her mother in the other room. She come back. 'I'll be out in the morning to have a look at you,' she said, 'though I'm supposed to be going back to London.' 'Oh?' I said. 'Please yourself! I shall be glad if *any*body comes to tidy up.'

On the Monday morning Ann was at the gate of Park Cottage with her bicycle. In she come and I introduced her to the dear old aunt who was sat in her armchair and knew her by her voice. It was all quite cheerful. Well, she stayed in a room to herself for the whole of that week and, of course, put the house in shape. Then she told me, 'I'll stay. I'll be your housekeeper for a bit.' Everything went well. Mary got on with her. Two or three months went by and she used to take the milk jug up to the dairy and see to my fowls and make life easier once more just the same as if I'd got another wife.

We was married in Brinsop Church in 1941. She was forty-nine, exactly five years older than I was. She was a real town lady, born in the town—she was born at Ross, in fact, before her parents moved to Hereford. How she took to the country at her age I do not know, but she adapted to everything. Sixteen stone, dark and stout, she had a smile for everybody and she was more interested in my day's work than what I was. 'Seen anything exciting today, Evan?' She loved me to tell her about everything. Oh, we had a lovely life together; never had a cross word. Nor with my first dear little wife— never did I have a quarrel with either of them. If we come to high words, 'Oh well,' I'd say, 'have it your way, my dear!' and out in the garden I'd go. I don't like quarrels; I detest them immensely; I say, 'Oh well, have it your way! Blow you!' and I'm off. When we moved up here to Ivy Cottage in 1955 and had electric installed we didn't agree over the Rayburn; Ann would only use the electric cooker and it's a lovely oven to cook in, the Rayburn. Since my daughter's been married she's been coming up to me for years with Charles and the children for Christmas Dinner and she's always cooked the turkey or the goose or whatever we have in the Rayburn, and—do you know? —it tastes sweeter, it tastes nuttier; out of the electric cooker it's tasteless. And there's several people agrees with me; they switch from the electric cookers to the Rayburns which is cheaper to run, too, than the electric. I, of course, never have to use coal, I can use logs which I don't pay for; I never pay for any wood, only give a man ten shillings on a Saturday afternoon for helping me to load a load from trees that have blown down or are windshook. There's plenty of wood on the estate for everybody—that's one of the perquisites.

I do not know of anything that Ann could not cook to perfection. She was in schools cooking and in hospitals cooking

142

before I married her; she cooked for thousands. I've still got twenty pots of jam in there now that she made before she died. There used to be three shelves of pots, about a hundred and forty pots in all—plum, damson, apple, blackberry, strawberry, blackcurrant, gooseberry; she made them as the fruit in our own garden come in season. That's where I've been very, very fortunate. Mary's mother, dear old Molly, she was another. I don't know, they had a different touch to the people of today. Brought up years ago with their mothers before them, they had this little touch of knowing what herbs to go and get to mix with the gravy and give it a flavour—mint sauce to have with your lamb, parsley sauce to have with your hot boiled bacon. They knew how to make pig and rabbit brawn—get the pig's head, clean it and cut the ears off and the tongue out and the jaws and the eye pieces and boil it all with a couple of nice half-grown rabbits, pick the bones out of the rabbits, and put it all through a mincer, and then put it in pudding basins, let it get set and cold, and cut it out like cutting pieces of cake. That and a lump of bread and you've got something in your tummy, you can go and do a day's work. Pig and rabbit brawn —you know, the old fashioned way. Good lord, people in the country today are as bad off as the townspeople. Seventy pence for one broccoli head! Lettuce two shillings a crown! They're not interested in gardening; they've no idea how to grow them; they've never done it! Growing vegetables isn't exciting enough for them; they get married with a tin-opener. They want to be bloody dancing, doing the Highland Jig or the Twist, I don't know what the hell they call it; *I* say it's going mad or up the wall —one of the two; you've only got to watch television for an hour and you'll have had a bellyful!

During the war, about four years before Sir Derrick bought the place, the deer got that numerous I had a big drive here; the War Ag [War Agricultural Committee]—the Ministry Department for keeping down vermin and so on while young workers was off the land and in the army—they helped me organize it; they distributed the meat and everything. Groups

143

of deer was coming out of the big coverts at night all round Herefordshire and they was doing that amount of damage that something had to be done; they was devouring mangels and swedes and going through the oat crops. So I organized this shoot and, in all, we had forty guns out by private invitation. I worked it so that there'd be twenty guns forward and twenty back, all spread out, no beaters, no dogs. I gave them the privilege of shooting pigeons or a hare or two for entertainment, and they used SG cartridges supplied by the War Ag, a very heavy load. That day we killed sixty-two deer; there was deer everywhere. There was two or three I'm sorry to say were never collected—they couldn't get the vehicles up the woods to load them. I'd invited five of my friend keepers in to shoot for the day and, at the end, the head of the War Ag, he said to the gentry, he said, 'Now all you gentlemen,' he said, 'that wants a piece of venison,' he said, 'a tip in the cap and you'll have a ticket, and when you bring your ticket to the slaughter-house,' he said, 'you'll all receive whatever joint you wish to have.' Well, it was all two shilling pieces, half-crowns and little red ten shilling notes, whatever everyone could afford. Then he said, 'Keepers that are here join round, please!' and he divided the money equal between us; I think we got eight quid apiece for our day's work. I didn't like venison then, but now I love it because my dear old Ann, God she could cook a piece of venison! It would melt in your mouth, boy! What a cook!

In the country during the war we could survive far better than the townsfolk. We could kill rabbits and eat our garden produce and, apart from all that, we could go out in the fields, dig a couple of swedes or a root or two of potatoes. Then we've always had our milk from Brinsop, and for our butter and cheese we could go as usual to the small farmers nearby, though we had to be careful, we had to conceal them, nobody had to see us do it; we was breaking the law. Restrictions on this, restrictions on that! I put in for a pair of Wellingtons to wade into the water for my wild duck. I goes in to the boot shop. 'I want a pair of nines, please. Wellingtons. Dunlop, if you've got them.' 'Yes, sir.' Then, after I'd paid for them—I think they was about fifty bob,—'Have you got a certificate?' I said, 'What for?' 'Oh, you can't have a pair of Wellingtons without a certificate with a Government stamp on it.' Not even a farm labourer going up to his knees in muck, *he* couldn't get a pair of Wellingtons, not unless some official signed a declaration that it was necessary! They tied you down left, right and centre! Them Wellingtons, believe me, was one year and three months on the shelf before I could get a certificate to have them. And I'd paid for them! I had to go to the MP of my constituency and get him to sign a paper that I needed them. And I *did* need them—badly, too!

One year we had German prisoners here harvesting. As I said, a lot of young men was in the army and we was short of labour for the harvesting and, as you know, there was no combines about then and all the corn was cut with horse-binders. There was a prison camp for Germans in Hereford and they distributed two or three to one farm, two or three to another. In fact, six came here and being that I was the odd-man-out keepering and in the Special Constabulary I was asked to look after them while they was doing the work. They was brought here about half past nine in the morning in a lorry and at four in the afternoon the lorry would collect them. One day I took my lunch out with me and I was with the men stooking corn, six sheaves to a stook in rows ready for the wagons to go between and load when they were dried out. They were very good at it; a fine lot of workers they were; they were as good as any Englishman. But it amazed me that when they sat down to lunch, all they'd got was just one round of bread each. That about fed me up, so I got in touch with the agent, H. K. Foster, and I said, 'Would you please find out if they've made a mistake with the rations for our German prisoners as they only had one round of bread for their lunch?' Next day I said to Ann, 'How much cheese have we got in the house?' She said, 'A couple of pound.' I said, 'Give me a pound and slice it up into six pieces,' and when they

145

got their bread I said, 'Come on! Help yourselves!' Then the agent come out to see me over our conversation the day before. I said, 'I want some rations for these Germans. You can't expect them men,' I said, 'to go stooking corn all day in twenty-acre fields on one round of bread!' 'I'll see as you have some,' he said and so he sent out rations and my wife controlled them —so much for each man which she wrapped up in little parcels —and I used to put them in my old pheasant feed-bag and take them to the fields. The agent he sent pounds of tea and everything, and the wife made tea and I took out bottles of it cold for them to drink. Everything went on lovely for the three weeks that they was here. One day I took them out a packet of cigarettes and they was that pleased they clapped their hands. I gave them a cigarette each at lunch and a cigarette each when they finished work before the lorry took them away. I smoked a pipe, and one of the Germans—how he did it, I don't know—I had an old spent .303 cartridge case, all brass, and when they was having their lunch he smiled at me and he made a movement like you'd strike on the wheel of a lighter, and next morning he brought me back the cartridge made into a lighter for my pipe; where he got his tools from in the prison camp, ask me another, I never knew. He brought me this lovely lighter and I had it for years, but one day I was chasing a rabbit and I lost it out of my waistcoat pocket.

Another job I had during the war was guarding the gate to the farmyard when we had foot and mouth disease. There was three of us policemen, including a regular, doing it four hours on and eight hours off around the clock for six weeks. Everybody as come into the farmyard had to put their feet in disinfectant and do the same as they went out. All the cows and bulls and calves had to be destroyed with a humane killer—one bullet right straight in the brain in the middle just above the two eyes—and put in pits down by the farm buildings, dug with a bulldozer, and covered with lime and earth. And while that was going on all the sheep was herded into a pen up in the orchard and killed in the same way. There was over a hundred

146

ewes heavy in lamb in a great mound all the way along and, until a great big hole was gouged for them in the bottom of the orchard, I had to go up in uniform with my gun and stay there five or six nights. I took an old chair to sit on and made a shelter with galvanized sheets and hung a chain with a big stick on up in an apple tree and, to keep myself awake and keep the dogs and foxes away, I used to pull this chain every now and again and it would go bang-bang-bang against the galvanized.

There was so much of this disease going about that men was fully employed by the War Ag to kill and bury. It cost the Government a lot of money. But there wasn't a loss of a penny to the farmers because they had the value of their stock to buy more, and Colonel Astley was no exception. That's a thing I never agree with—destroying a whole herd of cattle and a flock of sheep because one cow has got the disease. It happened here so simple. They lost a prize-winning cow when she was calving and they saved the calf. Well, to rear that calf they had to have another cow for it to go and suck so the bailiff went to Hereford Market, bought the cow and next morning the stockman said to him, 'That cow's got something the matter with her.' He sent for the vet. 'Foot and mouth disease!' Close the gates! Shoot 'em all! You've had it!

That was in 1941 or '42. As far as I remember, at the time of Lady Sutton's death in 1940 Colonel Astley was living with our MP—J. P. L. Thomas, First Lord of the Admiralty when Anthony Eden was Foreign Secretary—in Oak Cottage where the steward used to live and Mrs Henzell lives now. I know it wasn't very satisfactory. The Big House was now an empty mansion and all the old indoor staff had died or gone and all the Colonel had to look after him was a little butler, Bill Watkins, who's now helping at some big clubhouse in Herefordshire for men at nights—he's getting on in years like me. He was also in tow with a Major Scott over at Norton Canon and went there week-ends, going to dances and spending money like water. I remember I'd to erect a big kennel for the Colonel's alsatian bitch down by the carpenter's shop and she had ten puppies and I had to clean them out and feed them and take them for exercise, five in each hand on leashes—they nearly pulled my shoulders out. Well, I never liked this alsatian mother, and the Colonel, he always went to his dances with her in his car, and one morning I heard, 'Colonel Astley's got a broken wrist.' He'd opened his car door without speaking to the dog first, and she caught him by the wrist and broke it. Anyway, I hardly saw him between 1940 and 1947 because during that period he let the Big House to a French Convent School and the shoot to Colonel Thornycroft of Breinton and he left the farm in the hands of the bailiff and, after that, he sold the whole estate to Sir Derrick Bailey. I know I forecast the Second World War for him by twenty-four hours. I said, 'We're not many hours off war, sir,' I said. 'Look out!' I said. 'The band's going to play!' He said, 'Oh, don't talk so daft!' But the next Wednesday he stopped his motor-car outside Park Cottage, all dressed up in his uniform. 'By God, you was right, Evan!' he said. And *he* was one of the Intelligence Officers! I've had several omens in my life. Before I've gone up to a covert, I've thought, 'Oh, I wants to see Sir Derrick!'—I'd be ride-trimming or getting ready for the guns to stand—and I'd say to the wife, 'Oh, I won't worry to go down and see him now. I shall see him when I get to the yonder tree at the top of the wood.' When I got to that tree, Sir Derrick would be there on horseback, and I didn't know as he was going there: when I got there, lo and behold, there he was on his horse at a certain tree where we never met before yet I foreseen him before I went! I've pictured many a time when I've been going to meet somebody and, wherever I've focused where I thought I should meet him, lo and behold, I've always met that person at the spot where I've sort of foreseen. *Why?!* I wants to know! It's beyond me! I can't get over it!

As regards the Second World War, I've always said it and I'll say it again: Hitler made a big mistake. If he had put only one third of the force he put against Russia against Great Britain, we shouldn't have had a look-in. And if it wasn't for

Russia we shouldn't be here talking tonight, you and I. He chose the wrong party. I take my hat off to Russia. They can say what they like against her re-arming and her big navies and what have you, all for warfare, but she saved this little nation from being blown sky-high.

The Convent School was for a hundred young ladies, and they'd French cooks and all. They come here from Weston-super-Mare to be out of the bombing. The nuns used to go up and down counting their beads—'Dah dee dah dee dah dee dee'; you'd hear them talking to theirselves. It was a bit windy some days; the wind would blow their bonnets off and they'd be just bald-headed. I tell you, it's been the fun of the fair! The girls used to go out in groups all over the estate. What they was being taught I do not know. I never interfered. In fact, we was told to keep from them because they was all a private lot fresh to us and only squatting here for the duration of the war; we had enough to do going on with our own work.

I'm afraid I wasn't very popular with the nuns. This is what happened with them as regards me:—I was in blue three nights a week and one night I was doing my duty to see as all the cottages had drawn their blinds so as the aeroplanes couldn't spot any light anywhere and the Big House was lit up like a town. There's a hundred and eighty some odd windows all round Brinsop Court which runs, as I've told you, in a square all round a courtyard. Well, there was lights all round on the inside which lights up just like a big furnace and then lights again outside all the way around, kitchen and all. So I run round to the scullery door adjoining the kitchen and I bumped at it. I could hear the cooks shouting in French, then all of a sudden everything was still, out went all the lights and they come and opened the door. 'Ah!' I said. 'You're too late! Why aren't the blinds drawn?!' They gabbled away at me in French; I didn't understand a word. I said, 'The Mother Superior I want to see, please!' She wouldn't be seen to me that night so next day I went to Ben Thomas who was what they termed as our Air-raid Warden—air-raid warnings would be 'phoned through to him and he'd to notify all concerned. I said to him, 'Can you see the Mother Superior for me?' 'Yes, Evan,' he said. 'What's the matter?' 'Well, them lights last night,' I said. 'The Big House,' I said, 'was all lit up like a town all the way around! I went and hammered on the door,' I said, 'and out went all the lights a few minutes after!' I said. 'If I stand out of sight,' I said, 'will you try and get the Mother Superior outside?' I said. 'I wants a word with her.' So I stood round the corner and he went to the front door and rung the bell. I heard him say, 'Mother Superior, please!' A few minutes later out she came, twiddling with her beads on a string, and he started to talk to her about the lights the night before. She said, 'They were quite in order, quite in order!' I showed myself. I said, 'Pardon me, they weren't!' 'Oh, it's you again, is it?' I said, 'Yes, it's me. It's like this, madam,' I said. I'll always remember pointing at her with my finger. 'The ARP Warden have threatened me. I'm threatening you now,' I said. I said, 'He's threatened me by telling me that if I don't do my duty he's going to report me to the Chief Constable and,' I said, 'I'm not having that, and I'm not having you clicking your lights out when I comes to the door! Next time I see those lights on,' I said, 'I'm taking you to the police station!' 'Oh no, no, no! Don't do that!' 'Look after your lights, then, and we'll forget what happened!'

All the small windows, they'd got them blinded in a night or two, but—oh, about the end of the week—I went down and there was the lights again, all lit up eight o'clock at night; it had been dark for two hours. So I went round to the scullery door, tried the latch. No, that was locked. Went round to the front door and lifted the great big latch—he's still there—lifted him up. Lord, he was open! That was just what I wanted. I walked straight in. First room I come to, there was about a dozen girls sat down reading books. 'Put the light out or draw the blinds!' I went round all the rooms in the Big House like that till I come to the Mother Superior in the big sitting-room sat down reading some book beside the huge great fire. 'I'm reporting you in the morning!' I said. 'I've a good mind to do it tonight! You're not taking an atom of notice of me!' I said.

Well, it come the day that they had to appear at court. I had to go. I cycled over to Weobley Court and Police Station—it's all at Leominster now and Hereford. They sent a schoolteacher, an English girl, about twenty-three or four, and she was sat there too. I had to go up in the witness box. There was four magistrates on the bench. One of them said, 'Give your evidence, constable, please!' 'Very good, Your Honour.' I said, 'At such and such an hour . . .' I said, 'I want to be right, gentlemen,' I said. 'Do you mind me looking at my notebook?' 'Certainly. Carry on.' And I'd got it all written down there— what I'd said to the Mother Superior and what she'd said to me with the ARP Warden the following morning. So one of the magistrates on the bench, he said, 'Young lady, your name, please!' and she told him her name. 'Have you anything you want to ask the constable?' She said, 'Yes.' She said, 'Why was we never warned to put the lights out before we was prosecuted?' I said, 'Your ARP Warden had warned you. He told me himself,' I said, 'that he warned you about six times! *I* warned you three times. You took no notice of me and,' I said, 'the ARP Warden said he'd report me to the Chief if I didn't do my duty. Not only that,' I said, 'you were endangering everybody as is living in the district by having your lights on! You *were* warned!' I said. 'You cannot deny it!' 'Fined five pound!' And that was the end of the case. Do you know, there wasn't one of them used to speak to me, not the English girls or any of them after that?! That's what I got for doing my duty. But, to be fair to them, the nuns, they never done me any real harm, and one as was a doctor helped people in Brinsop when they was ill.

Looking at my notebooks for the period I see that most nights was without incident. One night I'd have to patrol to the top of Wormsley Hill where the big roundabout light was kept going as a signal for aeroplanes; or else I'd go to the cross at the tree at Credenhill; or it might be to Bishopstone or Norton Canon or Canon Pyon. You'd got a time to be at a certain point and you'd amalgamate, confer with the regular ranks. 'Is it all still on your beat all the way around?' 'Have you seen any flares or any lights?'—just to see that the country was abiding to the laws; every cottage, for instance, had to be blacked out as you was going and coming back. You might get new orders from a sergeant to look out for a stolen bike or go to The Railway Inn by Ivor's Brook Railway Bridge if the land-lord wanted protection at turning-out time. When drink is in, the wit is out. On Sunday, September the 5th, 1943, I see I was called to Foxley Army Camp because of a likely disturbance in the canteen. The soldiers used to go out in lorries to the small public houses and come back all cheery and bright and one night before we got this warning some of them went back in one Saturday and went into the canteen and drank the whisky and wine and pulled the taps out of the barrels and ate the sand-wiches as was cut and smashed the place to smithereens. Anyway, this Sunday the police was called in to be on the alert and I was one that had to go. There was fourteen of us in uniform. We went there in two private cars and was taken to a little block by itself—oh, they gave us a bust-up of a supper at nine o'clock; I had a good tuck in, I tell you. I had a glass of Guinness, I'll always remember that—perhaps two—and a plate of ham. If it was a dinner for a wedding it couldn't have been nicer. We all enjoyed ourselves. And in 1943! Afterwards, about half past ten, we all got in this big canteen, some under the counter, some behind the doors—the doors was locked, the windows barred—and we heard two lorries come in. The sergeant said, 'Get ready, boys! They're about!' Do you know, not a soul of them never come near?! We had a night out and a feast for nothing. They got the wind that we were there; no mistake about it, somebody told them. . . .

As regards my ordinary work I dug saffron one season for the Government—I've heard that they used it for dyeing the khaki uniforms. They advertised for the bulbs in the local paper. We wanted them cleared out of the woods anyway because if animals broke in and ate them they died straight away—it's a deadly poison. So I dug a couple of hundredweight and sewed them up in canvas bags and sent them away with permission from my master and was paid privately.

During the eight seasons that Colonel Thornycroft had the shoot I was so busy fencing and helping on the farm I never had the time to rear *and* kill vermin so I never reared one pheasant chick. But as a result of my labour we killed over two thousand wild birds. Colonel Thornycroft, he wrote me out a little reference which I was very proud of, and I still have it to repeat it now :

From Lt Col C. M. Thornycroft CBE, DSO

Dec 15th 1947

To all whom it may concern

I have known Mr Evan Rogers for about fifteen years and during the last 8 years he has been keepering a small shoot for me chiefly in his spare time. During that time (without turning any birds out) we have killed over 700 pheasants, increasing the number steadily each year, and a total of about 2,800 head.

Coming of a family of gamekeepers there is very little that Mr Rogers does not know about killing vermin. He is very hardworking, sober and honest and he delights in showing you the best sport possible.

C. M. Thornycroft

Lt Col

I was out partridge shooting with him one day, driving a patch of mangels, and I had Chappie with me, a golden cocker Madeleine Carroll gave me and I'd trained. There was two or three guns blazing off at the same time and Chappie was that excited seeing the birds fall around, he frothed at the mouth and Colonel Thornycroft, he said to me, 'Take that dog home, Evan! He's got hysteria.' So I put Chappie in the kennel, went back and joined the guns again and went on driving. When I finished shooting and went home, I thought I'd use some of a concoction Lady Kerr's kennelman had given her in-bred white fox-hound bitches when they were in whelp to stop hysteria and had passed on to me, being as I was a keeper with puppies.

So I got a tablespoon. The label on the bottle said, '1 table-spoonful for a small dog. 2 tablespoonfuls for an elkhound or a retriever'. I poured a spoonful in Chappie's water basin and he lapped it up and I closed the kennel door. During the night I said to Ann, I said, 'I'm going out to see how Chappie is.' I opened the door of the kennel. 'Come on, Chappie!' No response. He was cold and stiff. I'd killed him. No more partridge shooting for the little golden cocker that Madeleine Carroll gave me.

You can't beat Herefordshire soil; it'll grow anything—there's a farmer here grows seventeen ton to the acre of potatoes. The red clay brings the soil to look dark brick-red. It doesn't drain well but it throws some of the rain off the surface so the water can get away. When they plough a field and it gets very wet, they've got to wait for the soil to dry out a little before they can break it up; it's just like putty until the sun goes on it, then once the sun goes on it you can break it up as fine as if you'd put it through a quarter inch riddle. A seed can germinate in that fine soil and then, because of the clay, it holds the plant and the moisture doesn't run away from him. But the partridge don't like it; they like a dust-bath more so than pheasants. They will live but they don't do so well as they do in Ludlow where the ground's very light and sandy and loamy. I've been up with Sir Derrick in Ludlow shooting and we killed a lovely lot of partridge. I've often wondered why I didn't go up there to do some keepering but I've been that interested in the pheasant rearing and carrying through year after year that I never got around to it. I used to make my own dustbaths for the wild partridge with a big sheet of galvanized over four stakes up under a hedge. I'd take a bucket of wood-ashes and mix it with the soil and beat it up fine and spread it underneath and feed my partridge outside and when the sun come out you'd always see three or four run out from there and shake theirselves and fly away. Their season is a month before the pheasants', so if a pheasant gets up before the 1st of October when you're shooting partridge, you don't shoot him.

154

There's a photograph of me during the last partridge shoot I ever arranged for Colonel Thornycroft. It proved a big success because that one photograph shows me with eighteen brace in my two hands and they'd killed those before twelve o'clock in the morning—five guns—to say nothing about the birds they missed. That was the year I worked the Euston System which is a full time job in the spring—you don't want anything else to do during that period in the year from when the birds start to scrape out the nests where they're going to lay. By this system you collect your boundary eggs and bring them inland— to make larger coveys inland and not have coveys on the boundaries. When you're driving partridge in shooting, wherever they were hatched they'll always make for; then they'll fly over the boundaries into other people's roots and corn and you don't get the benefit. The Euston System stops all that and I'll tell you about it if you're interested.

There's the French partridge and the English partridge. There's a few of the French about in Herefordshire but it's the old English partridge I'm speaking about. I was stocked with about thirteen nests—thirteen couples, cock and hen; the cock pheasant will make eggs fertile with eight hen birds but a cock partridge, he has only one mate, one missus. Well, what happens is this: You find your scrapes, following your boundary hedges, banks and ditches all round the estate before looking inland—the birds scrape out a nest a month before they lay, it's unbelievable—and you mark each place with a secret mark, a little stick up in the hedge with a blue card on it. Next, you go round with two or three dozen dummy eggs, made of wood and painted green, the exact size of partridge eggs which are not much larger than a blackbird's. You go to the first nest. Perhaps you'll see three or four eggs, perhaps five; she's started to lay. Right. You take them all out and put dummies in their place—if you didn't put dummies in they'd forsake the nest and lay the remainder of their eggs elsewhere. Right. You open your shirt, tighten your belt and put the eggs in next to your skin. Always wear a blouse-jacket so that it doesn't rub against the eggs and break them if you happen to get over a stile or go through a gate and shut it a bit quick; you've got to do everything with care. Right. You go to all the nests like that and you have your little notebook and you write in separate columns '5 eggs No. 1, 3 eggs No. 2 . . .' so you know how many eggs you've had out of each nest; they never lay more than eleven or twelve eggs. This is just the commencement—you go round collecting every day; the hen partridge sits on the dummy eggs and lays more, and you can tell the dummy eggs from the new ones. Never go before twelve o'clock because they always lay in the morning. Go in the afternoon; if they're on the nest after midday you know they're going broody. But the main thing in the Euston System is to collect the last egg that the partridge lays for the simple reason if you leave her sitting on the dummies and one egg she'll hatch that one partridge and off she'll go.

Meanwhile at home you've got trays. You fill them with sawdust about two inches deep and you put in your little partridge eggs in rows—you can mix them all up because they're all fresh eggs and they haven't been sat on. Right. When you've collected all the eggs you put one bantam to sit today, one tomorrow, one the next day. If you put them to sit all at the same time you'd run your eggs off in one day; the eggs hatch to date when their twenty-four days are up. It's a marvellous thing; it's so interesting; it's unbelievable—whenever one egg is chipped underneath a bantam, the lot is chipped, every egg is chipped at the same moment. Take a clutch of *pheasant* eggs. One will chip or pip—the shell will crack—this morning. Well, not till late afternoon or perhaps the next morning the last chick will come out of the shell. But partridge are out together. And every egg as has been laid yet have got that little air valve I told you about where the chick gets his first breath of air from to give the strength to chip that egg. As he works his neck round, so he takes the top off the same as you take the top off a boiled egg when you're eating it. The top of the shell comes off and he just gives his little pair of wings a shiffle—they've no feathers on them, only a bit of fluff—and he rattles out and the warmth of the hen revives him and he'll run within eight hours as fast as you can walk. They're marvellous little birds, the partridge. They're only the size of your thumbnail when they're hatched, only just about three quarters of an inch long, the longest of them, from head to tail.

So, whenever the eggs are chipped, right, it's time to tighten your belt, put them in your shirt, and take them out around your estate and dispose of them by taking the dummy eggs out of your nests and putting the chipped eggs in. But you do this *inland*. You don't want eggs hatching on your boundary—you can knock the partridges off the dummy eggs on the boundary any time. No, you wants your partridge inland in the centre. You're following me nicely? So you go around with these chipped eggs inland and increase the clutches to twelve or fourteen chipped eggs. If the hen is on the nest, you don't make a noise, you just push a long hazel rod in, and she'll go out and cut all sorts of antics and run and turn over to attract you and take you away from the nest. Be as quick as you can. Up to the nest quick. Out with the dummy eggs. In with the chipped ones. Do that in the morning and in the afternoon she's happy, she's off into the growing corn crops or the hay fields or what have you with a brood of chicks. You've saved your eggs from the vermin; you've preserved them to the date of hatching. The stoats haven't eaten them, the magpies haven't sucked them. There you are. You know you've got them there. Right. It's up to you then to trap every hedgerow and kill all the vermin before they get to them.

The system worked. When the shooting day came for the partridge, Colonel Thornycroft was there with his three sons and so was Mr Goodwin from Burghill—he was there as an invite. We lined out fifty yards apart and I was driving all the stubble land where the corn had been cut into a big patch of mangels over the hedge. The partridge was getting up like flies because, of course, whenever you frighten a partridge he'll go straight to the root field. The first covey that got up was eleven and those eleven come straight down the line and the five guns—Bang! Bang!; Bang! Bang!; Bang! Bang!; Bang! Bang!; Bang! Bang!—they left me one bird and I always remember shouting down the line to them, 'Don't forget there's another season to come, gentlemen!' They could shoot, mind. They was wonderful shots. They never enjoyed theirselves more in their lives. There was only that one bird got away. And when it come eleven o'clock I said, 'Who'd like to moisten their mouths?'—they'd been walking and walking. And the sun came out nice and warm and I threw some eating apples I'd taken off the pippin tree in the orchard onto the bank and I see Colonel Thornycroft's three sons scrabble for them—it was lovely to be with gentlemen like it. But two of them we never seen again; they were killed in the war shortly afterwards.

Nine

When Sir Derrick Bailey bought the place, there was men
going to him with their written out references to make sure of
their jobs. I said to him, I said, 'I'm sorry I don't have a
reference from Colonel Astley.' He said, 'Colonel Astley gave
me a reference about you, Rogers,' he said, 'good enough to take
you to heaven if there is such a place.' I said, 'Thank you, sir,'
and it's been a lovely life for me ever since. Under the Astleys
I had Miss Tiddiman telling me what to do; I had the steward
telling me what to do; the farm bailiff would want me occas-
ionally; and Lady Sutton would send out messages with the
butler—I had four bosses and I didn't know whether I was on
my head or on my legs half my time. But after Sir Derrick came
here it was one dog, one bone. He was my master—and still
is today; no one gives me orders, only Sir Derrick; I'm personal
to Sir Derrick as his gamekeeper. I had chances to go head-
keeper on three estates as luck would have it, but I turned them
all down after a few weeks; I took to the gentleman straight
away. He knew nothing about me and I knew nothing about
him. He came to me, he said, 'Carry on the same as what
you've done for Colonel Astley.' I said, 'I'll try my best, sir, and
if I don't satisfy you it's up to you to tell me. And,' I said, 'if
you don't satisfy me, sir, I shall damn soon tell *you*!'

Well, I'd only used pheasant 'danger' nest eggs for rearing under
the Astleys, and the laying pen up Merryhill for egg production,
its posts had rotted and the wire-netting was taken off it by the
workers to go round their gardens to keep the rabbits from eat-

ing their green stuff. But there was an orchard in front of the Big House, and half of it was for ewes and lambs and half was the garden where Lady Bailey was always potching about among the daffodils and fruit trees, so Lady Bailey let me put up a pen in the fruit part—a hundred yards long and fifty yards wide—where the hen pheasants could lay among the raspberry, gooseberry and blackcurrant bushes and the small apple trees at the commencement of the season. I put netting over the top when I didn't wing-brail. Then, when I took my chicks off the meadow later, I put them in that pen with the net on and when they'd been in there for about a month I took the net off and let them go; there was plenty of large trees for them to roost in, trees nearby that I planted there myself in old Mr Astley's time—a patch of ash and a patch of Douglas. I had pheasants flying around the house and all round the estate and everywhere. That way I reared between two and three hundred every year and Sir Derrick was quite satisfied. It provided four good days' pheasant shooting around Christmas. After them, you've what they term as a 'cock shoot'—you go out and bag near every cock you can see. You've always killed more hens than cocks—cocks are wary old customers. The cock shoot is the last shoot of the season every year—generally on January the 31st or February the 1st; workpeople and all who's got guns is invited to try and reduce the cocks. You can never kill enough—always kill your cocks down hard. You see, a cock, he has what they call a 'harem'; he'll choose a meadow and he'll entice out four, five, up to nine hens and he'll keep parading round these hens when they're laying and, if another cock pheasant happens to light on that meadow, they'll fight till they nearly kill one another, and the danger is the cocks will be that intent on fighting and chasing one another they'll be missing the company of the hens, they'll not be paying attention to them, they won't tread them, and you'll have a lot of addled eggs. And even if they *wants* to tread the hens, they've knocked themselves about that much, they're not able to balance themselves to do it. So you can't kill too many cocks.

You rear every year if you can in order to keep up the stock on the estate, and, one year, Sir Derrick brought me in some six-week-old poults he'd been given. We only get one good June in seven here, as I've told you. When you've got tame birds as you're rearing in coops, the little chicks have got a chance to go in the coop and shelter in a thunder-storm. But the wild birds, if they're exposed to the weather . . . I had a thunder-storm the year before last and it would make you—well, I did, I shed tears. When you plant Douglas and Scotch and what have you, you always put down rabbit netting with a very small mesh to stop the rabbits taking the leaders out of them which they love to do if it comes a frosty weather with a bit of snow. The trouble is I've got three or four plantations all with wire netting to stop the rabbits going to the young plantings and the wild hen pheasant, she hatches her brood in the wood and they can't get through the meshes so they stop in the wood while she goes out to feed; then, when they're little fledglings and can lift off the ground, they fly out and follow her. So, she's down the corn-field with her brood of chicks. Down comes the thunder-storm. The year before last I was next door to drowning *myself*! I come home and the water was running out of the tops of my Wellingtons. Well, you see, the old hen bird, she'll go for shelter; she'll fly over your fence but the poor little chicks all runs up to the netting and in the deluge they can't lift off to get over. I could have went along and picked up five bucketful of my dead chicks and I cried.

Sir Derrick started a milking parlour. It used to take our old cowman from about six o'clock in the morning till eight to milk five cows into buckets with his two hands. With the all-electric milking machines it took about four and a half minutes to milk one cow and you put in six at a time. Well, talking about accidents, Sir Derrick had a silage machine bought for gobbling up the grass, and it's all put in a heap till it steams, and that is silage when it's pressed, what they feed the milking cows on, and it's a grand thing for cattle, no mistake. Well, I told you about the Euston System for rearing partridge and how I brought

161

big clutches into the centre of the estate . . . I went to the silage pit one day and I picked out of the grass little feet and wings and heads all chibbled up by the knives of the machine going round. Oh it was wicked, and, ever since, there's been very few partridge here. *Now* if I see a clutch of pheasants or partridge in the mowing field, I stop the man in control of the machine and get the old hen out so the little chicks will follow. But a little partridge is tiny when he's hatched and he'll hide if you make too much noise and won't run out of the grass till you're clear away.

Though Sir Derrick's very rich, he never had more than two indoor servants—the butler and his wife. I think his money came from interests in South Africa—he usually went there twice a year. He was in the Second World War as a pilot—he's a DFC as well as being a Bart . . . He used the aerodrome up at Shobdon and he's still, to my knowledge, got three of his own planes. He once offered to take me down to Poole in one to see my daughter but I like to stay on the earth with my feet: I don't want them dangling in the air, thank you! As regards the outside men with their residences on the estate, there was only about half a dozen workers left when he come, and he went round them, so I heard, and he said, 'Now what is *your* job on the place?' 'So and so and so and so,' they'd say to him. 'Right. Well carry on the same as you did for Colonel Astley until further notice!' 'Very good.' So they went on. Only a few weeks went by and I heard talk of one or two of them handing in their notices. Oh, they wasn't going to stick with a nigger-driver! Pickfords, the removal people, they was up and down the road like a blinking yo-yo! Coming from Africa, Sir Derrick was always used to having niggers working for him, you see, and of course he started, as I seen it, in a manner like, 'Go on! Do so and so!' and 'Do this!' and 'Do the other!' you know. But he was never like that with me; it's strange but it's correct. And whatever I asked for he never refused me; he was better than my father ever knew *how* to be. Maybe it was because I was brought up to obey. Always when he said, 'I want you to

162

be down to the house at two o'clock tomorrow (or "at twelve o'clock"). I want to see you for so and so or so and so (or "I've got a gentleman coming to see you")', I've gone down about five minutes before, but never five minutes after; and if he said, 'My horse broke the top rail of such and such a gate today, Evan. Repair it when you've got time, will you?' I said, 'Very good, sir!'; that was that; he knew it would be done. If it wasn't done the next day, it would be done the day after, according to how my hours worked out during the following two days; if a boss have got a man and asks him to do a job he should be able to come and inspect the job soon after. A servant is a servant; obey is the thing; you have to obey. *And* respect—'Very good, Sir Derrick. I understand. I know exactly now what you want.' I'd touch my hat to him, I'd say, 'Morning, Sir Derrick!' 'Morning, Rogers!' and then I'd talk to him after, the same as I'd talk to anyone; I didn't keep on saying 'Sir Derrick' all through my sentences; I just gave him that little respect when we met to prove that I was a servant and not his equal. He called me 'Rogers' in the first instance; then when he got used to me it was always 'Ev-*aahn*!' I can hear his voice now ringing in my ears; he could put on a very loud voice sometimes; and if I didn't hear it the first time he'd shout it lower down. That's how he always acted but he was a dear good man, there's no mistake about it; he's one of the dearest gentlemen that ever broke a bit of bread. Even when my dear old Aunt as was blind, a stranger to him, died at ninety-four only a year after he come here, he said, 'Oh, I'm sorry to hear of your loss, Evan,' he said, and he come upstairs and helped to carry her coffin down before it was taken to Brinsop Churchyard. Yet I've seen him in a rage with other workers. I'm sorry to say he was very fluent at swearing and of course I couldn't tell him to stop. He's even swore when he's been out shooting and Lady Bailey has come along. A pheasant fell in front of me and I was busy watching my dog to see as he didn't get too far away to flush too many birds, and Lady Bailey said to Sir Derrick, 'I know exactly where it dropped, darling!' I remember it quite clear. 'Well,' he said, 'tell Evan where the bloody thing is, then!' He said it to *her*—to Lady Bailey! Well, you know, it was extraordinary. I couldn't believe my own ears to think that he would ever speak to a lady like Lady Bailey, his wife, in those terms. I'd heard him swear at a workman though he'd never sworn at me.

Oh, I'm sorry, he did *once* swear at me. Before we started shooting one day I told him what parts of arable I was going to drive and what parts of woodland, and we worked it one, two, three beats before lunch and three beats after lunch, and we were driving a patch of kale for pheasants about the end of October just before the kale was finished cut—three guns: Sir Derrick, Colonel Thornycroft and Mr Goodwin from Burghill. Colonel Thornycroft hadn't got a dog so I got next to him with mine. Well, we'd finished shooting and the dogs—Sir Derrick had a very good one called Vod—couldn't find any more birds in the end of this patch of kale so Colonel Thornycroft, he said to me, 'Send your dog over here, Rogers,' he said. 'I've got a cock down here in the corner.' I said, 'Very good, sir!' I said, 'Sam!'—same name as the dog I've got now and the same breed—'Hi! Lost! Seek! Dead! Good boy!' and the dog went to where I pointed, to where Colonel Thornycroft had told me the bird fell, in front of Sir Derrick. Well, Sir Derrick never liked my dog going with his dogs in front of him—he liked to see his own dogs working. I understood that. But when I said, 'Hi! Lost! Seek! Dead!' he said to me, 'SHUT YOUR BLOODY MOUTH!' I said, 'VERY GOOD, SIR!', picked up the five or six brace of birds, coupled them together and started off towards the next beat, and the guns all followed me and the beaters up towards the big wood, Merryhill, where I was going to bring the bottom-half breast along. I opened the gate, the guns came in, and I said, 'Come along, beaters!' and Sir Derrick came up to me and he said, 'Which way are we going now, Evan?' because he'd forgotten the way I'd told him I was going to drive the wood. I took no more notice of him than if he hadn't spoken. He said, 'Have you gone deaf?!' he said. I said, 'No, sir,' I said. 'Didn't you tell me,' I said, 'about ten minutes ago, sir—it's certainly not a quarter of an hour, sir —didn't you tell me to shut my bloody mouth?!' and I looked him straight in the face. 'Oh forget it, Evan! Forget it!' he said, and tapped me on the shoulder. And he never swore at me again in his life, not in thirty years.

Well, as I told you, most of the old hands, they couldn't stick Sir Derrick at any price and they left and new men come in. The bailiff and Sir Derrick couldn't see eye to eye and after about two year *he* left and a new one come in—a slim, small-featured, cocky little bloke. Talk about Sir Derrick being a slave driver! This new bailiff, I could see him ordering the men about; they weren't allowed to light a cigarette hardly—'Never mind so much smoking! Get on with your work!' and all this bullshit to them, you know. Jim, the old stockman, had a cow calving and he went down to see him. He said, 'I want some help to draw the calf.' 'Oh, said the bailiff, 'we'll soon calve it!' he said. 'Go on back up to your job and get on with it. I'll be up there in a couple of minutes!' He jumped in the Land-Rover with a big waggon-rope; he went up; 'Where's this cow?'; put the rope in through the cow-house door, fastened it to the two front feet of the calf still half inside the cow laid down inside the cow-house, fastened it to the Land-Rover, jumped in the Land-Rover, and he pulled the calf, cow and all, out through the door. The old stockman said, 'I'd have killed the bugger,' he said, 'if I could have got at him with the pike in my hand,' he said, 'only he'd got the Land-Rover doors closed!' All the old boy could do was cut the rope off the calf and tell the bailiff to clear out of the yard. Then he went round the others who didn't like him and they all put their heads together and one of them even come to me. I was repairing the pheasant pen and the chappie said, 'Oh, I was to tell you you're to come in the yard in the morning,' he said, 'at nine o'clock. Sir Derrick wants to see us all.' So I come home and told the wife about it. Next morning I seen all the men going down across the orchard so I strolled down there myself at the time required. Lo and behold, here comes Sir Derrick along between the moats to all of us lined up in a row in front of the bailiff. He said, 'I hear things are not what they should be here,' he said. 'What's all these complaints I hear about?' He went to the first man; he made a note of his complaint. He went to the second man. He went to the third man—the stockman, that was. He told him he asked the bailiff for help. He said, 'He nearly killed your cow, sir!' He said, 'I'm not standing for that,' he said. 'I wants fair play,' he said. 'I'm looking after your stock and calving cows,' he said, 'and all the rest of it,' he said, 'and ask for a bit of help and then he come and tushed the calf, cow and all, out through the cow-house door!' He said, 'It's downright damn cruelty!' he said, and he said, 'If you don't stop him,' he said, 'I'm going to give you my notice!' He said, 'I'm sorry, but that's what will have to happen!' 'Right. Thank you, Jim,' says Sir Derrick. Next there was old Bob Eckley, the shepherd. Sir Derrick liked old Bob Eckley. He said to him, 'What have *you* got against him, Bob?' 'Oh,' he said, 'a proper bloody fool he is, sir,' he said. 'I don't mind working for a man,' he said, 'but I'm not going to work for a bloody fool!' 'Anything else?' 'No,' he said. 'That'll do for the time being!' Then Sir Derrick come to me. Now, he had bought the bailiff a nice sheep dog—I think he gave about £40 for it—but when he went for his holiday he just kicked the dog out of the house and let him find his own food; the dog was going round for a fortnight where anybody would give him a mouthful to keep him alive. The bailiff came back from holiday—he'd been back about a week before all this disturbance and distastefulness—but Sir Derrick had seen this sheep dog in the waste bins outside the Big House chewing a bone and a bit of old dry bread and he said to somebody on the place, I don't know who, 'Isn't that the dog I got for the bailiff?' 'Yes.' He said, 'Isn't anyone looking after him?' 'No, sir.' So Sir Derrick took this dog up to the kennels—Sir Derrick was Master of the Radnor and West up at Kington and rode with the North Hereford over at Bodenham; he hunted with the two packs, often three times a week in the wintertime—and this man as went out for the wounded and the dead cattle for to feed the dogs, he got him to shoot him with a humane killer. Well, the bailiff after his holiday went round the men and told them, 'Rogers is the cause of Sir Derrick putting my dog down'; he blamed me for it. So when it come my turn to talk to Sir Derrick in the row, and he said, 'Well, Evan? What's your complaint?' I said, 'There is *one* little thing in my mind.' He said, 'What's that?' 'Well,' I said, 'he's told the other men,' I said, 'that I was the cause of you killing his dog.' 'You certainly wasn't!' Sir Derrick said, and he looked at the bailiff who was stood about twenty yards away from us facing us all. 'I did it on my own initiative,' Sir Derrick said to him, 'because the poor thing was starved!' He said, 'You ought to be ashamed of yourself,' he said, 'for going away and leaving a dog without a mouthful.' The bailiff said, 'I'm sorry, Evan.' I said, 'Thank you. That's all I want.' So I said, 'Have you finished with me, Sir Derrick?' He said, 'Yes', and I come away and went off doing something up in the wood, and Sir Derrick said to the others, 'All right, men. Carry on,' he said, 'as if nothing had happened,' he said, 'and we'll straighten things out. I'm going in now,' he said, 'to make my mind up what I'm going to do.' So, when I came down out of the wood that night, Sir Derrick met me. 'Evan,' he said, 'after you've had your tea, will you do me a favour?' I said, 'I will if I can, sir.' He said, 'You've got a bicycle, haven't you?' I said, 'Yes.' 'Will you pop round,' he said, 'and catch the men,' he said, 'after you've had your tea?' he said. 'They'll be with their wives or in their gardens,' he said. 'Please to tell them that I'm giving the bailiff a minute's notice in the morning, and he won't be leaving his house to worry any of them in future.'

And that's what happened to him; that's how Sir Derrick acted with his bailiff. But it was laughable!—in the first two or three years after Sir Derrick came here the old furniture van was always coming. 'Hello! Here comes Pickfords! Pickfords it is! Wonder what's the name of the bloke coming in today!' The next bailiff was Hope and, after Hope, Edwards. The last was Bill Pritchard and he's farming half the farm now on his own. Everybody liked and likes Bill Pritchard and his wife—she cooked me a bit of dinner yesterday [Sunday, April 2nd, 1978]. The outdoor staff now is Mr Pritchard on his half of the estate—he does as much as any of them—and his tractor driver and stockman; and Master Tom Bailey on his half, he's got one tractor driver and a gardener that helps the tractor driver on the farm, and an odd friend or two who comes in and gives a hand. But, as I said, I'm just personal to Sir Derrick as his gamekeeper.

My other black labrador, Sam, he was a Christian of a dog—only a few months after Sir Derrick come into the house to live he held a couple of poachers for me up in the Sally Coppice Wood. They started funny business : 'parting'—you know, when you're on top of them before they know where they are and they see you, they split up. To start my story . . . One Saturday, I was in the yard with Sir Derrick and I heard a rifle go 'ping' up in the covert. I said, 'It's nearly dark,' I said. 'Who could be up that wood now?!' He said, 'Go up there!' I said, 'No. They'll be over the top of the wood and in somebody else's district before I get there, sir. They'll see me going up across the meadow.' 'Well,' he said, 'I want you to deal with them same as you do with whoever it is—' he said, 'the same as you did for Colonel Astley,' he said. 'I want you to do your duty.' I said, 'Very good, sir. That shall be done.' The following Saturday I said to the wife, 'Make me a ruddy cup of tea.' She made me a cup of tea. I went right away up through the boundary and down over the top of the hill to where I heard this shooting the Saturday before, and got in a hide, the old dog with me—I never went a yard at night time without him; he was a marvellous creature. The hide was under some elder bushes where I'd sawed a big oak tree off—I knew where it was; I only had to put a few more boughs to hide my head. I'm a great smoker and I struck a match to light my pipe, covered the match up and lit the pipe, turned the pipe upside down so that there'd be no red showing, and all of a sudden—I'd got the old dog and my eight fingers in his thick collar—all of a sudden the old dog went hughghghghgh. I whispered, 'Shut up, will you!' I give him a tap in the ribs with my fist. I told him, 'Don't you do that!' I looked down the bottom of the covert. I could just see there was two men getting over the gate in the bottom about a hundred and fifty yards from me, and between them and myself was a great big thick brake of briars—bramble briars, you know, blackberry briars, oh two foot high; you'd have a job to run through them but there was passages around. At the same time they got over the gate and the old dog growled, an old cock pheasant as luck would have it went up in the oak tree above my head. Up they comes. They got within thirty yards. One had got the rifle. The other had got a haversack on his back—he said, 'Go on! He's a beauty!' (Course, then, in the winter time, all the leaf was off; they could see the cock pheasant on the bough.) I stood up; I said, 'I wouldn't if I were you!' 'Oh!'—you should see them make for that gate! (They drove within a hundred yards of it up in a motor-car. I'd heard this car but it never tumbled to me it was the poachers coming.) I said to the old dog, I said, 'Go on now! Stop them!' He went for the first and—do you know what that dog did?—he jumped clean on his back and put him face first down in these briars! Over ninety pound weight that dog was. I went to him and I said to him, 'Hullo! What have you got in this bag?' I ripped it over his head—a hammer was in it. The other chap had nearly got to the gate. I said, 'Go on, Sam! Stop him!' He went to the gate and showed his ivories—hughgh! I said, 'Don't move or else he'll have you!' I run down to him. 'Here!' I said. 'What's it you've got there?!' and he was starting to tremble because the dog was wanting to get at him. I said, 'No, Sam, no! Friend! Don't touch!' Took the rifle off him.

The other chap had recovered then; he'd come down to us. I said, 'Now then, over that fence, please,' I said, 'and straight down to Brinsop Court, will you?!' I said, 'I'm going to give you a chance. I'm going to take you to my boss and whatever he decides will be done,' I said. 'He's my new boss and I'm doing for him same as I did for my old boss. Now,'

I said, 'it's up to you!' So one was starting to go one way and one the other when we got out on the meadow. I said, 'No, no funny business!' I said, 'I've got the rifle and I'm going to stick to it! I'm the one now that is armed, not you!' So the one said to the other, 'Oh, we'd better go.' 'I think you'd better,' I said, 'because if I snap my fingers you've had it! That old black man there,' I said, 'will have you by the throat!'

Goes down to the front door, rung the bell. The butler came to the door. 'Hello, Evan!' he said. 'What brings you here Saturday night, this time?'—quarter to seven; it was dark. I said, 'Is Sir Derrick in, please?' 'He haven't come back from shooting yet,' he said. 'He's gone out for a day's shooting.' 'Oh,' I said. 'That's a bit of a nuisance,' I said, 'but there,' I said. 'I've got a couple of men here,' I said, 'was up in the wood with this,' I said. 'Put this inside the door, will you?' The butler took the rifle and put it inside. I said, 'Lock the door. I'll wait till Sir Derrick comes.' I waited there till a quarter to ten with them two men and, them men, if they moved a foot, Sam went hughghgh like as if saying to himself, 'I'll have you!' Oh, he was a Christian of a dog! Only the Sunday before, me and the wife had been out to tea, and that dog had been playing with a little three year old girl with puffed sleeves and putting her hand down his throat playing ball with him. What a temperament for a dog!

About a quarter to ten, Sir Derrick put his car over in the big garage. There was room for four cars in that garage; mine was there; by then I had a Morris 8, a four-door saloon. I gave £250 for it; I paid £100 down and I paid the rest by instalments; I got it off the man who kept The Oak public house in Hereford by the old bridge going over the Wye—his son is the publican there today. I never used it a lot; I just used it to go out with the boys off the farm when darts started off full force all over the country, then I gave it to Charles in 1956. City dart teams had to play the county dart teams. In fact, I was in the dart team of The Traveller's Rest in Stretton—that was the public house we all used to go to on a Monday night.

We won the cup one year. There was the Moccas dart team; there was the Canon Pyon dart team, the Dilwyn dart team. Five of us on the estate was in the Stretton dart team . . . Well, Sir Derrick parked his car and come across the slab-stones between the moats to the house. He was waving a torch so as not to fall in. (Since then, I've put a good pathway four foot wide all in solid concrete, right the way through—fifty yards; I'll show it to you.) 'Hallo, Evan!' he said. I met him near the entrance gates at the front of the house with the lions on the pillars, not the Italian gates higher up the drive. 'What are you doing here?!' 'I've got the couple of clients,' I said, 'as you heard fire that rifle last Saturday!' He said, 'You haven't! Good for you! Where are they?' I said, 'At the front door, sir. They're waiting for your view on it.' I said, 'Your butler's got the rifle I took off them,' I said, 'inside the door as you go in.' 'Oh, come along, then,' he said. One man started crying; he said he'd got a family and was out of work. 'Oh,' said Sir Derrick, 'but who gave you authority to go in my woods?' 'No one,' he said. 'We seen the pheasants when we was here wiring the house,' he said, 'we was having lunch one day and we seen them out feeding on the stubble field.' *And that was the head electrician as re-wired Brinsop Court for Colonel Astley ready for Sir Derrick!!* In the end Sir Derrick gave in, he said, 'Well,' he said, 'just go and tell your friends,' he said, 'as I've got a man here,' he said, 'interested in a bit of sport for *me* and for *my* friends,' he said, 'and if you want shooting any time, if you come and ask,' he said, 'I can find you a bit, or rather my keeper can.' He was very fair that dear old gentleman. Long may he live. But the men never came back—they was too ashamed to come. People heard them talking about me in public houses and they all rushed to tell me how they broadcast the story.

That old dog Sam as held those poachers, he was ninety-two pound weight. My second wife, she used to take him up the Weobley to Brinsop Road for a walk on the lead and sometimes the school bus would come along and stop at the top of the drive for the children to get off and on. This was before Sir Derrick's time. The dog would be licking the children's faces— oh, he was a friendly old dog with children—but the butler's boy must have done something to him when Ann wasn't looking because whenever the children got off that bus and the boy went to touch him he growled. One day Charles took us to a place called The Bunch of Carrots on the River Wye down the other side of Hereford from here where he'd once built a flood-bank. There was an old gentleman stood up with the water nearly into the top of his waders with a fishing rod and I didn't notice in the old scrub on the side of the river bank as we walked down that he had a little lad there, the dead image of the butler's boy. My dog lifted his nose, showed his teeth and he was ready to spring and I just managed to stop him by holding his collar.

Labradors are wonderful guard dogs. I'm not afraid to go out in the dark up any wood if there's poachers about because I've only to snap my fingers and my dog's got them. But, I'm sorry, I can't tell you how that bit of training's done because that's to do with the law. It's like the training of the police dogs— they don't tell you how they train those dogs with the men with the bandages all round their arms. It's against the law for me to train a dog to capture human beings. Of course I can *shoot* a poacher, but only in the legs—I can only wound him : I mustn't shoot to kill. I know a little bit about the law; I was in the police for forty-two years! I do faintly remember a man-trap when I was a boy. It was a wooden structure up at the top of Merryhill with automatic springs made with bending poles and if a man got his foot in it he'd be lassoed up in the air. Another way they caught them was by digging pits.

Though I myself piped water into Park Cottage from a spring in Merryhill, we'd no electricity there till just before Sir Derrick. First there was a battery room down at the Court making the electric for the Court and the four cottages for the indoor servants. There was about a hundred and fifty cells all round one room and two Ruston and Hornsby engines. One engine was in action day and night, and when that one gave out they had the other ready for action. Then Colonel Astley said, 'We won't be bothered with this any more' and got joined on to the mains—at Credenhill, I think. He paid for all the poles and everything for the cable to come, and ever since there's been leads and—what do you call those big boxes on the poles?—distributors; electricity was put into one cottage and then another, all of them. That was the first time I'd ever had electric—just after the Second World War. But there's still places now in Hereford haven't got no electric. Does that surprise you? Only go up the road here half a mile; there's a man living there for the last twenty years and he's only got his candles and hurricane lamp.

Under Sir Derrick the old well and windmill wasn't supplying enough water for the Big House and the cottages and the water tanks in every meadow for the animals. So, to supply all that, he had a thirteen thousand gallon reservoir built by the side of Round Oak and another well sunk by the old one, and an electric pump forced water up into that reservoir and then it all come back down again for everyone in pipes by gravitation. As regards the tanks for the animals, the water comes to them in three-quarter inch reducers put into the mains at different angles. There's a ballcock in each tank and, when the tank is full, it can't overflow because the ballcock stops it; as the animals drink, so the ballcock lowers and the pipe fills it up again, and every animal is not short of water in a dry summer.

Oh, he was an outstanding master, there's no mistake; he was one of the loveliest minded men. When he engaged a man and the Agricultural Wage was three pound a week, well I had three pound ten and so did every man on the estate in addition to our cottages, rent free. He's been over-generous to me. That jacket lined with leather on the door—that's one of his own that he gave me. He's come to me many a time. 'Isn't it nearly time you had a new suit, Evan?' I said, 'I'm all right, sir, thank you. Save your money. Any old rags will do for this.' One year he came out shooting with a new light grey suit on. 'Ah!' I said to him. 'Looks very nice, Sir Derrick!' I put him on a

173

stand at the bottom of Merryhill and three more guns above him. A few birds went over; he knocked down a cock which was a bit of a runner. Now, Sir Derrick was a devil of a man to catch hold of a cock pheasant by the head and swing it round to kill it; he did it with this bird and it sprinkled him with red hot blood all the way up the waistcoat and the jacket and half way up the trousers. 'That's spoiled that suit! Another suit for you, Evan!' Well, he comes up the Arbour next day with this suit. I said, 'Don't be so silly, sir!' I said, 'You take it back down.' 'You're going to refuse it?!' I said, 'You tell Lady Bailey,' I said, 'to just get a bit of Robin starch and make it in a paste, moist, and wherever you see blood rub the paste in and put it out to dry.' I said, 'That Robin paste will suck every atom of blood out of that material, and all you want to do when it's perfectly dry is just give it a wriggle and use the brush on it and you won't see a speck.' He come up another time. 'Here you are, Evan. That's instead of the suit of clothes.' A five pound note! And he's still got the suit today! There you are! Lives are full of tales if only you can put them together. But it's like the bloke said—'You can tell a good tale. Can you sing?'

In the summer time you usually go out naturally dressed and that's why our gamekeeper's suits are always made on the green side to correspond with the green vegetation, so that if you're on top of an incline anybody watching can just see you, but when you're down and walking on the green and they're above you they can't; you can go along a meadow and you're not distinguished so easily because of the colour of your clothes. The tailors, as well as making you your gamekeeper's suit, they make you camouflage overalls for the wintertime out of a very light canvas like a mackintosh and painted all different colours—bluey green, brown and black. You stand in the shade of a tree and you can't be recognized—only your face—and the birds will 'light in that tree and you can shoot them—at least that's what you do if you're not a very good shot. You camouflage for different things. For instance, if you go shooting pigeons you just put your hand up the back of a chimney and smudge your cheeks and forehead which shine when the sun is shining. A pigeon and a carrion crow can see a shining cheek from a hundred yards. When there's snow on the ground I've gone so far as getting a sheet and I've cut three slits in it, put the one slit over my head and used the other two for my arms. A sheet is very pliable—it gives you arm-room to use your gun. If I have a gentleman come out to shoot woodpigeons in harvest-time when they're coming down in sixties and seventies to feed on the corn as it's ripening, what I do is if I've only got a little hedgerow that's just been laid, I make a hide with four tall stakes, put a bit of brown twine from stake to stake and twine honeysuckle all over save on the one side. Well, your gun can stand in there, or he can sit on a bale of straw, with a loaded gun and his box of cartridges and his lunch, and the birds can't see him with that canopy over him whether they come from the back or the front.

I wear brown plus-fours and a brown jacket and a cap to match with a peak in front and a peak behind on special occasions. A keeper don't wear plus-fours, not when he goes out shooting. But if I go to another estate to load for a gentleman, then I wears them. The gentleman has two guns and I stand behind with my bag of cartridges and my dog. I've got one gun in my hands and he's got one gun in his hands and I'm always feeding him with cartridges. As he shoots a bird and it drops to the ground I sends my dog and he brings it and puts it at my feet—if he knocks down twenty, thirty or forty, my dog does the work. It takes years of practice before you're a competent loader. No gentleman won't take anybody—he's got to have experience because there's been so many accidents with a novice as don't know what he's doing. I'd often go to Foxley and Ludlow, different places, loading for gentlemen. They'd send to Colonel Astley—'Could you spare your keeper for a day?' Colonel Thornycroft that had the shoot here for eight years, he invited me to Ludlow, pigeon shooting. He said, 'Come and have a day's sport with me and bring your gun, Rogers!' I

175

enjoyed myself. The owner of the shoot was Mr Goodwin who gave me a box of one hundred cartridges. 'Here you are, Rogers!' he said. 'I've enjoyed myself on your estate,' he said. 'Now I want you to enjoy yourself on mine!' And I did, I did enjoy myself. I remember Mr Goodwin alone, he bagged close on two hundred birds. Colonel Thornycroft, I think he killed a hundred and seventy. I killed sixty-three. Mr Goodwin had markets for them in Liverpool and Birmingham. Mr Pritchard as was bailiff here for eleven years and is now farming half of Brinsop, he's a wonderful shot. Master Tom Bailey who invites guns like his father did, well, he invited Mr Pritchard to come out shooting with us last year. I was very pleased. I put him on a stand with three other guns and he was knocking the birds down left, right and centre. Master Tom is very good some days; he'll never miss a thing. Another day he'll go out and he'll be missing all the time. You do get those turns; it happens with the best—I don't know if the weather affects your eyesight or what. Some of the guns as are invited here couldn't hit a barn if they was inside and the door shut . . .

But we was talking about Sir Derrick. Oh, he was a lovely gentleman. I've never met his equal yet. Once the cattle next door ruined a field of his corn, trod it all down; they was in all night running round it. He sent for the owner to come and see the damage they'd done. 'Oh,' the farmer said, 'I'm sorry about my cattle damaging your corn like that, Sir Derrick,' he said. 'I'd better get a valuer in.' Sir Derrick said, 'You can please yourself but,' he said, 'if you've got any money to spare,' he said, '*I* don't want it,' he said. 'You give it to the church.' And that's what the farmer done.

Except until just before he left for the Channel Islands, Sir Derrick came to church every Sunday morning of his life when he was in residence. He'd been a few times and he come up to me one day and he said, 'Evan,' he said, 'you don't mind my asking you?' he said, 'but I know you've been clerk,' he said, 'and my wife would like you to carry on.' I said, 'If it would please you, I'll certainly do it.' So at the next Parochial Church

Council Meeting he brought it up, he said, 'I'd like to make a little statement,' he said, 'and I'm going to foot the bill.' He said, 'Let's put everyone on the same level.' And that's when he rose my money from four pound to six pound a year for blowing the organ, ringing the bells and waiting on the vicar, and he paid the organist and the cleaner the same. But I still often wonder why with the money he had he never put in an electric blower for the organ when he had light bulbs put all round the church and, only a few year ago, spent pounds and pounds on re-roofing.

Otherwise I don't know how to praise him enough. Put him up against Colonel Astley who gave me a bloody box of fags for building up his shoot for him! The good he's done round here! And he never talks about it. All I'm worried about is I may be getting into trouble for mentioning his generosity in this book.

There's only one thing I've ever refused to do for him and that's use poison to kill the rats when we was infested with them after the war. It was like brimstone and it was mixed with crushed oats or flour and the rats ate it and took three or four days to die; it dried their insides up. I was catching a hundred rats in one night with traps behind pieces of board and roof-tiling in the farm buildings—when I'm destroying animals I like to do it the humane way, not for the poor things to suffer; if you find a rat alive in a trap you just press his two shoulders together with a grip of the hand to stop his heart beating, count one, two, three, four, five, six, seven, eight, nine, ten, and he's dead; you don't hit him with your trapping hammer or a stick or you'll smash your trap, then what are you going to do? Well, Sir Derrick went and got about seven seven-pound tins of this poison and he came to me and asked me to use it. I said, 'No, sir. I'm sorry but I can't do it.' He said, 'Fair enough,' he said, 'I'll get someone else to do it.' I said, 'Thank you, sir,' and a farm worker took on the job. Now, the bailiff, he'd got an elk hound puppy, a little bitch; he was offered fifty pound for her; and he thought the world of her—she slept in the kitchen in an armchair. He got up one morning and he gave her a pat. She was cold and stiff. When he accused me of poisoning her I said, 'Come on! The veterinary surgeon!' I made him take this dog to the vet in Hereford—I drove them in my Morris 8. The vet said, 'Hallo! Rat poison again!' So the bailiff said to him, he said, 'Will you come to Court?' he said. 'I'm going to sue the producers for my fifty pound dog!' 'No,' said the vet. Nor he didn't; nor he wouldn't, so what could we do about it? When we brought the dog back I opened her out and we found a rat's head in her stomach. You see an elkhound, when you come to rock bottom, was the only dog on the place that would touch a dead rat—like a fox who kills a hen and takes the head off because of the brains. A sheep dog would just smell it and walk on; a retriever would pick it up but he wouldn't go to eat it. By the way, did you know that a rat's *tail* is poison to anything that eats it? I always chops a rat's tail off before I throw it in the hutch to my ferrets. And did you know rats is intelligent? One night when Mr Hubert Delaval Astley first come here I was coming for home rather late at night down by the stables and I heard the groan of horses. I looked over the half-door of a stable and I could see a glimmer of light on the wall and Chris Waithe, the old waggoner, said, 'Hallo, Evan!' I said, 'Hallo, Chris!' I said. 'What's the matter tonight?' He said, 'These horses have got the strangles.' So I stopped to talk with him for a bit. He'd been using goose-grease on the throats of the horses because they had a job to breathe. He said, 'Have you ever seen anything like this in your life before?' I said, 'What's that?' He said, 'I'll turn the light down a bit,' he said. 'See up on that wall-plate there just under the roof?' he said. 'That half a jar of goose-grease there—you keep quiet a minute until you see what will happen.' Well, I sat down by the side of him on the mixing-bin where he mixed the chaff, and I kept my eyes glued up to this wall-plate underneath the rafters and, all of a sudden, out comes an old rat and trots along the wall, jumps up on this jar and he sat on top of it as if somebody was at the lavatory

178

and dipped his tail down in the fat and wiggled, wiggled, wiggled until his tail was all fat. Then he lifted up on his two hind legs and dangled his tail over the outside of the pot and another rat came and licked all the fat off. Then the other rat jumped up and he dipped *his* tail and let the one that he'd just licked lick him. I'd never seen a sight like it in my life before! And Charles, my son-in-law, he's seen them rolling an egg down steps—one lay on his back and the other rolled the egg onto him and so on following each other down to the bottom. Or so he says.

After the war, before myxie, the rabbits was so numerous I was gassing them with cyanide and leaving them dead underground. I had one large bank where there was about a hundred and fifty rabbits to the one burrow. You drove your rabbits to earth, then used your spade to block all the small holes of the burrow with turfs, leaving the main holes open till last. Then you opened your tin of cyanide and filled a tablespoon on the end of a hazel rod—or a bamboo cane—about three or four foot long, pushed your rod in one of the remaining holes and tipped your spoon. Before you could get your rod back you could see the fumes start to come out through the hole so you wanted to be quick putting a turf to the mouth and stamping it with your heel. You went on to the next hole as quick as possible, the next again, next again, doing the same till you'd put the gas in all of them and blocked them up. You could hear the rabbits bumping underneath the ground but that only lasted seconds, then they were gone. You're not allowed to use cyanide now by law—maybe because myxie is here to stay and that kills the rabbits instead (not all of them because some gets immune); maybe because children might open a tin and inhale the fumes and be dead in seconds, no mistake about it. One day, in Round Oak, the wind was blowing a little, I'd got my main holes ready, and I put my tin on the ground and took the lid off right in the way of where the wind was coming from. I reached for my rod, lifted up a spoonful of powder and, as I lifted it up, the wind blew the fumes from the open tin towards me. I was out for about three and a half hours. I'd rolled down the bank away from the tin. When I come to myself I was like something in a doze and my head was aching. I'm lucky to be here to tell the tale; thank God it didn't knock me out completely.

Ten

I moved from Park Cottage in 1954—Easter, I think. I'd had a row with the couple next door. The wife thought I'd killed a cat of hers and when you're a keeper, if people lose a cat or anything, the first thing they say is, 'Oh, the keeper's shot it!' whether we do it or whether we don't. One day she come out in her garden and she called me a bastard—I don't know why; thank God I'm not—and she was picking up cordwood and throwing it at me over the fence. I thought, 'You come over here, my lady, and I'll show you where your boundary ends!' The laughable thing about it was that I collected these lengths of cordwood and the next Saturday afternoon, when I'd eased off and more or less finished work, I brought the sawing-horse down from the woodshed by the pheasant pen, and her husband was digging his garden on the other side, not speaking a word to me, of course, and looking the other way, and there was I sawing up the logs as she'd thrown over the fence at me for my own use!

So I went to Sir Derrick and asked could I have Ivy Cottage up in the Arbour where I'd lived with Harry Darling, the old keeper, before I was married to my first wife. It had been empty for three years and every window was smashed but it now had running water laid on and electricity. The big ivy tree growing outside, it had grown so it was as big around as my thigh, about six inches through the root; I've never seen ivy grow like it; it was over the top of the roof and in under some of the tiles. Well, Sir Derrick said I could have the cottage and gave me a fortnight, I think, to square it all up. He said, 'Tell me when you wants to move, Evan!' I said, 'Very good, sir!' and got it in apple-pie order. I put five windows in and an extra big one where the front door used to be as is facing the garden; I cut back the ivy; I got the kitchen ready and one of the bedrooms. When I was ready I went to Sir Derrick and he come down himself with the old butler and the horse-box. Then, when me and the butler had carried out most of my belongings. Sir Derrick drove me and Ann up to the Arbour. Then, later, the bailiff and a couple of men helped me with the bedstead for the bedroom and my dog pen and the pheasant coops and runs and the ferret hutches—I made new hatching boxes—for the top garden; this time we used the horse-box and a tractor. My next job was to dig the bottom garden and plant new fruit trees. I planted gooseberries, blackcurrants and a Peasgood's Nonsuch apple tree. And I planted a William's Bon Chrétien pear tree—they call it for short a 'William pear'. Lovely pears they are, very juicy. I once had a pear off it weighing over a pound. It was three foot tall when I planted it; last year after I picked the fruit I'd to cut the leader out so it'll branch out and I'll only have to use a short ladder, it'll not be so high for me to get up in the air.

While we're on about planting I should tell you I've been more or less, as terms put it, 'woodman-keeper' for Sir Derrick! To introduce pheasant up by the Harlands Pool in the bottom of the horse-shoe of the valley between Vallet's and Merryhill I planted a covert of ash, larch and Douglas which has been very successful—three acres: a row of ash, a row of larch, a row of Douglas, all the way through. Then half way along Merryhill I felled a patch of oaks—about three acres—two thirds of the coverts here is oak—and re-planted it with Douglas. I planted six acres of ash in the centre of Sally Coppice, and in Stanks's Covert below Credenhill I planted poplars and Douglas, a thousand altogether, and only one died. I've lined the Arbour with ninety cypressus and planted them round the hard tennis court to have a background for the ball. Then there's the acre

182

of ash and half acre of Douglas I planted to make a covert in the Kitchen Garden. As regards the ash I've been told the grey squirrel will bite out the centre bud when it's throwing up his leader and make the tree branch out. Well, I can take you to Sally Coppie where the poles are thirty and forty foot long and if you'll find me one ash tree that's been spoiled out of that six acres I'll give you £5. And another thing I'll show you—they don't even nest in an ash tree because it's too bare; they always build their nests in large oaks or elms. You can go with a long pole and poke the dreys and you'll see the little squirrels jump—I love to see them—from tree to tree and bough to bough; it's better than going to a circus. As for to say they do damage it's a lot of bullshit. I never go desperate after killing them; I pick up a few in my stoat and weasel traps but I don't go out shooting them. I've planted in my time about forty chestnut trees from seed in Vallet's Wood to hold the game so if I'm taken ill and the pheasants don't get properly fed I'll find them there at the time of the year when the fall of the nut is—there's a fuzz protection that it grows in and it ripens and keeps the nut inside nice and mellow; well, the pheasants love that. *And* the grey squirrels love them. I was going up that wood one winter and just for the curiosity I followed a squirrel in the snow and, do you know?, he led me to his hoard of nuts in the butt of an old tree, all stacked there like a little larder. I had quite a few pound of hazel nuts and eating chestnuts. But you can't walk up Vallet's Wood now for timber lying on the ground; it's very sad to me. There's about eighty acres of it they've felled, including the chestnuts; they're leaving all the smaller trees to grow on into timber to follow for the next generation, *if* they don't bash them about too much falling the others in between them and disfiguring them. It's a bloody mess—no method; just trees plonked down one across the other.

Every autumn I'd to do about twelve miles of ride-trimming through the woods with my long-handled hook, because a gun is a dangerous weapon and you wouldn't expect a man to have to walk through *bushes* with a loaded fire-arm. One day I was having my lunch in the sun on the peak of Merryhill when, all of a sudden, I heard a sound just as if the wind was blowing the leaves—here comes a squirrel scurrying and hurrying right along by my feet and on past me and up an ash tree. And in a few moments here comes Mr Fox and he went to the butt of this ash tree and, blow me, he tried to get up after that squirrel! I shouted at him, I said, 'Reynard! What do you want?!' and he went down over the wood like a long-dog; he was soon away! But that poor devil must have been hungry, mustn't he?!

Only the year before last I planted two thousand of the trees on Merryhill—beech, Douglas, spruce and larch. It was Sir Derrick's idea to have it to be picturesque, not grown for timber, and to have different colours to make a better view from the house. They looks patchy at the moment but later on, in the summer, when they're all in full leaf it's going to be a very pretty covert; they're all there and all doing well. Some of them are only three foot tall yet but we'd a lovely bit of sport in among them last year; the birds love the sunny side under the bracken. I cut every briar twice over—that's twelve acres —in order to what I calls 'clean' the little trees and give them room to grow. I'll be doing the same this year again; in fact, I started last week [the week commencing 27th March, 1978].

See what I mean when I say my work is never done? Apart from the time Ann had a gall-stones' operation and I went with her to Poole so she could convalesce with Mary and Charles, I've been that interested in my work I've hardly troubled about holidays, only for the sake of giving *her* a holiday because it's very monotonous for a wife to be indoors day in, day out. What is their life if they don't have *some* entertainment? Share and share alike, I say—but, of course, you're a single man: you haven't had the feeling that I have. So I took her for a week once to Jack Redman's in Potters Bar, which is twenty mile out of London, I think, and I took her for another week to Bill Offa's in Lincolnshire.

When Molly was alive, Jack Redman was a sketcher and

184

drawer of bridges, touring round on a bicycle, seeing the country-side, and he went to Major Thompson, the steward of Brinsop, and Major Thompson came to Molly and he said, 'Could you put up a young man, Mrs Rogers, for a night?' 'Yes,' she said. 'I've got an extra bedroom.' So we put him up, and he was that taken up with the little valley that he asked could he stay longer. Well, Molly's sister's daughter came to stay with us too and they started keeping company straight away and within a few months they were married and they went to live at Potters Bar. I'm sorry to tell you that they got divorced but when Ann and me moved to Ivy Cottage he invited us to stay with him and his new wife for a week and offered to collect us and bring us back in his car. He was now living in a lovely little bungalow with a huge great garden, and about all he was interested in while we were with him was this miniature railway he had running right round the garden and into the front room. There was little bridges in the corners of the garden for the engines and the trucks to go down under, and the lean-to greenhouse was his station. I laid down some cement for him to run the rails in through the bungalow back door. I also planted him a couple of hundred quick-thorn to divide his bungalow from the next and I spent several days solid from seven o'clock in the morning till five digging and burying the turf.

Bill Offa used to be my neighbouring keeper for Major Devon-port on the Foxley Estate and we never had a mis-word. His father died in harness—he fell over a stile with a load of rabbits and that was his end, dear old boy: heart failure; fifty-five he was—mid-age I call it, though we're only supposed to live three score year and ten. Sir Derrick *made* us go to see Bill Offa one June for a change. Bill was working on this Lincolnshire estate with the new electric system for pheasant rearing. You take your hatched chicks from an incubator and put them in cubicles six by four by five foot high—a hundred chicks in each cubicle. And in each cubicle there's a foster bulb, what they call an 'electric foster-mother', about three inches off the floor, and there's just room to have a little teeny water-trough

185

all round made like a guttering on a greenhouse; the chicks are bound to have water to help them masticate their crumbs and pellets of special feed. They live in these cubicles till they're six weeks old, but there's a sliding door so that after three days they can go outside on the grass in four foot square pens; then when they're five weeks old they can go in pens twenty by ten by eight foot high built round the small ones. During the week me and Ann was visiting, Bill took me in the Land-Rover when he released a thousand six-week-old poults into a big pen in one of his coverts for his under-keeper to look after, and then we went and got another thousand chicks—hatched to date in the hatchery—to rear in the cubicles. So that's two thousand chicks he had! But there's one thing with the artificial method I'm dead against and that's the crumbs being thrown in the chicks' pappy droppings inside the cubicles during the first three days. Another thing—with a hundred to a cubicle and pen, the chicks start feather-pecking between five and six weeks old, especially round the back passage; when their little pin-feathers start to come, you can see the innards coming out of the holes of their little bottoms where the chicks have been pecking one another. You can't beat the old methods. The last lot of chicks I reared was under twenty-three bantams of my own with never more than twelve chicks to a bantam in coops and runs six foot long and four foot wide changed onto fresh ground every day out on the meadow. That way your birds are healthy. In keepering I've stuck to the same methods all my life for matters of importance. I've only changed what I've *had* to change, like it's illegal now to set the old steel traps though the new traps is more crueller than the old.

There's an incubator in the Big House in a private room by itself. Lady Bailey used to use it for hatching Aylesbury duck eggs. I'm telling a tale now about Master Tom behind his back. This is what actually happened: About five year ago I had sixty eggs spare; I hadn't got any more bantams—they was all sitting on pheasant eggs. 'Let's go,' said Tom, 'and I'll put them in Mother's incubator!' So that's what he did and he was taken ill and his mother took over. Then it come close on hatching day. About the twenty-first day that the eggs was in the incubator I went down through the yard and I was thinking, 'Oh well, another three or four days and they'll be hatching.' As I went by Pritchard's house, Judy—Mrs Pritchard—she came out and she said, 'I *am* sorry to hear the news, Evan!' she said. 'Lady Bailey tells me,' she said, 'all your pheasant eggs are a write-off.' I said, 'What's happened to them, then? Did the incubator go on fire?! Did she forget to fill the lamp with oil, or what?!' 'Oh no,' she said. 'There just weren't a chip in an egg.' 'Well,' I said, 'the damned things aren't ready to hatch yet for another four days!!' I ran breathless between the moats and straight into the Big House, down the passage and, as I got to the bottom of the passage, I run into Lady Bailey. I was that furiated I said to her, 'What's this story I hear,' I said, 'that my eggs are all upset—those sixty eggs?!!' 'Oh, they're a write-off,' she said. 'A write-off be damned!' I said. 'They're not due till next Wednesday! This is Monday!' She said, 'Oh! I am so sorry, Evan!' I went in. I put my hand on the eggs and they were just gone chilly. I put an egg up to my ear and you could just hear the little chick tapping its shell. I said, 'For Heaven's sake light that lamp!' She put it on. I said, *'I'll* come and see to them now,' I said. 'There *is* one or two alive in the shells!' I went in the next day and I got a basin, put some hot water in and then some cold and put my elbow in like you do for a baby before you bath it and put the eggs in and then put them back in the incubator. I thought, 'That will help the shells for the chicks to chip theirselves out if they're not too weak.' Anyway, on the day they should have hatched I went in in the evening and there was five little chicks out—all the other shells had dead chicks in. I put the five little live ones in my warm hat and I said to Lady Bailey, I said, 'I've got a bantam coming off,' I said. 'I can take these five little chicks to *her*.' Lady Bailey said, 'Oh let me take them first to show Tom in his bedroom!' As she was going along the corridor she tripped up and they fell out of the hat and one broke its wing and she stepped on another!!

It was an accident and I was very upset, but that's what we have to put up with sometimes—it's hard luck but I suppose it can't be helped. Out of sixty eggs, three chicks I had! She'd turned off the incubator three days before the chicks were due to hatch! Twenty-four to twenty-five days a pheasant egg is. She was going by poultry which is twenty-one days. Yes, that's the sort of thing as you've got to put up with in your life as well as do your work and settle down to it. Oh, it drives you up the wall. But I forgive everybody.

1954, the year we moved up to Ivy Cottage, I was notified that I was chosen to go to be reviewed on July the 14th with other members of the Regular and Special Police in Hyde Park, London, being as I was the oldest Special Constable in the Leominster Division of the Weobley Section. Then quite a month before the Review the sergeant from Weobley, he came over and he said, 'I want you to go to our Police Tailor in Hereford,' he said. 'You can't go in your present shabby clothes.' So I had to go first to be measured up and then they made me a lovely new suit of blue and I got a new hat and a new badge and new numerals, and my War Medals and my Police Bar was mounted on a rod—I was spick and span. And at the last moment another constable was taken ill so I was asked if I'd like to take my wife. I said, 'Yes, please!' I was the only one from Herefordshire that had his wife with him so I was highly honoured, I thought. Oh, they thought a bit of me when I was in the Police Force—but self-praise is no recommendation!

Two days before we went, Sir Derrick come up in the evening and he said, 'Oh, Evan,' he said, 'do me a favour!' I said, 'I will if I can, sir.' He said, 'My wife would like to see you in your uniform. If you don't show it to her here, she'll have to go to London.' I said, 'Oh well,' I said, 'I'll save you that expense anyway. I'll don my uniform last thing tonight,' I said, 'and knock at the door,' I said. So I dressed up. Ann pinned my medals on, and down I goes, done up like a dog's dinner. Knocked at the door. No one answered. I said to myself, 'Oh well, here goes!' So I lifted the big latch and in I went into the

188

hall and Sir Derrick shouted in that loud voice he used sometimes when he spoke, 'IS THAT YOU, EVAN?' I said, 'Yes,
sir.' 'COME ON IN!' In I goes into the sitting room. Lady
Bailey was sitting by the huge great fireplace and Sir Derrick was
stood by her and I was stood in the doorway with all the
electric lights shining on me and my numbers. 'Oh my good-
ness me! Thank you very much for coming down, Evan!' she
said. 'You've saved me a long journey!' I said, 'I'm very pleased
I can do something sometime.'

Next morning I got up, got my old feed bag and went and
done my rounds in the coverts and I was coming up the Arbour
and I seen Sir Derrick talking to Mrs Eckley, the widow of
his former stockman. Well, she called up later with an envelope
he give her saying, 'Don't forget to give that to Evan, will you?,
when you calls on Mrs Rogers today. He may want it tomorrow
and he may not,' and when I opened this envelope there was
enough notes in it if we needed them to give us a damn good
time. *That's* the sort of man Sir Derrick was.

The day of the Review we was up at five o'clock: PC
Williams, a regular from Weobley booked on the coach for to
go to London, he picked us up at seven and drove us to Hereford
in his little car. I was the only one in full uniform—the others
were wearing civilian jackets so as not to get dust on their
tunics. My wife wore a nice blue silk blouse, and a white under-
blouse under it, with a white collar and a little bit of old-
fashioned braid around her neck and some white beads to
match, and she had a brown skirt like a scotch plaid with pleats
in and brown stockings to match and brown shoes to match,
and on her head was a red, close-fitting hat—she looked ever
so bonny. Anyway, we left Hereford on the coach at eight and
got to Oxford between twelve and one and sat down in a hall
at one big long table, the Herefordshire constables and myself
and my wife, and enjoyed a lovely dinner. Then after a little
brush up and wash and something we got on the coach again
and straight to London to just outside Hyde Park where my
wife was taken to her seat near the Queen and Prince Philip's

rostrum while the rest of us formed up to fall in at a quarter to two, ready for three o'clock.

We stood to attention at two o'clock and the Queen started at about ten to three. The ambulance men, they was rushing to and fro, less than every ten minutes, taking constables off the parade ground that had fainted because they was too stiff and didn't relax enough. The Queen was in a rostrum looking down at us, and there was a lot of people sat around her including Prince Philip. Then a little coach came along like a little tractor with a box on it at the back, and there was seats and cushions in it and she drove up and down the ranks at a walking pace, not driving fast, and reviewed us all. She started at the front and worked her way to the back and round and up into the rostrum again. Then the band began to play quick march and, two files at a time, right turn, quick march, left wheel, we wheeled round and straight up in front of the rostrum and off the parade ground. When you got within about thirty yards of the rostrum the sergeant of police as was leading each section, he shouted, 'Eyes right!' and so, whenever he said 'right', you brought your head sharply right. Then after we passed her we got 'Eyes front!' and kept on and the band was giving us the step. It was magnificent. My wife was sitting on the level on the Queen's right in some rows of seats close to the rostrum —I spotted her in her little red turban. On our way out there was a sergeant dropped dead at the gate. Loudspeakers said, 'Section So and So will meet at So and So' and men who knew the ground directed us 'This way, please!' and we marched there and stood till our coach come along. My wife was looked after and brought to the coach. It was all organised beautifully; there wasn't a hitch. The ceremony ended at a quarter past four. A lovely day that was; I've often thought about it.

On the way home, by the time we got to Ross it was dark and, at the bottom of the pitch just outside, the coach had to stop because we saw a motor-car as had overturned. The others were back in their civilian jackets so one of them said to me, 'Hey! What's your name, constable?' I said, 'Rogers.' 'Come on

Rogers! Do your stuff! Get down to that car!' A sergeant said to him, 'Slip your tunic on! You can't expect a stranger to know this district like you knows it. Give him a hand!' So the pair of us got the driver out of the car and took him to Ross Police Station—the cooler—while some of the others in their sports jackets put his car upright. I never heard nothing of what happened to him afterwards. He was paralytic drunk.

When the coach stopped at Hereford the constable from Weobley as had his little car, he drove me and my wife out here and we invited him in and I gave him a drop of whisky and thanked him for his day's work. Ann only had a cup of coffee —she was next door to being a teetotaller, dear old soul. I'm not a big whisky drinker but I've always kept it in the house in case I'm a little groggy and in case I have a friend in, to give a drink to him just for old time's sake or for new time's sake. And I like a drop with a teaspoonful of sugar in it and some hot water at night when it's a frost because this old house, you know, is only one brick thick. And I find it keeps my pecker up if I have a teaspoonful in my cup of tea first thing in the morning. Anyway, the constable asked me, 'Have you enjoyed yourself?' I said, 'It's a day I shall never forget.'

I didn't retire from the police till 1962 when I was sixty-five but the main incident I'd to deal with after the war happened while I was still at Park Cottage. It concerned the stealing of some wine-glasses. About once a month all of us Specials, we had to congregate at Weobley Police Station for practising this and practising the other such as crawling on our bellies through a fire lit in a tent. Well, two of us Specials and two regulars happened to be standing talking at the gate of the car park of The Unicorn public house at turning-out time when all a sudden Mrs Walden, the landlord of The Salutation a hundred yards away, come running up the road after a lot of Welshmen boarding a bus in the car park and shouted, 'They've stolen some of my wine-glasses!' One of the regulars, his name was PC Harvey, he was only five foot four inches but he was ten stone and very strong and a ju-jitsu man—he could throw a sixteen stoner up against a wall and knew how to hold a prisoner so as he couldn't retaliate. He said to me, 'PC Rogers?' I said, 'Yes?' 'Stand in the gateway! Don't let the bus or any motor-cars out! I'm going to find those glasses!' Up he goes, runs to the end of the bus and I seen him questioning one of these Welshmen. All of a sudden he caught hold of him, twisted his arm up over his back and dragged him down the steps. He said, 'Here, Rogers!' and he gave me two little wine-glasses with legs to them. 'Take these and come with me down to the station!'—and he put the other two constables on the gateway to stop everything coming out. And as we reached the police station another Welshman come along and said he was this man's brother-in-law and put his hand in his pocket and said, 'I've got another glass!' I said, 'Come on in! We want you, too!' The sergeant took all the details and let them go that night but in about twenty-eight days they was carted up from Wales and was fined £12 each for being disorderly and stealing, and they had to compensate Mrs Walden for her glasses because she'd lost more than three—the rest of the chaps on the bus said, 'Come on! Search us, brother!' but no more could be found.

The year I moved up to Ivy Cottage, I was working in the garden one Saturday afternoon and I heard a rifle shot from the direction of the meadow by Brinsop Road. I jumped on my bicycle, rode down the Arbour and up the drive and when I got up the drive I seen a little car on the road by the side of the meadow and this fellow going up the meadow to collect this hen pheasant he'd shot. When he seen me coming he went down and he somersaulted the fence and into the car and away with his pal, and by the time I pedalled to the main bottom road there was no sign of them. So I came back and went on with my work through the next week. Starting in my garden again on the following Saturday afternoon, all of a sudden, pinnng— I heard the rifle. I jumped on my bicycle and on the way down I met the bailiff. I'd told him all about the previous Saturday. 'They're here again!' I said. He said, 'Right!' he said, and we jumped in his car and we was lucky enough to get their car number. The bailiff come back into Brinsop Court and he rang the police while I went up the meadow and picked up a cock pheasant shot through the neck with a single bullet. I walked back to the top of the drive and by the time I got there here comes a sergeant and a constable with the two culprits in their car. So the sergeant said, 'Do you recognize these men?' 'Too true I do!' I said. '*And* their clothing!' One of the little blighters was a boiler-stoker from Burghill Mental Hospital. The police caught them in their car going down Ladylift Hill just before you get into Weobley. Well, they was summoned to Weobley Police Station and Court and they was fined £12 each. I was hoping their gun would be confiscated but it wasn't.

The Law is so uncertain you don't know what they'll do next. If a man goes and stabs his wife—he haven't *killed* her—right, he's prosecuted. 'Is there no way to join you two people again for you to hold the peace?' The wife says, 'No,' but the people in the court, they do nothing about it. 'Oh, well, we'll discharge you on condition as you don't molest your wife, and see how you go on for the next twelve month.' Right. That court will do that. That man can call himself free though perhaps he wanted to get rid of his wife, perhaps he'd got another fancy lady somewhere. Now *another* poor bloke as goes up, he blacks his wife's eyes and they have a row and the wife sues him, they'll put *him* behind the bars, they'll give him twelve months—a simpler case but they give him the harder penalty, and the man as ought to have had the heavy sentence, they let him go scot free. Do you call that Law? *I* don't. We can't shoot plover—they're protected. So are the swan, heron, golden eagle, buzzard, hawk . . . Why the hawk is protected I do not know. Ask the government. It's worse than daft. He's one of our greatest enemies. We gamekeepers, we've *got* to break the law if we're going to put a good show of game up. Say it's discovered I kill a buzzard. I may be fined or I may be put in behind the bars. It all depends on the judge. *That* is what's so unfair. There's been many a man prosecuted and I've been able to help him out and get him off, even in a courtroom when I was in blue. 'Pardon me, your Worship! . . . So and so and so and so, so and so and so and so.' 'Is that so, constable?' 'Yes, sir.' 'Case dismissed.' My voice has touched the people on the Bench. Who are those people on the Bench? No more than what you and I are. Judge ye not lest ye be judged.

Eleven

In 1965 the Agricultural Minister presented me with a Long Service Medal at the Three Counties Show at Malvern. Then, in 1967, when I was seventy, The Country Landowners' Association presented me with another one at the Game Fair— it has a dog and a gun and a bag and a boat on it. I can't remember where the Game Fair was that year, but they always pick a piece of the countryside where there's some woodland and they can demonstrate so people will understand perfectly where not to set traps and where to set traps and how to make a tunnel. The young generation, if they go to the Game Fair, can see all the appliances that a gamekeeper uses, and the suppliers have stands for selling patents and 'humane' traps and biscuit meal and pheasant coops and so on. There's clay pigeon shooting too.

I didn't take my pension at sixty-five—I was still proper athletic and I loved making sport and I had a dear good master; I thought, 'No, I'm not going to be bothered with no pension yet,' and I didn't take it till I was seventy. And when I was seventy Sir Derrick wrote me out a cheque of a thousand pound. I could have fainted! He said, 'You're deserving of all I can give you and a damn sight more, Evan. You've been a faithful servant.' I said, 'Thank you, sir, for the compliment. I like to do my duty.' He said, 'You've certainly done that!' and he said to me, he said, 'There's the house,' he said, 'for as long as you like to live in it. You've got nothing to worry about.' I've no rent to pay, no rates to pay. All I've got is a blessed high electric

195

bill and, now,the telephone as well. I'm one in a million to be treated as Sir Derrick's treated me in old age; I've never wanted for a thing. He said, 'Don't do any *heavy* work on the place, Evan! Just walk around the coverts and look after the game if you'd like to carry on!' I said, 'I'd like to carry on to the end, sir, if I'm able!' And even though he's gone to the Channel Islands he still gives me an allowance every week for tobacco money —and a glass of Guinness if I need it. He said again, before he went three year ago, 'You go and put your gun under your arm,' he said, 'and take your dog round the estate so that people can see you're around,' he said, 'and I'm damned sure that they're not going to interfere with Tom.' Twelve weeks ago was the last time I seen him. He said, 'Don't forget, Evan,' he said, 'I still hold myself responsible for you!' I said, 'Thank you, sir. It's very kind of you.' I said, 'For the couple of pounds that I'm getting I'll see that I continue to do a fair amount of work for your son.' Sir Derrick's agent, he sends the money to Tom every week and Tom brings it up to me.

I suppose one of the reasons for Sir Derrick being so generous to me is that everything I use I buy myself. I've told you it already. Every trap—I've still got dozens of them—every tool I've got—axes, hackers—I've always paid for them personally. I expect my employers have offered to buy them but I said, 'No, I'll get my own, thank you.' I even buy my own guns. The only thing they've supplied to me is cartridges. They wouldn't get a lot of keepers like that: I'm one out of a thousand. You'll think before we've finished that I've been a funny old quist in my life, but I've always worked by myself and I like to have a tool the minute I want to catch hold of it; I've had so many jobs and needed so many tools I didn't want to have to go and ask someone who'd say, 'Oh, I'll find it for you next week. I don't know where so and so put it.' That's no good. Before I'd be bothered going asking and waiting, I'd go to town and buy a spirit level or buy a long-handled hook or buy an axe or buy a saw or buy a hacker if I wanted one. The trouble is the bailiff would send up: 'Oh go up to Evan! He's got some tools!' and you like to keep friendly with people. They'd take my hacker; they'd chop away through stones and all with it. Before I lent it, I could shave with it. When I got it back I could ride to London on the damn thing!

To celebrate my seventieth year I took everybody off the place and gave them a big dinner—beef and all the trimmings— at The Kerry Arms in Hereford. The bailiff, Mr Pritchard, he took me in his car. Master Tom Bailey and William Bailey, they had their car. Then there was the chappie up the top of the Arbour and two or three that have left now—I let the lot come, the more the merrier. There was five cars—nearly every workman's got a car these days. It cost me £18 near enough, the food alone. They were late cooking the beef for us so after a song or two—I sang my favourite: 'If You Were the Only Girl in the World'—we missed the sweet and we all came out and got into the cars and went up country right over on the Hay Road leading to Brecon to a lady that I know well, we call her Flo. I said, 'Come on! Let's go and see Flo!' Right! We all got in the cars at Hereford and we got to Flo about half past nine and we was there till about eleven. I think I gave a couple of recitations and a couple of songs and introduced the others to sing. I was one over the eight. We had a jolly night and none of us was sober when we got home, I tell you! The wife didn't come with us that night; she wasn't interested. But she knew what we was doing. I never do anything deceitful. No—open and straight! I don't care a damn what people talks about— or what they say! Sticks and stones may break my bones but words will never hurt me!

I had another good evening about six year ago when I went to Leominster to the dinner after the annual Ploughing Match. We had duck and all the trimmings and it cost me a guinea. Lady Bailey was there but Sir Derrick had gone to Africa. Their son, John, spoke in his place and then Mr Pritchard got up and gave an address about the farming situation, and someone from Africa staying at Brinsop gave a version of the agriculture business in Africa and made it very amusing. A party had been

197

engaged to put up a play but the play ended an hour before closing time and there was no one to carry on to entertain. A chappie that came with me, he said, 'I'll bet you a pound you don't go up on the stage, Evan!' I said, 'I'll bet you I *will*!' and I went up the steps and onto the stage of this lovely big hall and I went across to Bill Pritchard sat in a row of seats there with Lady Bailey and I said, 'You don't mind if I gives them a song?' And as I turned around the audience started singing my song: 'If You Were the Only Girl in the World'. It just gave me a lift and I was away, gones.

If you were the only girl in the world,
And I were the only boy,
Nothing else would matter in the world today,
We could go on loving in the same old way.
A Garden of Eden, just made for two,
With nothing to mar our joy;
I would say such wonderful things to you,
There would be such wonderful things to do,
If you were the only girl in the world,
And I were the only boy.

Everybody was aroar in the place. The claps, they echoed. I won my pound but me and the chappie as bet me, we spent it between us before I come home.

I'm sorry to tell you that before Sir Derrick went to the Channel Islands he and Lady Bailey parted. It makes my heart ache to think of it. They made such a lovely couple. He's a well-built man, an easy fourteen stone as looks very fine in hunting or shooting clothes, and she looks tall, slim and lovely, like Mrs Thatcher—when I see Mrs Thatcher on the television I very often says, 'There's Lady Bailey!' I used to make horse-jumps and all for them to train their horses on when they was out— rails of birch, fifteen foot long, five foot high. And she used to have great trouble getting her horses into the boxes when she was going to the hunt until I told her not to stand in front of the horse and try to pull him but to stand back by his shoulder, catch hold of him by the bit and hold her arm out stiff and then he'd walk up with her like a little soldier, no trouble at all, because he'd got his freedom. She was amazed when I told her, and *I* didn't know till *I* was told, but that's how news gets around, isn't it?—from one to the other. Sir Derrick's now bought her house up in Lyonshall, a lovely place, everything there she needs. Before he left I noticed he wasn't coming to church. I said, 'I'm sorry you can't make it to church, sir.' 'No,' he said, 'I can't do it, Evan,' he said. 'I don't want to sit in church by myself,' he said. Then, because he didn't come, I thought, 'Well, I'll give up too,' and we talked heart to heart, me and Sir Derrick—he was, as I've said before, better than ever my father was to me. I could howl over their parting. When I talked to him I said, 'I'm thinking of retiring as clerk.' 'Just the job, Evan!' he said. 'Don't you think you've done enough for that church?' I said, 'Well, I'm asking you because you're my superior and I'd like to have your view,' I said. 'I don't want to let anyone down. I've done it for fifty-three years.' He said, 'It's damn long enough!' he said. 'Let some of the youngsters do it!' So, as I've told you, I retired two years ago this April and no one's rung the bells since.

About the same time as I retired from the church, the doctors were trying to get my wife, Ann, to go on a diet. But no, she wouldn't, though her legs was nearly as big as my waist. When she got so lumbersome she couldn't lift her legs to go upstairs I brought a bed down for her and put it in the front room. My son-in-law, Charles, had already put a division in the old wash-house adjoining the cottage and put a new bucket-lavatory indoors there and a contractor built a glass shelter with a flat floor outside so that she could get to it without getting wet or tripping up—the old bucket-lavatory used to be ten yards across the yard by the end of an old pigsty. Then, last year, Ann had the first of a series of little strokes so I put a commode at the head of the bed and put an extra light over the bed with a switch for her to put her thumb on. I done everything possible; I even bought her a coloured television and arranged to have a telephone put in and paid a pound an hour for a Home Help lady to come twice a week, an hour each time.

One morning during Ann's last illness, in mid-December last year, I come downstairs and she was sitting in the middle of the room. She'd dragged the bedclothes off the bed, broken a box, knocked a table over, pulled the tape out of the arm of an arm-chair; there she was, sat with half the bedclothes all around her and every pillow and every cushion off the settee. I tried to pick her up by her arms but, no, she was that big she couldn't get on her knees, she couldn't get her legs behind her body. I had to go down and get Master Tom and he went and fetched his gardener and the tractor driver and *they* had a job to lift her. Expect me, a man of eighty-one—eighty then—to pick up six-teen stone, nearly dead weight, by myself! At nineteen years of age I was fourteen stone two and five foot eleven and three quarters but now I'm only ten stone and five foot ten. I got the doctor straight to her and, of course, she had to go in to Hereford General immediately. Mr Pritchard used to take me to see her every night in his car, and night after night we had to slow down the car as we neared the hospital so as not to smash up children on their skate-boards. Dozens of them! How dangerous! Scoot, scoot all over the road! Let them have their sport and their enjoyment in the right place where they're doing no harm to nothing or anybody; let them get on with it; that's me! But to go on the highway where there's traffic—bicycles and pedestrians and cars—and them scooting and bump-ing into you, what is more aggravating?! In the City of Here-ford, night after night when I visited my dear old wife—*and* Sundays and Saturdays! No, it's all wrong! Where's the law of the country?! Keep things in order! Everybody's complain-ing. One week they run into an old lady about eighty years of age doing a bit of shopping. They're on a bit of board and away they go! It's because there's no police on foot today; they're all in motorcars with loudspeakers and what have you! When the *old* policeman was on the beat he was allowed to give a boy as done wrong a good smack and that boy never forgot it and there was order kept; boys knew how far they could go! But now, give them an inch and they'll take a mile. You give them one bit of playground and they'll soon be over the hedge and making a playground somewhere else. They get dissatisfied; they wants a change all the time. I can't understand it. Well, yes, I *can* understand it—it's because their parents are at work. They comes home from school, they go in the larder—a piece of bread and butter or a lump of cake—and then, 'Where shall we go tonight, kid?' I'll always remember I went to Hereford one night recently, not above eight or ten year ago, at the time they was advertising a different kind of television set in the first instance. I was stood there waiting by The Horse and Groom, a public house, and just opposite was the television shop —it's still there—and I heard two little boys. The one said, 'Let's go over there and have a look at that new television, kid!' 'No!' said the other one. 'That's stale!' And the television hadn't been in the window a month! He wanted something fresh. You can't satisfy them.

Ann died on January 15th this year after a severe turn which altered her face and took away the use of her right arm and right leg completely. She was eighty-five. Now she's gone Sam whines every day of his life for her; you never heard him whining before in his life. 'Oooooh.' I open the window at nights when I've gone to bed and I say, 'All right, Sam! I'm here!' and then he'll cool down till morning. He knows she's gone. After I'd had my tea and shut up the fowls I'd give him a run across the meadows here and bring him straight back in to the cottage and the wife had got a bowl of milk for him, always, always. And the last words she said to me the night before she failed to recognise me the last time I went in to see the dear old soul—do you know what her words was? 'How's Sam?' That's the second time I've been through it—I shall be getting used to it if it happens again. I know two or three dear old souls—they'd be only too pleased to have a home. I'm not swanking or boasting—it's only an ordinary home as you can see—but, you know, I'd have no trouble, even now at my age.

There's one, she'd throw up her house tomorrow if I said, 'Would you like to come and live with me?' Being without a woman is too lonely a life for me. Since Ann passed away Mary and Charles persuaded me to have a telephone, but I have a lot of friends who haven't got one so I can get in touch with them only by corresponding with letters. And with those that have one I may be up in the woods when the telephone rings so I must arrange to tell them when I'm indoors and when I'm not. I hope when I'm taken ill or anything that I'll be able to scramble to ring up Mary and Charles. They come to me, thank God, almost every other week-end and every time they have a holiday. The last time they was up here, they decorated the kitchen—they changed the walls from pink to green and painted the ceiling white and the beams black. They'll be doing the bedrooms this summer. Bill Griffiths who used to work in the skinyards, he comes to see me—it's nice to have a little chat, one to the other. Then there's the Home Help twice a week and I also get two cooked dinners—Meals on Wheels—Tuesdays and Thursdays. Well, I've got no one to cook for me; what am I to do? I can't live on bread and cheese all the week round, every week of the year, can I? I pay 15p for the meal but I don't pay for the delivery; ladies without husbands and all the rest of it, they do it for a hobby; I give them the money every day they come. And the Pritchards and the new gardener and his wife, they've been very good about Sunday dinners when Mary and Charles aren't here. The gardener and his wife—they've only been on the estate six months—they didn't come to my dear little wife's funeral but, do you know?, the first Sunday after, up they come. 'How are you off for dinner?' 'Oh,' I said, 'the bailiff's wife has asked me down for my dinner today, thank you very much.' 'Oh well, next Sunday. Don't forget! Next Sunday you're coming to *our* house!' The governor's gardener and his wife, strangers to me! Well not quite strangers —they'd only been here about a fortnight and they was having a look round and I said, 'Come on up with me. Come in!' and in they come and on with the tea things and they sat down to tea. My wife was housebound and I've always liked to entertain her as well as myself and equalise the amusement with new people and hear about what they've been doing before they came here and have a little conversation to keep her mind lively. Women, you see, they get very low spirited and you must try and rise them up, cheer them up a little bit. He was a sailor and he's been out of the navy for about six years. He's only a young man, about thirty odd. They've only been married a few years and they've no family yet. He's a very handy chap as I see him; he wanted a place in the country and now he's got it. Next Sunday [April 9th] I've got to go to dinner with them. That's their attitude.

I haven't had the bill yet for putting in the phone but I think I can manage it; I'm going to try to if the Social Services don't. A big hole's been made in Sir Derrick's £1,000, I can tell you, but I don't owe anyone a penny bar that bill as I recollect at the moment; I've always paid my way. I spent nearly four hundred quid for that coloured television set in the front room and Ann never had the pleasure of seeing it and *I* rarely look at the damn thing—it disturbs the quiet mind. Before that one we had a black-and-white but it conked out and they wanted forty pound to have it repaired. Everything's going up, up, up, up. I should like to see Margaret Thatcher get in tomorrow—she can't make a bigger balls-up than what *these* rebels have! Rebels they are and nothing else—they don't know what they're doing half the time. They tax my few extra earnings when I'm drawing the pension! Can you beat it?! Is it fair?! They tax the income on my few savings! What for?! Why the hell should *they* come by it?! *I* worked for it! *I* saved it! They never told me to save it, did they? I could have pissed it all against the wall—there you are, you've got it in plain English! No. Give Mrs Thatcher a chance! If she's got the courage to go ahead, well, let her have a go! See if she can put *something* right!

About eleven year ago I bought a two-barrelled gun, 5¼lb, for £50 off a keeper friend of mine at Harewood End. Do you know, a gentleman come here on a shoot three seasons ago and he begged me to sell him that gun for £100?—that was a pound on a pound! No man can tell the value of *anything* because the prices are changing so quick! There's a greenhouse outside I gave £98 for. The catalogue today—only two years older—is asking £160—the same sized greenhouse, the same wood, the same glass and all! I had the wind come here recently; it blew out twelve panes of glass—down, crash! I went in to Hereford. Do you know what they wanted for twelve panes of glass to replace the broken ones? £33 for twelve panes, two by two! There's thirty-two panes I got for £98 and the whole greenhouse as well, yet for twelve panes you've got to pay £33! Does it stand to common sense?! I don't want to bore you stiff but there's an old friend of mine down in Credenhill, I called on him the other day because all his greenhouses went head-longs in the same gale and he lost all his plants and everything. I said, 'Of all that glass of yours as got smashed have you any as was saved? It's the same calibre of glass as what is in *my* greenhouse.' 'I let my son-in-law,' he said, 'have a hundred and fifty panes,' he said, 'but I still think I've a few,' he said, 'at the back of the shed. Come on up,' he said, 'and we'll have a look,' and he pulled out these lovely panes of glass—I've got them in my greenhouse now out of the wind up against the door so that whenever the woodwork gets dry enough I can put them in . . . So—to cut a long story short—he says, 'How many do you want?' I said, 'Have you a dozen there?' He said, 'Yes.' I said, 'What's the damage?' He said, 'They tells me, you know,' he said, 'that glass has gone up!'—he's an old fashioned codger as you may think I am. I said, 'How much do you want for them?!' He said, 'Give us £9.' I'd got a spare £10 note in my wallet, I said, 'Well, I've got a couple of V's to cut,' I said. 'I should like another pane or two.' 'Right-oh!' he said, and he gave me three more panes and I gave him £10 for the lot and he was as pleased as anything.

I bought a pair of shoes five weeks ago for £23! That would have been my wages for half a year's work under old Mr Astley.

Before the First World War, when I was a boy, you could get a pair of clogs for winter wear in the snow for two and nine-pence. In those days cigarettes was one penny for a packet of five and I brought home many an ounce of tobacco for my father—thin twist, all in a coil—for threepence an ounce. Now I pays £1.57 for a two-ounce packet of Gallagher's Condor, long cut. My week's grocery bill for the 31st March was £11.36 —and that's before I start feeding the dog. Oh my God, how the Old Age Pensioner lives on a pension in the town where he can't grow his own vegetables I can never understand! The whole world's crazy—I'm always saying that but it's true. Yes, I want to see Mrs Thatcher in power. I shall die happy then.

Gilbert and Page, they used to send you a nice catalogue showing you the kind of traps they were selling, the kind of pheasant coops and runs they were selling . . . None of that now; you've got to surmise all that! They just tell you the price of coops is so much and your runs is so much—all in this new coinage and you don't understand a thing of it. And the prices! Oh my hat! They've gone up terrific! It's the same with their pheasant meal and their dog meal. It makes your hair stand on end! The Income Tax People, they send all keepers and workmen on estates like Brinsop Court a form—'What is your occupation?' 'What is your wages?' and so and so, and so and so, and so and so. Then you *try* to get a rebate. After I officially retired, Charles used to help me. 'Going to make your list out, Dad, for your rebate claim?' 'Yes,' I said. 'Here's the old one.' 'Oh, but don't you need a mack?' I said, 'Yes. Mine's getting torn.' 'Well, you can get a mack,' he said. 'Oh!' I said. 'Put a mack down, then!' So later he put down the price of the mack. Or he put down for waders and Wellingtons. We were honest and put down exactly, didn't fiddle. I kept the receipt every time I got anything from a merchant—even dog biscuits. But they always cut out my most expensive item—what I claimed for feeding the dogs. They said, 'We're informed that a retired gamekeeper needn't keep dogs.' What the hell's the good of any keeper without a dog?!!

With the expense of everything, even the gentleman owner, he's got to make money to make everything pay. For several years now they've formed syndicates on some large estates—so many guns joins in and pays so much per year. Major Devonport's son next door on the Foxley Estate, he had a syndicate from Germany last season—five of them I believe it was; it's hearsay evidence that I'm divulging now—and they paid so many hundred pound per gun for about eight days' shooting. It do allow him a chance to pay his way, and on the big days he had the privilege of inviting his friends in to shoot with the German party. Master Tom doesn't do it here at Brinsop—he just invites three or four guns three or four times a year around Christmas and we have some very nice shooting and everything goes well. The Foxley Estate is five thousand acres. They only used to keep one keeper; now they can afford to keep two. But the vermin problem, they cannot cope with it, so they must have a tremendous loss of their reared pheasant chicks.

I didn't rear last year because my bantams died from some disease at the end of '76 after they'd reared the chicks, and this year, I'm afraid, I shan't be able to do it either. Luckily, as I've told you, we're well stocked—I'm relying on the weather in June, the critical month of the year, when the chicks of your wild game can be washed out. I've got most of the stock in the covert right by the Big House and it's close to home to look after. I don't know the name of the disease but the bantams, they stopped picking, drank a lot of water and moped about from place to place and wasted away to a frame of bones and then dropped dead. There was one estate in the same year over the other side of the River Wye where they reared about five hundred chicks and when they got them to six weeks old the keepers had to go and kill them all which would have broken my heart. I know it's true because the gentleman as owns the estate, his keeper came with him to load when he was here shooting and he told me with his own lips. He said, 'You're a fortunate man not to have the disease.' Then at the end of the year mine caught it. Could it be in the air, because I'm miles away from that estate?—there's the River Wye between us and miles and miles of landscape. There's a big noise at the moment about badgers carrying a disease that cattle gets. They're going so far as blowing gas into their burrows with gassing machines.

In 1976, as well as the eggs from my danger nests, I had a hundred eggs off Lord Portman who lives up underneath the Black Mountains. I thought it was a good thing to bring in new blood so they all would mix up and I'd get stronger pheasants for flying. I heard about Lord Portman's keeper through Mr Pritchard who drove me there in his car and I paid for them with my own money. I put fox-snares round the release pen that year and I'd already released one lot of pheasants, and they were roosting lovely. I'd another lot in there—and a week or two longer than I should have done because they were starting to hit their heads against the wire netting and taking their feathers out—when Master Tom told me to take my snares up because of his dogs. I obeyed him of course. Next morning I went down there. There was my little chicks—seventy odd out of the hundred I had in there—all in heaps, all dead and their heads off in the pen. A fox had got in; he'd scratched underneath the wire netting and he hadn't stopped at the chicks, he'd killed one of the two or three bantams I'd put in there as well. Tom's dogs was not under control then. He's controlled them since because didn't I bully him! I went down to him. He was on a tractor. I said, 'Come on along with me, young man!' I was in tears and I was mad. He come up. 'Oh, Evan!' he said. They were for him and his friends to shoot. I said, 'Yes! If I hadn't taken them blasted wires up,' I said, 'I'd have had the fox!' That's life, you see; it's just one of those things that happens in your life. You take notice of others. And I was going to release them the next morning because there was a man over the boundary, he had a patch of late corn and I was hanging on to my birds for them not to go across and go into that corn or else I should have lost half my birds as I'd reared when he cut it.

The pen is still intact in the gardens and I could use it to-morrow if I needed it, but I'm not capable of doing so at the moment. Tom's interested; I mustn't say he's not; he loves his bit of shooting and I never let him down last season. I think he'll want to raise birds later on. He's too interested in horses now, and racing, but when he's older he'll get past being jogged about on a saddle. He's about five foot ten, the smallest of the family. We always said, 'Hello! Here's going to be another jockey for the Baileys!' and we were right. But he's had to diet to compete with these weights on the horses and I don't think that's doing his health any good; it's getting too much for him; and he's knocking himself about a bit, having some tumbles. Oooh, he's had several falls! I lost a pound on him the year before last when he raced a little mare—the first racing horse he ever bought, at a point-to-point over the other side of Hereford. The tractor-driver took me in his car. Tom had to go twice round this circuit and, do you know?, he was about seven hundred yards in front of any one of them and on the last lap round and, the third jump from home, the horse just ran up to it and threw back and he went arse over head. Betting on horses is a bloody mug's game. I've only bet about three times in my life and I've only won once down at The Bell when I drew Mahmoud out of the hat for Mary when it was running in the Derby in 1936.

Tom's got six or seven racehorses, and a lady groom that lives in the Big House. Good luck to him! What a man fancies, let him do it! He hasn't got used to his surroundings yet; he's only been in charge of half the estate for two year. A deeper interest in rearing pheasants will come, but I don't think it will come in my day because I'm eighty-one now and I don't think I shall be young enough to carry on. I'm going by Sir Derrick. He was a youngish man when he come here and he gave up horses just like snapping your fingers, just like closing a book, and it was all shooting though he'd been hunting two or three days a week. At the moment Tom's got too much on his mind—he spends half his time on horse-back and the other half organising the cattle and the sheep on his half of the farm. He's only got two men working for him and it's no good using the incubator unless he can get someone else to look after the chicks. But I'll say this for him: although I don't always see eye to eye with him, whenever he knew I was bad the other day, he was up here. I sent my Home Help that comes in for an hour, I said, 'Pop down and tell Master Tom,' I said, 'that I'm not well today and I can't do anything.' He was out at the time, but he was up here as soon as he come back home to see what he could do.

I've given him my .303 for shooting deer—for shooting deer you use an army rifle-bullet. Since the last war we've only killed one deer here now and again. I've shot and dressed many a deer on this estate and taken him in the house for eating. I used to dress sheep and all off the farm to go in the Big House for Lady Sutton and Sir Derrick. If there was a young lamb wasn't fit for sale—was damaged with a broken leg or anything—I had to go and bleed it and skin it and then, when it was cold, quarter it up for Lady Sutton and Sir Derrick's guests. I generally did the sheep in a shed at home. For the deer I went outside the Big House where I'd got plenty of water to wash the blood away down the drains.

Everything's changing in this whole world and it's changing too fast, we can't keep up with it—and I'm not just saying this because I'm getting so damned slow. Old binders, old mowing-machines—they're littered about and pushed in gaps in the hedges. It's a new world we live in today. I wonder what it will be like in the future! If I could only come back after, oh, say fifty years' time when I'd see the changes! I remember when I was a boy going to school it took a sheep-shearer three quarters of an hour to an hour to shear one sheep. Now a champion shearer can do one in three and a half minutes—zzzzzzzz. A combine will sweep up eighteen acres in a day and all the corn will be in the granary by night. That used to take three days' cutting and then there were women stooking the sheaves and the sheaves had to be out in the weather for three Sundays clear before hauling them into the barns to be thrashed. Now it's already thrashed, it's ready, if it's dry, for the miller within forty-eight hours from the time it was stood in the field. Look at the milking machines! Look at the tractors! A tractor will go out and plough ten acres in two days when it took a waggoner with his two horses ten days at the very least. Men used to be on the potato field picking and forking and digging and scratching the potatoes in the rain and the mud and in mess up to their bottoms—it would take you a day to dig one row, two hundred and eighty yards long. Now they've got a machine that'll dig about ten acres a day; the potatoes go, earth and all, into a box—the potatoes one way and the earth and stones through riddles another—and then they go down a tube into the trailer and you can take your trailer to the barn, three ton of potatoes at a time. But mechanization have ruined the countryside as regards work—W-O-R-K! When I come to think that there was twenty-two men kept on this place and now it's run with four—two farmers with two men each—and most of the cottages, that used to be filled with farm workers all getting a living, let to strangers! And the young people who go in the factories, they're bored stiff! There's men who went off the land here from Brinsop into Wiggins's factory in Hereford. There they go, about six miles a day in their motor cars from the council houses in Weobley. They get more money, but what good is it to them?! What good is money today?! Everything's so expensive, they're buying less with their extra wages! Whenever the hooter goes in the evening—you can hear it from this distance—you'll see about twenty-six cars come up here, vzzzz vzzzz, and go right away over to Weobley; they're straight from the factory home. Down in the morning again— and if you're on the road they knock you arse over head. And when they get there, they're only a number, and they come out as a number. 'Number so and so. Pay packet!' 'Number so and so!'—no 'Mr Jones,' 'Mr Roberts' or nothing else! Then at the week-end they go to the football match at Hereford. That's all they can do—rub shoulders and watch! God man,

I'm sorry for them! My heart aches for them! They've got no outlook. After they've given their wives sufficient to run their homes, they're either spending the bit of money they do earn on the horses or sat in the public house. You'll see them in the public house Friday night when they draws their pay, then Saturday night. Then, Sunday lunchtime, 'Oh, I must get on! I shall be in a row with the missus!' Five past two, 'So long, Bill! See you tonight!' Then they're there till ten o'clock on the Sunday night. Then, off they go on the Monday morning down to Wiggins's again. Week in, week out. And, oh, holiday time—they must have that by the sea! 'Seaside donkeys' I call them! They save all the year round for their holiday by the sea and they spend what they've saved in a week. Then they carry on the next year just the same. Thank God I've got a *little* bit behind me. I *have* looked after it! It'll come in for my grandchildren if *I* don't want it. You'll excuse me getting aeriated (sic) like this but I'm giving you my idea of what is all nonsense and can be done without . . .

To get back to mechanization. Look at the thousands of pounds that we've spent on implements to take the work away from hundreds of human beings! Wouldn't it be better to keep those men in interesting work and stop making so much of this old iron? There's about two thousand men working at Wiggins's. Do the foremen of that factory know any one of them? No, they're there as numbers, I know that for a fact. When the human being is just numbered in and numbered out, when you come to numbers instead of names, my God, it's a sad story! Thank God, when we was in the army, even, we had more than a number! '24973—Private Rogers!' I knew I was a person! But God help them in the factories today! There they are, one screwing a bolt and the other taking him off and another placing him some- where and another screwing him up again and so on into the next section, into the next section, on rollers, passing through —why, it's a wonder half of them isn't daft! Of course, I'm an uneducated man—but I've been a man working all my life by myself and as your years go by you think a lot. It's impossible maybe to stop mechanization now because things have got into such a state. But if you've got unemployed and more unemployed and Britishers because of that are having fewer children, are we still going to let the foreigners come over by the hundred like they've been coming? What's the good of birth control if you're going to let the natives come in here and take over like they're taking over in Manchester and Birmingham?! There's streets of them living there! The more vacancies there are, the more foreigners there are to fill them! Because of mechanization we're over-populated already. And it's no good saying 'grow more this and grow more that!' if we're going to use hundreds and hundreds of acres of arable land every year to put up bricks and mortar. If they have to build, why don't they get up in the big derelict woods and bulldoze there, build on old woodland and leave the agricultural land as is producing wheat and oats? Now they're trying to keep children on years and years at school because of the unemployment situation. *We* left school at twelve before mechanization and went straight to work—country children, healthy little boys and girls. I've seen a little boy of twelve after he's left school go out and drive a pair of horses harrowing down ready for planting in front of the drills. I think some of us even in *my* day were kept on at school too long! It happened in our little school that boys reached standard six when they were eleven and had to stay on till they were twelve. I've seen Mrs Jones get the little infants— five, six and seven—and put these boys as had passed their exam to teach them little things: twice one are two, twice three are four, I mean six—Oh, I'm going on fine, ain't I?! *That'll* make good reading, won't it?! They had to dally their time away. They would have been more useful at home, weeding the garden or chopping the morning wood, doing something *useful*. There was plenty of jobs the farmers wanted done— they'd have been glad of their assistance.

You can tell I'm no town man! Some people are born citizens: I'm a born countryman. After I've been with my daughter in Poole for a few days I want to come back home.

I'm a proper duffer when I get to town. I've never even been properly acquainted with Hereford. No, there's nothing to beat the countryside—the magnificent sight of autumn when one little frost tips the leaves and the woods are changed and one variety of tree turns yellow and another turns red, another gold, another bronze, and you've got that view of the scenery of the hills, that wavy effect like the waves of the sea before the winter comes and the leaves all go withering, flying down in the wind . . . I've loved this old place all my life and my object is to end my days here so as I can be buried by the side of my two wives. Early in the morning I like best, when you hear the blackbirds and the mistlethrushes up at the tops of the trees putting in their little notes of praise for the lovely morning. And I'm still getting up six-thirty to seven o'clock and feeding my game birds round about the near parts after my cup of tea. I do my scattered coverts after breakfast. But I feed each of the long distance ones only every other day—the poplar bed down by the church and the one up Merryhill and the others up Red Bar and the Vallet's and Round Oak Hill and the one by the Harlands Pool as we shoot duck on. I like to feed till April comes in—the pheasants always keep in the woodland this time of year, though they come out if there's any bit of green stuff about; one thing they love is turnip tops, kale tops or anything like that. I take them what quantity of corn I like in my carrying bag, my corn bag, as I've free access to the granary. I walk quite six mile a day but I ride part of the way up the roads on the bicycle to save my legs. My feet have got a hard skin on the bottom from so much twisting them about and walking up hill and down dale. I've to use Vaseline with an old pair of socks to try to keep the skin moist and soft. Then at night I sometimes gets the cramp. The only preventative I've got at the moment is to give the egg of cramp sinews underneath my knee a rub, get my feet on the carpet, go round the bottom of the bed and out onto the bare oilcloth and, with that sudden coldness of the oilcloth and a couple of walks back and forth—just a couple of strides—I can get back into bed and I don't have

213

it again. That extra chill seems to satisfy the nerves or some-thing. It *is* the nerves and sinews, isn't it, with cramp? I found that was the remedy—hot water bottles are useless. Now my father, he suffered from cramp terribly and he always had on the locker by the head of his bed a bar of yellow brimstone, and all he had to do if he had the cramp was just grip that brimstone in one hand, and the cramp left him immediately. I've tried it and it don't take no effect of me. That proves we're not all the same, don't it?

In addition to the feeding I'm killing vermin every day, and I've done more housework this last eighteen months than ever I done in my life. Then I've got that twelve acres of planting as I planted two years ago that wants cleaning as the briars are holding the little trees down. Then I've to replace those twelve panes of glass in my greenhouse. It's been a very, very wet spring and I've not even touched my garden yet. Here I am talking to you with the sun shining, yet the ground's too wet to go digging on it and making it solid. If I went out there and messed, I'd only be making work for myself, though I see that Mr Pritchard's working his ground for the corn. After three or four dry days I can get on the ground and do twice as much digging as when it's wet. I'll catch up when we've finished our episode. I want to get a row of broad beans in and a row of early peas. I grow in the garden nearly everything you can mention—broad beans, peas, carrots, parsnips, onions, cauliflower, broccoli, cabbage, sprouts . . . and I haven't planted a seed yet. Tom this morning [6th April, 1978] asked me to build a pit with breeze-blocks—it's five foot six deep, eight foot six wide and fourteen foot long. The pit's already dug but I've to cement the bottom with four inches of concrete and breeze-block the sides and plaster them to hold the water in—all the juice from the silage pit will run into it and then, you see, we'll pump it out and spread it on the ground and it will make the grass grow better. He knows I can do it and the ex-pense it would cost to get a contractor in if I wasn't working for my bit of tobacco money from Sir Derrick—I'm one of the family. I've got to measure how many breeze-blocks it will take before I start—they're not ordered yet. That's my latest job. I put a pen up recently for Mrs Henzell's poultry. Then there's . . . oh, I could go on for ever talking about my work, but I think we've covered a big part of the acre, don't you?!

I hope my life story have been interesting to those of you who read it, so bye–bye and God bless you all!

Evan Rogers,
Ivy Cottage,
Brinsop.
Herefordshire.

Evan Rogers died peacefully on March 23rd, 1983.
He was 85.

ELAND

61 Exmouth Market, London EC1R 4QL
Email: info@travelbooks.co.uk

Eland was started thirty years ago to revive great travel books that had fallen out of print. Although the list soon diversified into biography and fiction, all the books are chosen for their interest in spirit of place. One of our readers explained that for him reading an Eland is like listening to an experienced anthropologist at the bar – she's let her hair down and is telling all the stories that were just too good to go in to the textbook.

Eland books are for travellers, and for readers who are content to travel in their own minds. They open out our understanding of other cultures, interpret the unknown and reveal different environments, as well as celebrating the humour and occasional horrors of travel. We take immense trouble to select only the most readable books and therefore many readers collect the entire, hundred-volume series.

You will find a very brief description of our books on the following pages. Extracts from each and every one of them can be read on our website, at www.travelbooks.co.uk. If you would like a free copy of our catalogue, email us or send a postcard.

ELAND

'One of the very best travel lists' WILLIAM DALRYMPLE

Libyan Sands
RALPH BAGNOLD
An heroic account of an infatuation with the
Model T Ford and the Sahara

An Innocent Anthropologist
NIGEL BARLEY
An honest, funny, affectionate and
compulsively irreverent account of fieldwork
in West Africa

Memoirs of a Bengal Civilian
JOHN BEAMES
Sketches of nineteenth-century India
painted with the richness of Dickens

Jigsaw
SYBILLE BEDFORD
An intensely remembered autobiographical
novel about an inter-war childhood

A Visit to Don Otavio
SYBILLE BEDFORD
The hell of travel and the Eden of arrival
in post-war Mexico

Journey into the Mind's Eye
LESLEY BLANCH
An obsessive love affair with Russia and
one particular Russian

Japanese Chronicles
NICOLAS BOUVIER
Three decades of intimate experiences
throughout Japan

The Way of the World
NICOLAS BOUVIER
A 1950's road trip to Afghanistan,
by a legendary young sage

The Devil Drives
FAWN BRODIE
Biography of Sir Richard Burton,
explorer, linguist and pornographer

Travels into Bokhara
ALEXANDER BURNES
Nineteenth-century espionage in Central Asia

Turkish Letters
OGIER DE BUSBECQ
Eyewitness history at its best: Istanbul
during the reign of Suleyman the
Magnificent

An Ottoman Traveller
EVLIYA ÇELEBI
Travels in the Ottoman Empire,
by the Pepys of 17th-century Turkey

Two Middle-Aged Ladies in Andalusia
PENELOPE CHETWODE
An infectious, personal account
of a fascination with horses,
God and Spain

My Early Life
WINSTON CHURCHILL
From North West Frontier to Boer War
by the age of twenty-five

A Square of Sky
JANINA DAVID
A Jewish childhood in the Warsaw
ghetto and hiding from the Nazis

Chantemesle
ROBIN FEDDEN
A lyrical evocation of childhood
in Normandy

Viva Mexico!
CHARLES FLANDRAU
Five years in turn-of-the-century
Mexico, described by an enchanted Yankee

Travels with Myself and Another
MARTHA GELLHORN
Five journeys from hell by a great
war correspondent

The Trouble I've Seen
MARTHA GELLHORN
Four stories of the Great Depression,
offering profound insight into the
suffering of poverty

The Weather in Africa
MARTHA GELLHORN
*Three novellas set amongst the
white settlers of East Africa*

The Last Leopard
DAVID GILMOUR
*The biography of Giuseppe di Lampedusa,
author of* The Leopard

Walled Gardens
ANNABEL GOFF
*An portrait of the Anglo-Irish: sad,
absurd and funny*

Africa Dances
GEOFFREY GORER
*The magic of indigenous culture
and the banality of colonisation*

Cinema Eden
JUAN GOYTISOLO
*Essays from the Muslim
Mediterranean*

Goodbye Buenos Aires
ANDREW GRAHAM-YOOLL
*A portrait of an errant father,
and of the British in Argentina*

A State of Fear
ANDREW GRAHAM-YOOLL
*A journalist witnesses Argentina's
nightmare in the 1970s*

A Pattern of Islands
ARTHUR GRIMBLE
*Rip-roaring adventures and a passionate
appreciation of life in the Southern Seas*

Warriors
GERALD HANLEY
Life and death among the Somalis

Morocco That Was
WALTER HARRIS
*All the cruelty, fascination and
humour of a pre-modern kingdom:
Morocco in the 19th and early 20th century*

Far Away and Long Ago
W H HUDSON
*A childhood in Argentina, and a hymn to
nature*

Palestine Papers 1917–22
ED. DOREEN INGRAMS
History caught in the making

Holding On
MERVYN JONES
*The story of a London dockland street,
and the families who lived there*

Mother Land
DMETRI KAKMI
*A minutely observed Greek childhood on a
Turkish island in the 1960s*

Red Moon & High Summer
HERBERT KAUFMANN
*A coming-of-age novel following a
young singer in his Tuareg homeland*

Three Came Home
AGNES KEITH
*A mother's ordeal in a Japanese
prison camp*

Peking Story
DAVID KIDD
*The ruin of an ancient Mandarin
family under the new communist order*

Scum of the Earth
ARTHUR KOESTLER
*Koestler's escape from a collapsing France
in World War II*

The Hill of Kronos
PETER LEVI
A poet's radiant portrait of Greece

A Dragon Apparent
NORMAN LEWIS
*Cambodia, Laos and Vietnam
on the eve of war*

Golden Earth
NORMAN LEWIS
Travels in Burma

The Honoured Society
NORMAN LEWIS
Sicily, her people and the Mafia within

Naples '44
NORMAN LEWIS
*Naples, surviving the horrors of war
through her talent for life*

A View of the World
NORMAN LEWIS
*Collected adventures of a lifelong
traveller of genius*

An Indian Attachment
SARAH LLOYD
*Life and the love of a Sikh temple servant in
a remote Indian village*

A Pike in the Basement
SIMON LOFTUS
*Tales of a hungry traveller: from catfish
in Mississippi to fried eggs with chapatis
in Pakistan*

92 Acharnon Street
JOHN LUCAS
*A gritty portrait of Greece as the
Greeks would recognise it, seen
through the eyes of a poet*

Among the Faithful
DAHRIS MARTIN
*An American woman living in the holy
city of Kairouan, Tunisia in the 1920s*

Lords of the Atlas
GAVIN MAXWELL
*The rise and fall of Morocco's infamous
Glaoua family, 1893-1956*

A Reed Shaken by the Wind
GAVIN MAXWELL
*Travels among the threatened
Marsh Arabs of southern Iraq*

A Year in Marrakesh
PETER MAYNE
*Back-street life and gossip in
Morocco in the 1950s*

Sultan in Oman
JAN MORRIS
*An historic journey through the still-
medieval state of Oman in the 1950s*

Hopeful Monsters
NICHOLAS MOSLEY
*A passionate love story at the birth of the
atomic age*

Full Tilt
DERVLA MURPHY
*A lone woman bicycles from Ireland to
India in 1963*

Tibetan Foothold
DERVLA MURPHY
*Six months with recent exiles from Tibet in
Northern India*

The Waiting Land
DERVLA MURPHY
The spell of the ancient civilisation of Nepal

Where the Indus is Young
DERVLA MURPHY
*A mother and her six-year-old daughter
explore a wintery Baltistan*

In Ethiopia with a Mule
DERVLA MURPHY
By mule across the mountains of Abyssinia

Wheels within Wheels
DERVLA MURPHY
*The makings of a traveller: a searingly
honest autobiography*

The Island that Dared
DERVLA MURPHY
*Three journeys through the landscape and
history of Communist Cuba*

The Caravan Moves On
IRFAN ORGA
Life with the nomads of central Turkey

Portrait of a Turkish Family
IRFAN ORGA
*The decline of a prosperous Ottoman
family in the new Republic*

Sweet Waters
HAROLD NICHOLSON
A turn-of-the-century Istanbul thriller

The Undefeated
GEORGE PALOCZI-HORVATH
The confessions of a dedicated, Hungarian communist, tortured by his own regime

Travels into the Interior of Africa
MUNGO PARK
The first – and still the best – European record of west-African exploration

Lighthouse
TONY PARKER
Britain's lighthouse-keepers, in their own words

The People of Providence
TONY PARKER
A London housing estate, its secrets and some of its inhabitants

Begums, Thugs & White Mughals
FANNY PARKES
William Dalrymple edits and introduces a true portrait of early colonial India

The Last Time I Saw Paris
ELLIOT PAUL
One street, its loves and loathings, set against the passionate politics of inter-war Paris

Rites
VICTOR PERERA
A Jewish childhood and a portrait of Guatemala

A Cure for Serpents
THE DUKE OF PIRAJNO
An Italian doctor and his Bedouin patients, Libyan sheikhs and Tuareg mistress in the 1920s

When Miss Emmie was in Russia
HARVEY PITCHER
Six adventurous British governesses, caught up in the Revolution

Nunaga
DUNCAN PRYDE
Ten years among the Eskimos: hunting, fur-trading and heroic dog-treks

Ask Sir James
MICHAELA REID
The life of Sir James Reid, personal physician to Queen Victoria

A Funny Old Quist
EVAN ROGERS
A gamekeeper's passionate evocation of a now-vanished English, rural lifestyle

The Pharaoh's Shadow
ANTHONY SATTIN
In pursuit of Egypt's past, through her teaming, mysterious and enchanting present

Travels on my Elephant
MARK SHAND
Six hundred miles across India on the back of the much-loved Tara

Valse des Fleurs
SACHEVERELL SITWELL
A day in the life of imperial St Petersburg in 1868

Living Poor
MORITZ THOMSEN
A Peace Corps worker's inside story of Ecuador

The Fields Beneath
GILLIAN TINDALL
London revealed through a micro-history of Kentish Town

Hermit of Peking
HUGH TREVOR-ROPER
The hidden life of the scholar and trickster Sir Edmund Backhouse

The Law
ROGER VAILLAND
The harsh game of life played and enjoyed by the southern Italians

Bangkok
ALEC WAUGH
The story of a city, a monarchy and a
nation

The Road to Nab End
WILLIAM WOODRUFF
A story of poverty and
survival in a Lancashire mill town

The Village in the Jungle
LEONARD WOOLF
A dark novel of villagers struggling
to survive in colonial Ceylon

Death's Other Kingdom
GAMEL WOOLSEY
The tragic arrival of civil war in an
Andalusian village in 1936

The Ginger Tree
OSWALD WYND
A Scotswoman's love and survival
in early twentieth-century Japan